A Supplement to the Authorised English Version of the New Testament

Γαδαρηνῶν is sanctioned by only eleven MSS (although B C M are among them), and five Evangelisteria, or extracts from the Gospels for ecclesiastical purposes; but into the latter a variation would easily be admitted, which removes the apparent discrepancy between the narrative of St. Matthew, and those of the other Evangelists. Origen says ἐν ὀλίγοις εὕρομεν εἰς τὴν χώραν τῶν Γαδαρηνῶν, and both the Peshito and Philoxenian Syriac, together with the Persic version (see note on ch. vi, 13), and one or two Fathers, favor the same side.

Γεργεσηνῶν, on the contrary, is the reading of the vast majority of manuscripts of both families; of the Coptic, Æthiopic, Armenian and some less important versions, as well as of several ecclesiastical writers of various ages, down to the time of Theophylact. Indeed there would have been little scruple respecting the authenticity of the received text, had it not been imagined by Wetstein, and after him by Michäelis and Scholz (Proleg. N. T. § 15), that Γεργεσηνῶν originated in a gratuitous conjecture of Origen. Now not to insist on the glaring improbability of the supposition, that the unsupported influence of *Origen* was sufficient to procure the insertion of any reading his capricious taste might dictate, into nearly all the manuscripts of Scripture scattered throughout the world; we may reasonably doubt whether, on an attentive examination, his words will bear the construction put upon them by Wetstein. They occur in his commentary on St. John, Tom vi (Opera, Paris. 1759 Delarue, Vol. iv, pp. 140—1). He had taken up a notion (a very idle one perhaps) that the etymology of certain names of places mentioned in the Bible, was prophetically significant of the great events, of which they were hereafter to

Library of The Theological Seminary

PRINCETON · NEW JERSEY

PRESENTED BY

Samuel Agnew

BS186
.S434
Copy 1

A

SUPPLEMENT TO THE AUTHORISED ENGLISH VERSION OF THE NEW TESTAMENT

BEING A CRITICAL ILLUSTRATION OF ITS MORE
DIFFICULT PASSAGES FROM THE SYRIAC LATIN AND EARLIER
ENGLISH VERSIONS WITH AN INTRODUCTION

BY THE REVEREND
FREDERICK HENRY SCRIVENER, M.A.
OF TRINITY COLLEGE CAMBRIDGE ASSISTANT MASTER OF THE
KING'S SCHOOL SHERBORNE

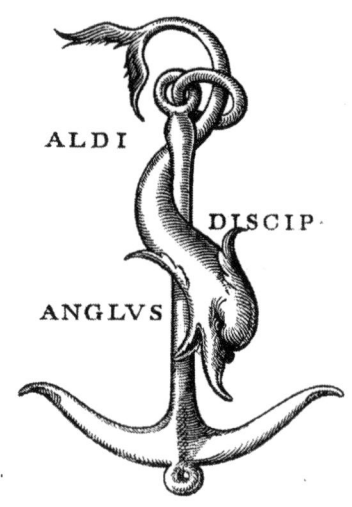

LONDON
WILLIAM PICKERING
1845

"As nothing is begun and perfected at the same time, and the latter thoughts are thought to be the wiser: so, if we building upon their foundation that went before us, and being holpen by their labors, do endeavor to make that better which they left so good ; no man, we are sure, hath cause to mislike us, they, we persuade ourselves, if they were alive, would thank us. The vintage of Abiezer that strake the stroke, yet the gleaning of grapes of Ephraim was not to be despised (Judges viii, 2). Joash, the king of Israel, did not satisfy himself till he had smitten the ground three times; and yet he offended the prophet for giving over then." Preface of the Translators to the Reader, Authorised version of the Bible.

Table of the Contents of the Introduction.

	PAGE
DESIGN OF THE PRESENT WORK	1
Division of the whole subject into THREE general heads	5
I. ERRORS OF CRITICISM in the Authorised version, arising from false readings of the Greek text. Account of the Textus Receptus	ibid.
Text followed by our common version	7
Griesbach's edition, and theory of recensions	9
Archbp. Laurence's "Remarks"	12
Scholz's edition, and theory of recensions	16
Lachmann's Nov. Test. Græc.-Lat.	23
Tischendorf's Nov. Test.	30
General result of the preceding review	31
II. ERRORS OF INTERPRETATION in the Authorised version	32
(a). Errors in the signification of single words. Lexicography	ibid.
(b). Errors in the grammatical construction of one or more words in the same clause. The article. Bp. Middleton's theory	36
On the exact rendering of the Greek tenses	44
(c). Errors in the dependence of clauses on each other	46
On the punctuation	47
On the divisions into chapters, verses, and paragraphs	48
III. ERRORS OF EXPRESSION in the language of the English version, arising	
(a). from want of uniformity in rendering the same Greek word	50
(b). from grammatical inaccuracies	53
(c). from ambiguous, obscure, and obsolete expressions	55
On the marginal renderings in the Authorised version. Dr. Blayney	57
On the use of the Italic character. Dean Turton	59

Contents of Introduction.

	PAGE
Application of other versions to the Illustration of our own	63
THE PESHITO SYRIAC VERSION	ibid.
The Philoxenian Syriac version	68
THE LATIN VULGATE VERSION	70
Modern Latin versions of Beza and Castalio. Boisii Collatio	72
EARLY ENGLISH VERSIONS. Their internal character	74
Wickliffe's Bible, A.D. 1380	75
Tyndal's New Testament, 1526, 1534	78
Coverdale's Bible, 1535	83
Cranmer's, or the Great Bible, 1539	87
Sir John Cheke's Translation of St. Matthew, about 1550	88
Geneva New Testament, 1st edition, 1557	92
The Bishops' Bible, 1568, 1572	94
Laurence's Critique	96
Rhemish New Testament, 1582	97
King James's Bible, 1611	101
LATER ENGLISH VERSIONS. Doddridge's Family Expositor, 1739—1756	102
Campbell on the Gospels, 1788	104
Macknight on the Epistles, 1795	106
Archbp. Newcome's Translation of the New Testament, 1796, &c.	108
Dr. Boothroyd's Bible, 1823, 1836	110
Holy Bible with 20,000 emendations, 1841	111
Dr. Symonds's Observations on the Authorised version, 1789—1794	113
Pr. Scholefield's Hints for an Improved Translation, 1836	115
PRINCIPLES OF INTERPRETATION. Grinfield's Nov. Test. Hellenisticum, 1843	117
Bp. Jebb's Sacred Literature, 1820	119
THE GREEK COMMENTATORS, Chrysostom, Theophylact, &c.	122
Modern Commentators, Kuinöel in Libros N. T. Historicos	125
CONCLUSION	126
NOTES ON THE AUTHORISED ENGLISH VERSION OF ST. MATTHEW	131
Appendix A. On the principal Greek Manuscripts of the Four Gospels	327

INTRODUCTION.

Design of the present work.

IT is generally agreed among competent judges that a new translation of the Holy Scriptures, for public use, is both needless and inexpedient. Assured that our present admirable version faithfully conveys to the English reader the general sense of the original Hebrew and Greek, they rightly judge it at once unnecessary and dangerous to unsettle and perplex the simple by attempting to improve it. The Bible of King James's translation is cherished as their best treasure by our countrymen and kindred, in every spot on the globe where our language is spoken or our name respected. It is the only bond which unites our Dissenters at home with the Church of their fathers. These are advantages which could not be expected to accrue to any modern version, were its superiority to the old one ever so decided; even were it to embody the results of all the Biblical learning and critical research of the last two hundred years.

Yet however excellent our common translation as a whole, like every other work of man, it is far from being faultless. During the short period of eighty years which had elapsed between the commencement of the English Reformation and its publication in

B

1611, at least five separate versions of Scripture had appeared—to omit several less important editions—Tyndal's, Coverdale's, Cranmer's, or the Great Bible, the Geneva, and Parker's or the Bishops' Bible; each of them perhaps superior to its predecessors in faithfulness and perspicuity. All these earlier versions our translators were instructed to keep in view (the Bishop's Bible especially, which was then read in Churches); and comparing them diligently with the original tongues, to amend them where they were inaccurate, and studiously to retain their renderings wherever they were correct (*See King James's first and fourteenth Instructions to the Translators*). To this holy task a large body of the best divines in the kingdom devoted themselves for above three years: translating, revising, and debating with each other on the numerous difficulties that arose: till at length they produced our authorised translation; a work of such surpassing merit that it at once superseded all previous attempts, and closed the older versions for ever on every one save the Biblical antiquarian.

Now it were unreasonable to suppose, that if our authorised version is so great an improvement on all that went before it, during the short space of eighty years, the current of improvement is here to stop, and that no blemishes remain for future students to detect and remove. More than two centuries have passed since that version (or, to speak more correctly, revision of former versions) was executed, and they have been centuries of great and rapid improvement in every branch of knowledge and science. So amply furnished were King James's translators with all the theological learning of a learned age, that there was no risk of their falling into errors which could seriously affect the belief of their readers, on any of the great points of Christian doctrine. Still it must be confessed, that in their time, Scriptural criticism was but in its infancy. Few manuscripts had been collated in order to settle to original text; the *Greek* language, in particular, was studied rather extensively than accurately; the peculiar style of the writers of the New Testament was little understood. The general sense of Holy Writ was apprehended by them at least as well as by ourselves: they drank deeply (how much more deeply than we are wont to drink!) of the waters of life: and if they knew little respecting the critical niceties which characterise high scholarship at present, it was no fault of theirs that they could not anticipate the results of the long labors of those who were to follow them. As well might we impute it as a defect to Newton, that he did not presage the discoveries of Herschel or of Olbers.

It is the design of the present work to collect and review those passages of our authorised version of the New Testament, which a diligent collation with the original may shew to be inaccurate or obscure: and such an undertaking will perhaps be approved by many who would earnestly deprecate a formal revision of the translation itself. A production intended for the use of the student in the closet can give no offence to the weak or ill-informed Christian; and may, if carefully executed, prove the means of exciting in the intelligent reader an interest in the cultivation of Biblical criticism; and a well-grounded admiration of the version, whose merits form the subject of our enquiry. In a performance like the present it would be worse than idle to aim at originality. The interpretation of the Bible has tasked the intellects of the ripest scholars in Christendom for many ages; and in theology all that is *really* new is certainly false. Hasty and presumptuous conjecture, indecent as it is in every case, becomes positively sinful when we approach the Scriptures of truth. It was chiefly with the view of checking a rash spirit of criticism that I determined to annex to *every* correction I shall propose the renderings of the earlier English versions; and (if they be corrections which concern the sense) those of the Peshito Syriac and Latin Vulgate also. It will thus be visible at a glance, how far the changes I suggest are favored by the weighty authorities above mentioned: and I am sensible that where the interpretation of the common translation is supported by the united testimonies of the Syriac, Latin, and former English versions, a very strong case must be made out, before I can hope to convince my readers of the propriety of disturbing the received rendering. Such instances, however, will be found exceedingly rare.

It is almost superfluous to state my reasons for adopting the versions I have named as my models and guides in the task I have undertaken. The earlier English translations, independently of their intrinsic excellence, are the basis of King James's Bible, which resembles several of them to an extent of which nothing short of actual inspection will enable us to form a notion. The Peshito Syriac and the Vulgate are among the most precious monuments of Christian antiquity; they are the productions of an age little posterior to that of the Apostles; and have been constantly used in the public services, the one of the Oriental, the other of the Western Churches, from that period down to the present hour. But the character of each of these venerable translations will be more conveniently discussed hereafter.

<small>Division of the whole subject into three general heads.</small> The texts whose renderings in our authorised version I have presumed to examine, are arranged in the body of my work according to the order in which they stand in the volume of the New Testament. But it will be proper to state fully in this Introduction the principles on which I have acted, and to which perpetual reference will be made in the course of my review.

It would appear then that the inaccuracies of our common English version of the New Testament may be comprehended under THREE general heads.

I. ERRORS OF CRITICISM, arising from false readings of the Greek text.

II. ERRORS OF INTERPRETATION, which originate from mistaking the sense of the original Greek.

III. ERRORS OF EXPRESSION, where the language of the English translation itself is ambiguous, ungrammatical, or obscure.

Each of these leading divisions of the subject will now be considered in such detail, as its relative importance shall seem to demand.

I. ERRORS OF CRITICISM, arising from false readings of the Greek text.

<small>The Textus Receptus.</small> By the Received text of the New Testament we usually understand that printed in Robert Stephens's third edition of 1550, or that of the Elzevirs, published in 1624. These two editions differ from each other in about 130 places,* but

---

* Tischendorf enumerates 115 variations (Præf. N. T. 1841): but exclusive of stops, accents, and manifest typographical errors, I believe 130 to be nearer the truth.

their general character is the same; though Stephens's peculiar readings may perhaps be considered preferable, on the whole, to those of the Elzevirs. Mill's Greek Testament (Oxon. 1707) professes to be a reprint of Stephens's text (Proleg. p. 167), though it departs from it in several places, without giving any intimation to the reader.* Professor Scholefield's Greek and English Testament of 1836 (which I have constantly used for the purposes of this work), although stated to be an exact reprint of the Stephanic edition of 1550, differs from it in Luke vii, 12; x, 6; xvii, 1; 35; John viii, 25; xix, 7; Acts ii, 36; Eph. iv, 25; James v, 9; 1 Pet. iv, 8; 2 Pet. ii, 12; 2 John v. 5; Rev. vii, 10. In most other reprints of the received text, the Elzevir edition is adopted as the standard.

It is not necessary at the present day to enter upon a prolix discussion respecting the sources of the Textus Receptus. It will now be admitted on all hands that the learned persons who superintended the earlier editions of the New Testament, both possessed a very limited critical apparatus, and did not always avail themselves as they ought of the resources which were within their reach. It is therefore most satisfactory to discover that the text which they formed bears, in all probability, a closer resemblance to the sacred autographs, than that of some critics very much their superiors in Biblical science; who, moreover, had access to a vast treasure of materials, which was entirely unknown to their

---

* Tischendorf refers us to Luke vii, 12; John viii, 25; Acts ii, 36; xiv, 8; xv, 38(?); Eph. iv, 25; 1 Pet. iii, 11; 21; iv, 8; 2 Pet. ii, 12. But I doubt not that several more might be added: e. g. Luke x, 6; xvii, 1; 35; John xix, 7.

Introduction. 7

predecessors. I hope it is no presumptuous belief, that the Providence of God took such care of His Church in the vital matter of maintaining His Word pure and uncorrupted, that He guided the minds of the first editors, in their selection of the authorities on which they rested. It is easy to declaim on the low date and little worth of the manuscripts used by the Complutensian divines, by Erasmus, or Stephens; but what would have been the present state of the text of the Gospels, had the least among them conceded to the Cambridge MS. or Codex Bezæ, the influence and *adoration**** which its high antiquity seemed to challenge? But we shall be better able to appreciate the excellency of the received text, when we have examined the principal attempts that have been made to supersede it.

Text followed by our common version. Theodore Beza's several editions of the Greek Testament contain a text essentially the same as that published by Stephens, from whose third edition he does not vary in much more than eighty places. But his critical labors claim our especial notice, from the deference paid to them by the translators of the English authorised version; who, though they did not implicitly follow Beza's text, yet have received his readings in many passages where he differs from Stephens. I subjoin a list of those places, in which our translation agrees with Beza's New Testament, against that of Stephens. Matth. xxi, 7; xxiii, 13, 14; Mark viii, 24; ix, 40; xii, 20; Luke i, 35; ii, 22; x, 22; xv, 26; xvii, 36; John xiii, 31; xvi, 33; xviii, 24; Acts xvii, 25; xxii, 25; xxiv, 13; 18; xxvii, 13; Rom. vii,

---

* " Codices vetustatis specie pæne adorandos." R. Stephani, Præf. N. T. 1546.

6; viii, 11; xii, 11; xvi, 20; 1 Cor. v, 11; xv, 31 (where however Beza's 1st edition of 1565 coincides with Stephens); 2 Cor. iii, 1; v, 4; vi, 15; vii, 12; 16; xi, 10; Col. i, 24; ii, 13; 1 Thess. ii, 15; 2 Thess. ii, 4; 1 Tim. i, 4; Hebr. ix, 1; James ii, 18; iv, 13; v, 12; 1 Pet. i, 4; iii, 21 (?); 2 Pet. iii, 7; 1 John i, 4; ii, 23 (though the clause is inserted in italics); iii, 16; 2 John v. 3; 3 John v. 7; Jude vv. 19; 24; Rev. iii, 1; v, 11; vii, 3; 10; viii, 11; xi, 1; 2; xiii, 3; xiv, 18; xvi, 14; xix, 14. In 33 out of the above 60 texts Beza was followed by the Elzevir edition of 1624. The passages in which our translation agrees with Stephens against Beza are Mark xvi, 20; John xviii, 20; Acts iv, 27; xvi, 7; xxv, 6; Rom. v, 17; 1 Cor. iii, 3; x, 28; 2 Cor. iii, 14 (?); viii, 24; xi, 1 (?); Gal. iv, 17; Phil. i, 23; Col. i, 2; Tit. ii, 7; Hebr. x, 2; Rev. iv, 10. In Matth. ii, 11; x, 10; John xviii, 1; Acts xxvii, 29, our version adopts a reading found neither in Stephens nor Beza; in the last two cases on the authority of the Latin Vulgate. After this examination (which I trust will be found tolerably accurate*) we may safely determine the character of the text received in our translation: and it will be seen that Mr. Hartwell Horne is not quite correct in his statement (Introduction to Scriptures, Vol. II. Pt. ii, p. 13) that "Beza's edition of 1598 was adopted as the basis of the English version of the New Testament published by authority in 1611." It does not appear that the translators adopted any particular text as their standard, but exercised their own judgment

---

* Besides Stephens's 3rd edition of 1550 and the Elzevirs' of 1624, I have used Beza's New Testaments of 1565, 1582, 1589 and 1598.

on the several readings, as they passed successively under review.

But whatever might be the minute diversities of the early editions, they present to us a text in substance the same: for what are eighty or a hundred variations (many of them so unimportant as not to affect the sense in the slightest degree), in such a book as the New Testament? And though, more than a century later, Mill and Wetstein spent their lives in the collation of Greek manuscripts, they both felt that the time was not yet arrived when they could securely introduce any changes into the textus receptus. It was reserved for Griesbach to publish an edition of the New Testament (1796—1806), exhibiting a totally new revision of the text, into which numberless various readings were admitted from manuscripts, versions, and ecclesiastical writers: no preference being given to the received text as such, where it was not supported by what he deemed competent authority. It is my present purpose to investigate the correctness of the principles on which Griesbach proceeds: and the celebrity which his work has attained, coupled with the magnitude of the alterations he has made in the inspired volume, will perhaps give me a claim to the reader's indulgence, if I prosecute my enquiry at some length.

Griesbach's edition, and theory of recensions.

The main feature of Griesbach's scheme of revision is his theory of families or recensions, the first slight draught of which was sketched by the learned and amiable Bengel; and which, after receiving some improvements at the hands of Semler, was applied to the criticism of the New Testament by Griesbach, in his "Curæ in Epist. Paulin." and his "Symbolæ Criticæ." Every one who has consulted the materials collected by Wetstein and his successors must have observed, that certain manuscripts and versions bear some affinity to each other; so that one of them is seldom cited in support of a various reading (not being a manifest and gross error of the copyist), unaccompanied by one or more of its kindred. Now it seems a very reasonable presumption that documents which are thus closely connected, have sprung from a common source, quite distinct from the great mass of manuscript authorities, from which they thus unequivocally withdraw themselves. And if these families could be shewn to have existed at a very early period (that is to say, within one or two hundred years after the death of the Apostles); and were it to appear moreover that certain peculiarities characterised the manuscripts of certain countries; it is plain that we should then have made important advances in our knowledge of the history, and consequently of the relative values of the various recensions. We should thus have some better guide in our choice between contending readings, than the very rough and unsatisfactory process of counting the *number* of authorities alleged in favor of each. I believe that Griesbach has entirely failed in his attempt to classify the manuscripts of the Greek Testament; but I am not blind to the advantages which would ensue from such a classification, were it possible to be accomplished. His was a noble ambition; and if he did not achieve all that he aspired to, " magnis tamen excidit ausis."

The researches of Griesbach, prosecuted with unwearied diligence during the course of many years, led him to the conclusion that the several families into which manuscripts are divided, may be reduced to three great classes, the Alexandrian, the Western, and the Byzantine recensions. The standard of the Alexandrine text he imagined that he had discovered in Origen, who, though he wrote in Palestine, might be fairly presumed to have brought with him into exile manuscripts of the New Testament, similar to those in ordinary use in his native city. The text of the Western Church would naturally be drawn from the Italic version and the Latin Fathers; while the large majority of manuscripts, versions, and ecclesiastical writers followed the readings which prevailed in the Patriarchate of Constantinople. He then proceeded to attribute to each of these three families an equal influence in correcting and settling the text; or rather, he considered the testimony of the Byzantine class inferior in weight to that of either of the others. Consistently with these principles, the evidence of the very few antient manuscripts of the Alexandrine class which are yet extant (e. g. Wetstein's A, B, C, &c.); or of the Latin versions, and one or two old Latinising manuscripts (e. g. D of the Gospels; E, F, G of the Pauline Epistles), if supported by the Fathers of the two families, and sufficiently probable in itself; may balance or even outweigh the unanimous voice of hundreds of witnesses of every kind, should they happen to belong to the unfortunate Byzantine recension. Indeed the agreement of the Alexandrine and Western families is pronounced by Griesbach (Proleg. N. T. Vol. I. p. lxxx) to be a sufficient proof of the high antiquity of the reading which they favor; and " si internâ simul bonitate suâ niteat," of its genuineness also.

Let us now see the practical effect of this ingenious and refined theory on the text of the New Testament. I select one example out of multitudes which occur in all parts of his edition. In Rom. xii, 11, the fol-

12   Introduction.

lowing words appear in the Textus Receptus, τῷ κυρίῳ δουλεύοντες. Here instead of κυρίῳ Griesbach reads καιρῷ, in which alteration he is supported by no modern editor; and of the earlier by Stephens alone. In defence of this change (by no means a trivial one), what authorities appear in Griesbach's note? The evidence of three uncial manuscripts (D F G) of the 8th or 10th century, and the Latin translations contained in two of them (D G); some Latin manuscripts spoken of by Jerome, Rufinus and Bede; a Latin inscription prefixed to this chapter, quoted by Lucas Brugensis at the beginning of the 17th century; a remote and possible allusion in Ignatius ad Polycarp. (c. 3. see Mill *ad loc.*); and two passages of Gregory Nyssen. Ignatius and Nyssen must be presumed to represent the Byzantine family, as all his other witnesses are clearly Occidental. And on such evidence Griesbach rejects the reading sanctioned by all the versions, by the Fathers who have quoted the text, and by about 150 manuscripts of all ages and countries known to him, which contain the Epistle to the Romans. Where the external testimony is so decided, the intrinsic goodness of a reading is a matter of secondary importance. Knapp however refers us to ch. xiv, 18; xvi, 18, in favor of the common text; while Wolf (Cur. Philol. *ad loc.*) quotes Col. iv, 8 in support of καιρῷ, and shews that the expression καιρῷ δουλεύειν is occasionally met with in Greek authors. The variation in all probability arose from the custom of representing a familiar word like κυρίῳ in an abridged form (κρῷ), a practice which would scarcely have been adopted in the case of καιρῷ.

Archbp. Laurence's "Remarks."

It certainly seems astonishing that a theory which built so vast a superstructure on foundations thus slight and precarious, should have commanded for a considerable period the assent of the learned throughout Europe. But it was not till the year 1814 that Archbishop Laurence published his " Remarks on Griesbach's Systematic Classification," which at once, and almost without an effort, laid his whole edifice in the dust. As this masterly production has finally settled the question respecting a triple recension of manuscripts, it may be convenient to give a brief analysis of the principal arguments which Dr. Laurence employs in the course of his investigation.

In the first place, he observes (" Remarks" ch. ii), that whereas Griesbach expressly confesses in his " Curæ in Epist. Paulin." that five or six different texts might be formed from the manuscripts now extant; still, in the full consciousness of the doubtful and imperfect nature of his hypothesis, he confines himself to the use of the three above-mentioned recensions, the Alexandrian, the Occidental, and the Byzantine. Thus he satisfies himself with a coarse approximation to the truth, and substitutes conjectural probability in the room of certainty. Yet it is easily seen how extremely fallacious every system of classification must be, which excludes from our consideration half the families of manuscripts, which are known to exist.

But, waiving this preliminary objection, fatal as it may well be deemed to the whole theory, and conceding that all possible recensions are reducible to three; let us examine Griesbach's mode of determining the class to which a particular manuscript or version belongs. This point is of great importance; for if he possesses no accurate means of classifying his authorities, it is obvious that his scheme, even if true in itself, can never be safely applied to the criticism of the New Testament. Now I have before stated, that his Alexandrine family is discriminated from the rest, by comparing each manuscript separately with the readings found in Origen's works; the quotations of that Father being made the standard of the Egyptian recension. Thus, inasmuch as in St. Paul's Epistles Griesbach reckons that the places in which the Codex A of Wetstein and the quotations of Origen agree with each other against the received text amount to 110; while the places in which the Codex A disagrees with the received text and Origen united amount to but 60; he concludes that the Codex A belongs to the Alexandrine, and not to the common or Byzantine recension, for the simple reason that 110 is greater than 60. Admitting for a moment that Griesbach's calculations are accurate (which is far enough from being the case*), he has nevertheless committed an oversight so enormous, as to be perfectly incredible if it were not self-evident. It requires no argument to show that the true character of the Codex A as much depends on its agreements with the received text, as on its disagreements. Let us see how far this new element, essential as it is to the formation of a right judgment on the subject, will affect the result at which our critic has arrived. Still adopting Griesbach's own numbers (Symbol. Crit. i. p. 134), it appears that the Codex A agrees with the received text against Origen in 96 passages, which, added to the 60 places given above, will make the

---

* Archbp. Laurence, in his Appendix, has shewn from an elaborate collation, that the Codex A agrees with Origen against the received text in 154 places, and disagrees with Origen and the received text united in 140. The total sum of the agreements of the Codex A with the received text against Origen he proves to be 444.

Introduction. 15

sum total of its differences from Origen 156; whereas it differs from the received text only 110 times. Hence the conclusion to be drawn from Griesbach's own premises would unavoidably be the very opposite to that which he seeks to establish: viz: the Byzantine character of the Codex A.

It is unnecessary for us to follow Archbishop Laurence in his exposure of many other errors both in reasoning and computation, of which Griesbach's critical writings furnish a luxuriant crop. Still less need I indicate the grounds of that Prelate's opinion, which he distinctly intimates, but with characteristic caution refrains from expressing: that the Alexandrine text is a nullity, although the Western is really different from the Constantinopolitan; the Latin version, like the Latin Church, being " that mighty rod of Aaron, which is ever prepared to swallow the feebler rods of Egypt." (Remarks, p. 90). From the very first Laurence's refutation was felt in this country to be unanswerable.* With all our gratitude to Gries-

---

* Yet as late as the year 1840, a revision of the authorised English version of the New Testament, conformably to Griesbach's text, was executed by a " Layman," now deceased. The reasons which induced him to adopt that text shall be given in his own words. " It is one which the general opinion of critics throughout Europe has long fully approved. At any rate it is a known and well-recognised standard—resting, in every part, on reasonable, well-weighed and probable evidence: and though there may occur in it, as there must in any such undertaking, instances of nicely balanced testimony, in which other minds may come to different conclusions from Griesbach's on the same evidence, or as to the mode of weighing and classifying the authorities, yet that is a difficulty from which there never can be means of escape." Preface p. ix. It is not a little remarkable that this modest and amiable writer failed to perceive, that " the mode of weighing and classifying the authorities" is precisely the point at issue between Griesbach and the advocates for the received text. How far that

bach for what he has really effected for the criticism of the New Testament, his theory of recensions has been tacitly and universally abandoned. In Germany, indeed, the "Remarks" on his classification appear to have experienced the strange neglect, which English divinity seems fated to meet with there; but which we, I trust, are too wise to resent or retaliate. Yet within the last few years, they who have clung to Griesbach's main hypothesis, have advocated it on grounds widely different from those propounded by its author.

As a specimen of the practical results of Griesbach's system, Dr. Laurence refers us to John vii, 8; 1 Tim. iii, 16; important texts which I shall be called upon to discuss in their proper places. Hardly less striking are the following instances, to which I invite the reader's attention: Matth. xix, 17; Mark iv, 24; Acts xi, 20; Col. ii, 2.

Scholz's edition, and theory of recensions.

The next considerable attempt to form a consistent theory of families (for that of Hug is but a modification of Griesbach's) was made by Professor Scholz of Bonn, in his edition of the New Testament, 1830—36.* If the value of a production is to be estimated by the

---

critic's recension "rests on reasonable, well-weighed, and probable evidence," the arguments I have alleged will by this time have enabled my readers to judge for themselves.

* I have not alluded to Dr. Nolan's "Integrity of the Greek Vulgate," 1815, because I have been compelled to arrive at the conclusion that his scheme of recensions is radically erroneous. Few things perhaps are more sad to the honest enquirer after truth, than to see a learned and single-hearted man like Dr. Nolan, by assuming as certain what is barely possible, and setting ingenious conjecture in the room of historical fact, led on step by step to adopt a theory, which (to use the words of Dr. Turner of New York) " is sufficiently condemned by its own extravagance."

amount of labor which has been spent upon it, Wetstein alone can enter into competition with this Romanist divine. For twelve years he was engaged in searching the chief libraries of the continent in quest of manuscripts of the New Testament, and its principal versions. He has even extended his Biblical travels to the Archipelago and the Greek monastery of St. Saba near Jerusalem. By these means he has nearly doubled the list of manuscripts of the Greek Testament named by Griesbach and his predecessors. To the 674 MSS which had been collated or referred to by others, Scholz has added no less than 607, which he enjoys the honor of first making known to the world. It must not, however, be supposed that any large portion of them has been carefully examined by this indefatigable editor; we ought rather to wonder that a private individual could do so much, than to murmur at the slight and cursory manner in which the great bulk of his documents has been inspected. The following table will convey some notion both of what Scholz has effected in this matter, and of what he has been compelled to leave undone.

Scholz's new MSS.	Collated entire.	The greater part.	In select places.	Cursorily.	Merely named.	Total.
MSS of the Gospels	10	11	159	7	20	207
Evangelistaria	1	5	27	29	61	123
MSS of the Acts and Cath. Epp.	4	14	28	10	27	83
MSS of the Pauline Epp.	4	2	11	66	32	115
MSS of the Apocalypse	1	3	1	20	13	38
Lectionaria	2	1	11	15	12	41
Totals	22	36	237	147	165	607

I cannot help observing that Scholz's collation of select passages is of a very hasty and superficial character, being sometimes limited to two or three chapters, and seldom extending beyond twenty. He does not seem to have been guided in his choice of manuscripts for closer examination by the relative value of the documents themselves, so much as by the pressure of external circumstances. His chief attention appears to have been devoted to the manuscripts in the libraries of Paris and the North of Italy; those which he inspected least carefully are deposited in Palestine and—England. His neglect of the manuscripts of our own country, however mortifying (six MSS in the British Museum, Evan. 444-49, are collated only in the 5th chapter of St. Mark) I do not so much regret. The time cannot be far distant when we shall be ashamed to depend on foreigners for our acquaintance with a vast store of our own intellectual wealth, much of which has lain untouched since the days of Mill. Respecting the Oriental Manuscripts, which naturally excite our ardent curiosity, Scholz affords us less information than would be contained in a good catalogue. Nor can we discover any intelligible plan in the selection of his materials, with reference to their *subject-matter*. The number of the extant manuscripts of the Gospels is very great (about 745 in all); those of the Apocalypse are few (103) and inaccurate: no book either of the Old or New Testament so urgently needs the care of a critical editor. Yet Scholz contents himself with a cursory view of all his new manuscripts of the Apocalypse except four, only one of which has been collated throughout. Nor will the *quality* of his documents aid us in accounting for the course he has pursued. It will hereafter be seen that he was specially bound by the hypothesis he had adopted, to give a distinct explanation of the nature of the later or cursive Alexandrine manuscripts; particularly of those which were designed for the public services of the Church. Yet monuments of this kind, the very existence of which is barely reconcileable with his theory of recensions (e.g. Ev. 354; Evangst. 71; Lect. 22; 46), he passes by with as little scruple as the crowd of Constantinopolitan codices, in which he scarcely meets with a single variation from the received text once in a chapter! (Proleg. N. T. § 55). On the whole, therefore, we cannot but conclude, that though Pr. Scholz is entitled to our thanks for having opened so many veins of precious ore, he has in a great measure left the task of working them to other hands. In truth, so far is his edition from realising his confident boast " omnibus fere, qui adhuc supersunt, testibus exploratis, *eorumque lectionibus diligenter conquisitis* " (Præf. N. T. p. 2), that it has rendered further investigation on a large scale more indispensable than ever.*

From Scholz's performances as a collator of manuscripts I proceed to consider his success as the author of a new scheme for their classification. Like Archbp. Laurence, he can trace no such fundamental difference between the Egyptian and the Western documents, as to justify his arranging them in distinct classes. Hence *his* Alexandrine family comprehends the Latin versions, and the Greek manuscripts which resemble them, as well as the authorities named Alexandrine by Griesbach. He moreover contends that the Constantinopolitan or common text (which is not far removed from our printed textus receptus),

---

* When Scholz states (Proleg. § 37) that he has collated more than 100 MSS entire, and 200 in not less than twenty chapters each; he must be understood to include his re-collation of many manuscripts used by his predecessors: a very valuable portion of his labors.

approaches much nearer to the sacred autographs than does the text of Alexandria: both on account of the internal excellency of its readings, and because it has been the public and authorised edition of the Greek Church, from the earliest ages to the present day. On a subject of so great doubt and intricacy, it would ill become me to pronounce a positive judgment; but if I may venture to express an opinion formed after long and repeated consideration, I believe that in its main features Scholz's theory is correct. The distinction between the Alexandrian and Byzantine texts is too broadly marked to be controverted; and no hypothesis which has yet been suggested is so simple as Scholz's, or so satisfactorily explains the leading phenomena of the case. At the same time I am unwilling to commit myself to the reception of all his details; and his historical demonstration of the truth of his system (Proleg. N. T. cap. i—iv; ix) is likely to carry conviction to few, who really know what historical demonstration means. The chief objection to his whole scheme (as I hinted above) is the existence of a few late codices of the Alexandrine recension, furnished with liturgical tables and directions, as if designed for the services of the Church: whereas we have no reason to believe that the Egyptian text was ever used for this purpose within the Patriarchate of Constantinople. It is of course very easy to say that such manuscripts were transcribed merely as curious relics, and not for actual use (Horne's Introduction, Vol. II, pt. i, p. 60), but till we are possessed of more information respecting them than Scholz has afforded us, we shall scarcely acquiesce in this mode of evading the difficulty. At all events, one thing is clear. If we consult the monuments of the Byzantine class, we find their testimony regarding the sacred text uniform and consistent; exhibiting no greater degree of variation than is sufficient to establish the independence of the several sources whence it is derived. Whereas the Alexandrine manuscripts and versions, on the contrary, abound in the most serious discrepancies; many of them are full of interpolations, omissions, and critical corrections; so that they often agree as little with each other, as with their adversaries of the rival family. I assent, therefore, to Scholz's conclusion (Proleg. § 58), " nihil ex textu illo, quem refert classis Constantinopolitanorum codicum, demendum aut mutandum, nisi quod falsum aut improbabile esse apparet." And this falseness or improbability can spring only from considerations of internal evidence.

But it is chiefly on the point of internal evidence that Scholz's edition is a decided failure. Although he is so far from undervaluing its importance, that he alleges it in favor of his own system (Proleg. § 55), yet he seems quite unable to apply it, even in cases where it is most necessary to be thrown into the scale. Few other critics would have introduced into the text the anomalous form ἀπεκατεστάθη (Matth. xii, 13),* and that too chiefly on Alexandrine authority, after it had been rejected on account of its inherent improbability† by Griesbach, who professes

---

* Scholz's text actually contains the word ἀποκατεστάθη, but if we look to the inner margin, this appears to be a misprint. Other examples of scandalous inaccuracy in the typography of Scholz's volume will be found in the Introduction to Bagster's English Hexapla, p. 163.

† ἀντεπαριτάξατο however is found in several manuscripts of Chrysostom, Hom. in Matthæum. II. p. 20, where see Mr. Field's note. I recollect no other examples of such a form.

to make that family his standard. Again, in Matth. xi, 8 Scholz's reading βασιλείων is so very inferior in sense to βασιλέων, which is given by the received text and by Griesbach, and so much resembles a marginal gloss, that its Byzantine advocates, however numerous, ought in this case to be disregarded. In ch. x, 8 of the same Gospel, there is some variation in the MSS as to the order of the two clauses λεπροὺς καθαρίζετε, νεκροὺς ἐγείρετε; and Griesbach, in compliance with his usual Egyptian guides, places the raising of the dead before the cleansing of the lepers. Scholz solves the difficulty by omitting νεκροὺς ἐγείρετε altogether, on evidence which I will not call weak (for numerically it is far from being so), but certainly insufficient in a passage of so great importance. How much more wisely would he have acted, had he borne in mind the observations of Vater (himself no warm friend of the textus receptus); " omissio oriri potuisset oculis scribarum ad simile λεπροὺς delapsis; *vel ex dubitatione de hac facultate Apostolis concessâ;* saepiusque ex propositionibus ejusmodi accumulatis una alterave a scribis omissa reperiretur." I may here remark, that Vater's practice of compressing in a few words all that can be said concerning the internal evidence, stamps a value on his edition of the New Testament (Halle, 1824) which it would not otherwise possess.

The foregoing instances have been designedly taken from three consecutive chapters of St. Matthew's Gospel, and the reader will perceive from them that Scholz, after his own fashion, makes almost as great havock with the received text, as the redoubtable Griesbach himself. A large list of passages might also be drawn up, wherein Scholz has followed Griesbach's example in tampering with the sacred original,

Introduction. 23

in a manner which no strictures of mine can adequately condemn. The Lord's Prayer seems to be the special object of their attacks. They agree in expunging the doxology in Matth. vi, 13, on grounds which (as I hope to shew in the sequel) are miserably insufficient; and on evidence which Scholz, at least, might have remembered is exclusively Alexandrine. And as if this were too little, they unite in rejecting the last petition ἀλλὰ ῥῦσαι ἡμᾶς ἀπὸ τοῦ πονηροῦ in Luke xi, 4, on the authority of the Latin Vulgate, and the manuscripts most suspected of Latinising; but mainly I suppose on the presumption that the clause in question was interpolated from St. Matthew.

After these slight specimens, which might be multiplied a hundred-fold, I may be allowed to express my regret that Scholz's edition should have been received in England with a degree of consideration to which it has slender claims, and which was never accorded to it at home. I freely admit the value of this critic's exertions as a collator of manuscripts; I admire his diligence, and venerate his zeal. His theory of recensions I conceive to approximate very near to the truth. But he seems disqualified by a lack of judgment for the delicate task of selecting from the mass of discordant readings the genuine text of Holy Scripture.

Lachmann's N. T. Græc.-Lat. The first edition of Lachmann's New Testament, 12mo, 1831, attracted much notice throughout Germany. In the Preface to his enlarged edition (8vo, Tom. i, 1842) he inveighs against the critics who reject his theory in a tone so bitter and arrogant, that however it may remind us of the controversial licence of by-gone times, it is little creditable to his character as a scholar and a

Christian.* Whether true or false, it must be confessed that Lachmann's scheme of recensions is perfectly novel. Its two main features are a total disregard of internal evidence (concerning which I shall speak presently), and the absolute rejection of all manuscripts, versions and Fathers, of a lower date than the fourth century. For what reason this particular epoch should be assigned, beyond which all authorities are to be treated as worthless, Lachmann has not troubled himself to explain; but so rigorously does he act upon this arbitrary rule, that the evidence of Chrysostom, the prince of the Greek Fathers, is excluded from his work, " ne ad quintum sæculum descenderemus" (Præf. p. xxi); because forsooth, though he flourished in the fourth century, he happened to die in the eighth year of the fifth.

The consequences of this strange restriction may soon be told. Of the 745 manuscripts of the Gospels, or of portions of them, known to preceding critics, Lachmann retains but *seven:* the Alexandrine

---

* His periodical reviewers, three in number, are courteously compared to the three Phorcides of Æschyl. Prom. 795; and throughout a Preface of 44 pages he wears out this sorry witticism, ringing the changes on the spite, and impudence, and folly of the hags (Γιææ). It might almost be said that Lachmann speaks well of no one. Scholz he does not condescend to name. The judicious Vater he termed " homo levissimus." Tischendorf's New Testament is " tota peccatum." Fritzche, the excellent commentator on the Gospels, is a fourth Græa. But the most amusing case of all is Dr. Barrett's, who was guilty of editing the facsimile of the Dublin palimpsest of St. Matthew (Z of Scholz). After duly thanking the *engraver* for his workmanlike skill, Lachmann kindly adds, " Johannem Barrettum, qui Dublini edidit anno 1801, non laudo; hominem hujus artis, ultra quam credi potest, imperitum."

MS (A of Wetstein); the Vatican (B); the Codex Ephremi (C); the Dublin uncial palimpsest of St. Matthew (Z); the Wolfenbuttel fragments published by Knittel (P; Q); and the Borgian fragment of St. John (T). The readings of two of the most important out of the seven were very imperfectly known to Lachmann. Angelo Mai's long-promised facsimile of the Codex B has not yet appeared; and Tischendorf's excellent edition of the Codex C not being published in time, Lachmann was compelled to use Wetstein's inaccurate collation of that document. To the preceding list we ought perhaps to add the Cambridge MS, or Codex Bezæ (D), whose testimony he admits for certain purposes (Præf. pp. xxv; xxxvii), although it is posterior to the fourth century; as indeed we may reasonably suspect are most of the other seven.

Very similar is the effect of his system on the versions of the New Testament. The Sahidic indeed, he quietly observes, may possibly be of service to those who understand that language; but why should *he* learn Syriac, when the most faithful and antient manuscripts of the Peshito are still uncollated (Præf. p. xxiv)? Having thus disposed of the two great Eastern versions, nothing remains but the old Latin translations; upon which, however, he has bestowed such diligent care, as entitles him to the gratitude of the Biblical student. Following for once the example of the early editors, he annexes to the Greek original Jerome's Latin Vulgate; and that too not the common authorised text of the Romish Church, but one which he has formed for himself, chiefly by the aid of two antient manuscripts of that version. To the Italic, or as he would call it, the Afric translation,* he devotes a large share of his attention; anxiously collecting its fragments from such of the older manuscripts as, in his judgment, present it in an unadulterated state; as well as from the Scriptural quotations found in Irenæus, Cyprian, Lucifer of Cagliari, and Hilary of Poictiers, the only Latin authors whose testimony he deems trustworthy on this point. Of the Greek Fathers he cites Origen alone; and by means of this slender apparatus of critical materials, Lachmann hopes to supersede the labors of all his predecessors, and to establish on a firm foundation a pure and settled text of the Greek Testament.

Whence then, it may well be asked, this deliberate rejection of the great mass of authorities? Whence this voluntary choice of poverty, when we might freely take possession of a rich harvest, which others have toiled to gather in? " Ante omnia," Lachmann replies, " antiquissimorum rationem habebimus; fine certo constituto recentiores, item leves et corruptos recusabimus." (Præf. p. vi). Let us endeavor therefore to discover the causes, why the oldest manuscripts should *necessarily* be the best, while the more recent are to be despised as " corrupt and of little consequence." Now Lachmann would perhaps be slow to assert that the more recent Byzantine documents are but bad copies of the Alexandrian, Vatican or Paris MSS; yet no supposition short of this will

---

* This is not the place to investigate the truth of Dr. Wiseman's conjecture, which Lachmann implicitly adopts, that the first Latin version was made in Africa; and that, being subsequently corrupted in Italy by various hands from Greek manuscripts newly imported from the East, the interpolated copies received the name of *Italic*, and are those alluded to by Augustin in the celebrated passage De Doctrin. Christ. II, 22.

answer the purpose of his argument. The remark is so trite that one is tired of repeating it, that many codices of the ninth or tenth century were probably transcribed from others of a more early date than any which now exist: and the incessant wear of the uncial Constantinopolitan manuscripts in the public services of the Church will abundantly account for their general disappearance at present (Scholz, Proleg. N. T. § 56). We all know the reverential, and almost superstitious care with which their Synagogue rolls are preserved by the Jews; yet scarcely one of them has been written so long as a thousand years. The Alexandrine copies, on the contrary, having fallen into disuse at the æra of the Mohammedan conquests in Egypt and Northern Africa, have been buried since that time in the recesses of monastic libraries, until they were disinterred on the revival of learning, only to be prized as valuable relics, and jealously guarded by their fortunate possessors.

Again it may be observed, that Lachmann claims for his best manuscripts no higher antiquity than the fourth century. But we have the strongest proof the nature of the case will admit, that no important change has taken place in the received text, since the rise of the Arian heresy, and the final recognition of Christianity by the Roman Emperors. The deep anxiety to procure correct copies of Holy Scripture (see Euseb. de Vit. Constant. iv, 36, 37), and the perpetual watchfulness of rival parties, seem to preclude the possibility of extensive alteration from the fourth century downwards. It was far otherwise in the earlier history of the Church; when its scattered branches were harassed by persecution, and maintained no regular intercourse with each other. During the cruel reign of Diocletian more especially, when fresh copies of the New Testament must often have been produced in haste, to supply the places of those destroyed by the enemies of our Faith; when such manuscripts were secretly circulating among persons whose lives stood in jeopardy every hour: it is easy to see that many errors may have imperceptibly crept into the sacred text, which the well-meant criticism of subsequent correctors would tend only to aggravate and confirm.

In what way, then, does Lachmann meet the obvious suggestion that our present cursive manuscripts are but the representatives of venerable documents, long since lost? He grants that it might possibly be true, but denies that in fact it is so. " Since the oldest manuscripts still extant," he says, " wonderfully agree with the citations of the most antient writers; why should we think that Irenæus and Origen used more corrupt copies than Erasmus or the Complutensian editors?" (Præf. p. vii). With Lachmann's last statement I cheerfully join issue. We need only refer once more to Archbp. Laurence's " Remarks" (see above, p. 15) to prove that Origen at all events does not agree with his favorite authorities against the common Byzantine text. With respect to Irenæus, if Lachmann alludes to the small portion of his work yet preserved in Greek, it would well become him to demonstrate what he so readily assumes. But if (as is more probable), he refers to the old Latin version of that Father, I answer, that the semibarbarous renderings of an unknown translator may very properly be applied (as Lachmann often does apply them) to the correction of the Italic; but can lend us no certain aid in determining the readings of the Greek Testament adopted by Irenæus.

The exclusion of internal evidence, which is another peculiarity of Lachmann's system, arises partly from his misapprehension of the duties of an editor, and partly from a reverential fear lest his own fanciful opinions should be obtruded in the room of the oracles of God. He seems to imagine (Præf. pp. v, xxxiii) that the province of a reviser of the text of Scripture (" recensere "), should be kept quite separate from that of a corrector (" emendare "). The former he would limit to a bare representation of the readings of manuscripts and versions, while he permits the latter to exercise a critical judgment upon them. It will probably be thought that this distinction is too nice to be reduced to practice. The application of internal reasons, *when external authorities are almost evenly balanced*, is surely very far removed from wanton conjecture. At the same time we cannot be too much on our guard against substituting ingenious speculation in the place of positive testimony, and treating as a co-ordinate power what is useful only in the character of a subject-ally.

Where the foundations are unsound it is fruitless to dwell too minutely on the superstructure; yet it ought not to be concealed, that Lachmann develops his false principles with rare acuteness and logical skill. The few authorities he admits are marshalled in two families; the Eastern, comprehending nearly all the uncial manuscripts; and the Western, which is composed chiefly of the Latin versions, supported in the Gospels and Acts by the Codex Bezæ. These classes respectively correspond with Griesbach's Alexandrine and Occidental recensions; his Byzantine documents being rejected by Lachmann in one promiscuous mass. This editor has also constructed a graduated scale, containing six degrees of probability, in some one of which a place is assigned to each various reading, according as it is supported by the witnesses of one or both families, wholly or in part. On a general view it will perhaps appear that Lachmann's text is somewhat preferable to Griesbach's; but a list of variations from the textus receptus, covering 43 pages of his first edition, will shew the formidable effects of his daring and mistaken theory.

Tischendorf's N. T. The researches of Scholz have done much towards removing the obloquy and undeserved contempt which had been cast on the received text by critics of the last century. A desperate effort has recently been made by Tischendorf (Nov. Test. Lips. 1841) to retrieve the credit of Griesbach's theory, or at least to vindicate the principal changes which he introduced into the text of Scripture (e. g. Matth. vi, 13; John vii, 8; Acts xx, 28; 1 Tim. iii, 16). His own sentiments on the subject of recensions seem to be the following (Proleg. N. T. p. 49). The great bulk of various readings in the New Testament arise from accident and the errors of copyists. If a formal revision of manuscripts ever took place (which he will not undertake to deny), we are so totally ignorant of the country, and age, and plan of the editors, that it would be wrong to concede to it any practical influence in determining questions of criticism. Assuming the characteristic differences between Scholz's Alexandrine and Byzantine families as a simple fact, for which he does not pretend to account, he gives the decided preference to the Alexandrine readings, whenever some serious obstacle does not oppose their reception. For this preference he assigns one, and (so far as I can observe) but one reason,—the high antiquity of the manuscripts which follow that recension: an argument on the validity of which I have already delivered my opinion (see p. 28). Corrected therefore by nothing but the operation of a few sensible canons relating to internal evidence (Proleg. p. 50), Tischendorf's text is completely Alexandrian. A large portion of his Prolegomena is aimed against Scholz, whom he criticises in a thoroughly hostile spirit; and accuses (I fear with some truth) of disgraceful negligence in the execution of his edition, even to repeating the typographical errors of Griesbach (Proleg. p. 52). Tischendorf's New Testament may be found useful by those who wish to possess, in a small compass, the latest information on the subject of various readings.* As an original work its value is very questionable.

General result of the preceding review. My design in the following pages limits me to the examination of such various readings of the original, as in translation affect the sense of the passage in which they stand. The deviations of our English version from the textus receptus I shall never intentionally leave unnoticed. In other cases, I by no means purpose to confine my observations to those passages, in which I acquiesce in the propriety of a change in the Greek. So many important places in the New Testament have been rashly mangled by the German editors, that I shall only be discharging a plain duty in protesting against their innovations, and in stating my reasons, as briefly and distinctly as I may, for abiding by the readings of the common text.

The leading principles by which my criticisms are directed may readily be gathered from the foregoing

---

* He is the first to apply the St. Gall MS (Δ of Scholz) to the criticism of the Gospels.

remarks. I would adhere as much as possible to the text of the editions of Stephens, Beza and the Elzevirs; not indeed because it is the received text (as Lachmann so unfairly insinuates); but because I believe it to bear, on the whole, a close resemblance to the best manuscripts, which have been used by the Greek Church from the earliest ages. The schemes both of Griesbach and of Lachmann I feel bound to reject, since their direct tendency is to overthrow the testimony of the vast majority of our critical authorities, on grounds too precarious to admit of satisfactory defence. By conceding some weight to internal evidence, and by following out Scholz's hypothesis more consistently than he has done for himself, we may hope to purge the received text of its grosser corruptions, and to approach more nearly to the Apostolic autographs than any of the illustrious scholars whose attempts have passed under our notice. Those who best know the difficulties of my task, will be the most disposed to allow my claim on their candor and indulgence.

II. We now come to our second general head, comprehending errors of interpretation, which arise from mistaking the sense of the original Greek. Of this class there are several varieties, which may be distributed as follows:

(II, a.) When the inaccuracy consists in the mistranslation of a single Greek word. This is the Lexicographical branch of our subject, and has been assiduously cultivated by some of the best Biblical critics on the continent: Fischer, Schleusner, Tittmann and Wahl being the great names in this department of literature. Errors may arise in the rendering of single words in several ways. Either the sense of the word may be totally mistaken, as

Introduction.

πυγμῇ in the *text* of Mark vii, 3 (one of the marginal interpretations is probably correct); ἐνταφιασμός, Mark xiv, 8; ἀπογράφεσθαι, Luke ii, 1; πωροῦν, 2 Cor. iii, 14; and perhaps also φαιλόνης, 2 Tim iv, 13. This source of error is happily very rare in our version. Or a transitive verb may be wrongly used intransitively, as σκανδαλίζειν, Matth. v, 29 (where the margin is right); κατοπτρίζεσθαι, 2 Cor. iii, 18. Or a word is rendered in its ordinary sense, where the context requires a less usual one to be adopted; as πίστις, Rom. xiv, 23; χάρις, 2 Cor. viii, 6; 19 (it is right in the margin of both verses, and in the text of v. 4); ὑπόστασις, Hebr. xi, 1 (where again see the margin). This is probably the case also with νεανίσκοι, Mark xiv, 51; ἤκουσαν, Acts xxii, 9; καταχρᾶσθαι, 1 Cor. vii, 31. Or the strict literal sense may be brought out more fully than the sacred penman seems to intend, as συκοφαντεῖν, Luke iii, 14; xix, 8. In like manner, diminutives are sometimes expressed as such in our version, when it is by no means certain that the writer designed them to convey a notion different from that of the word from which they are derived. Thus for example, Peter is said by all the Evangelists to have cut off the ὠτίον of the high priest's servant, and some commentators have supposed that only a part of the ear is here meant; whereas St. Luke, in speaking of the very same act in the preceding verse (ch. xxii, 50), uses the word οὖς instead of the diminutive ὠτίον.* So again, St. Matthew (ch. xv, 36) calls the same fishes ἰχθύας, which in v. 34 he had named ἰχθύδια. The word

---

* And the best Classics constantly use diminutives, in speaking of parts of the body: e. g. ὀμμάτια, ῥινία, &c. See Lobeck's note on Phrynichus, p. 211.

θυγάτριον is twice used by St. Mark (v, 23; vii, 25); yet since in the former case it is applied to a damsel of twelve years old, it must like κοράσιον (Mark v, 42) be rather a term of endearment than a diminutive in its proper sense. Παιδίον also frequently occurs in the New Testament, being used nine times in the second chapter of St. Matthew with reference to our Saviour: yet it is remarkable that neither the Syriac, Vulgate, nor English versions before the Bishops' Bible express the diminutive. For further information on this point I may refer to Campbell (Prel. Dissert. xii, 1, 19); whose judicious observations nearly exhaust the subject.

It only remains to say a few words respecting the force of prepositions when compounded with verbs. I must here observe that Schleusner's practice in this matter seems neither just nor rational. He first enquires for what Hebrew word a particular Greek compound verb is used in the Septuagint, or other Greek version of the Old Testament. If the same Hebrew word be rendered in another passage in these versions by the corresponding simple Greek verb, he concludes at once that in Hellenistic writers the simple and compound verbs in question are identical in signification. Thus, because Aquila in Psalm cxxx, 5 renders the Hiphil conjugation of יָחַל by καραδοκεῖν, but in Psalm xxxvii, 7 the Hithpahel conjugation by ἀποκαραδοκεῖν, he infers after Fischer " substantivo ἀποκαραδοκία (Rom. viii, 19; Phil. i, 20) non ampliorem notionem subjiciendam esse, quam simplici καραδοκία;" although Chrysostom expressly paraphrases the word by ἡ μεγάλη καὶ ἐπιτεταμένη προσδοκία; and Tittmann, in his beautiful fragment on the Synonyms of the New Testament (Vol. I. p. 187 English translation), has since proved the in-

Introduction.

tensive force of ἀπὸ in composition from such instances as ἀπεκδέχεσθαι in Rom. viii, 19, and ἀποκαταλλάσσειν Eph. ii, 16. Now Schleusner's process is open to this manifest objection; that even supposing the style of the writers of the New Testament to resemble that of the Alexandrian and later versions of the Old so closely, that they all uniformly use the same word, in precisely the same sense (an assumption which may well be doubted); yet the principle of interpretation here described would compel us to tie down *original* authors in a varied and copious language like the Greek, to the meagre vocabulary of the Hebrew. But if we turn from the Hellenistic translators to the Greek classics, we find an exquisite array of compound verbs, scattered in lavish profusion over every page, but never (I am speaking of the best writers) without their apt and proper meaning; gently and concisely insinuating some limitation or collateral idea, which, though not absolutely essential to the sense, gives completeness to the image which is preserved to the mind of an intelligent reader. No one who has imbibed the spirit of Thucydides, or Plato, or the Attic orators, will be soon persuaded that the Greek prepositions in composition are idle and superfluous prefixes; though he must often despair of expressing them in a modern language without straining the sense by giving undue prominence to the incidental and subordinate notions which they convey. The rule I have proposed to myself on this point is the following. Whenever I conceive that the writer's meaning is rendered obscure or imperfect by neglecting the force of the preposition, I have invariably suggested its adoption, even where it may produce a degree of awkward circumlocution (e. g. Matth. xvi, 22; Mark iii, 2; Luke viii, 40; Hebr. xii, 2). But when, on the contrary, (as in the case of ἀπέρχεσθαι, ἀποκρύπτειν, ἀποβλέπειν and many other verbs of frequent occurrence), the preposition is manifestly a dispensable accessory, I have thought that the *spirit* of the original is best preserved, by wholly suppressing the particle in translation.

(II, b.) The next sub-division of my second general head treats of inaccuracies in the grammatical construction of one or more words in the same clause. On this important and comprehensive branch of the subject I wish to make a few preliminary observations relating to the article, and to the tenses of the verbs. It is obvious that the great mass of errors of this description are too miscellaneous in their character to admit of more minute classification.

On the subject of the Greek article I must profess myself a disciple of Bishop Middleton, whose work has taught us more concerning the use of this important little word, than former scholars had thought it possible to attain. His treatise is a perfect model of close argument and accurate learning, applied to the support of a most ingenious and elaborate hypothesis. The reader is probably aware that Middleton does not agree with the majority of grammarians in considering the nature of the Greek article demonstrative, but pronounces it to be the *prepositive* relative pronoun (the common relative ὅς being retrospective), which is anticipative, and whose relation to its adjunct (noun &c.) is supposed to be more or less obscure. It is, in fact, the subject of a proposition, whereof the adjunct is predicate, and the participle ὤν the copula. Thus the expression ὁ ποιμήν " the shepherd" would be called by Middleton elliptical, the full form being ὁ [ὤν] ποιμήν, " he-who [is] shepherd." Now although this definition is far less simple than that of Matthiæ and the great body of critics, and though the direct evidence urged in its behalf may be slight and precarious, it is difficult to study the beautiful process of analytical reasoning by which its author deduces from it the principal phænomena of the use of the article, without feeling a growing conviction, that the theory which satisfactorily accounts for so large a body of philological facts cannot be entirely false.* Still, the peculiar excellence of Bp. Middleton's volume arises from the circumstance, that its value as a practical guide to the interpretation of the article is nearly independent of the correctness of his hypothesis. We may, if we please, entirely reject his speculations, without impairing, to any considerable extent, the usefulness of his grammatical canons. If subsequent researches have taught us that he sometimes makes too little allowance for the varieties of idiom or the license of spoken language, and has erred in exacting an universal observance of rules which are only *generally* true; it would be unjust to forget that this has ever been the besetting fault of the most eminent scholars; a fault from which Dawes and Elmsley, nay even Porson himself, were by no means free. Above all we are bound to bear in mind the Bishop's acute distinction, that while examples of the insertion of the article in a manner irreconcilable to his principles would constitute a serious objection to the validity of his theory, or if numerous must overthrow it; instances of its omission, where it might justly be

---

* The examples of a purely demonstrative sense of the article given by Mr. Green (Grammar of the New Testament Dialect, p. 136) are all *capable* of another solution. But I am not at all inclined to dogmatise on the subject.

looked for, ought to produce no such effect: since the natural tendency both of poetry and common discourse is to abridge the fuller forms of expression which are required in written and periodic prose, *where no ambiguity results from such abridgement.* No one will doubt the accuracy of his distinction, who, with a view to this enquiry, will compare a few pages of the Greek Tragedians with a short passage from Xenophon or Isocrates. The prose writer will probably be found to repeat the article five times, where the poet employs it once. Yet it is obvious that if this variation in usage be a real obstacle to the reception of Bp. Middleton's system, it must prove equally fatal to every other hypothesis that may at any time be devised.

I have endeavoured, therefore, in the course of my review, to give its full force to every article contained in the sacred text, whenever it can be expressed in English. On this point, as is well known, our translators have not exercised their usual care. Instances abound in which the English indefinite article is wrongly substituted for the definite; sometimes to the injury of the sense (1 Cor. v, 9; Hebr. ix, 1); but more frequently to the suppression of some minute circumstance, or delicate intimation, which tends to give an air of freshness and reality to the original (Matth. xiii, 2; xvii, 24; Luke xii, 54; John iii, 10; v. 35; Acts xvii, 1; 2 Cor. xii. 18). In several cases I have been compelled to dissent from the views of Bp. Middleton; with the greater confidence whenever I had the advantage of treading in the steps of Professor Scholefield or Mr. Green: but they I believe would cheerfully admit that nearly all they know on the subject is derived from our common master's " Doctrine of the Greek Article."

For myself I must confess that I have studied his work earnestly and repeatedly with ever-increasing admiration. So subtle yet so exact were his habits of thought; so deep and comprehensive his learning; with so much singleness of purpose did he devote his best powers to the defence and elucidation of God's Holy Word, that I cannot but regard Bp. Middleton as one of the brightest ornaments of his age, and of the Church in whose service he sank into a premature grave. Yet this is the man of whom Moses Stuart of Andover, in a tract which he is pleased to call " Hints and Cautions respecting the Greek Article," thus modestly expresses himself: "I have read his book until I despair of getting to the light; so often does he deal in the claro-obscure, and so often utters unguarded assertions, or at least such as are incapable of solid defence." Those who happen to be acquainted with any of Mr. Stuart's publications, will readily conjecture to whose account the blame of this claro-obscurity should be placed.*

Before we quit the subject of the Greek article, it is proper to notice an important theological discus-

---

* To name but one instance of this gentleman's fitness for compiling Grammars of the New Testament Dialect, will it be credited that he is perplexed at the very common construction of $\pi\alpha\acute{\upsilon}o\mu\alpha\iota$ with a participle? At least the following in his *whole* note on Hebr. x, 2. "'Επεὶ οὐκ ἂν ἐπαύσαντο προσφερόμεναι; 'for otherwise, i. e. if the sacrifices could have perfected those who presented them, would not the offerings have ceased?' To προσφερόμεναι most critics subjoin εἶναι understood [it would be worth while to know what critics, since the days of poor Lambert Bos], which would be equivalent to the infinite προσφέρεσθαι, rendering the phrase thus 'They (i. e. the sacrifices) had ceased to be offered.' The sense of the phrase, thus explained, is the same as I have given to it. But προσφερόμεναι (θυσίαι) ἐπαύσαντο seems to me more facile than the other construction." *Facile* with a witness!

sion to which its use in the New Testament has given occasion. In the year 1798 the excellent Granville Sharp first published his " Remarks on the uses of the Definitive Article in the New Testament, containing many new proofs of the Divinity of Christ, from passages which are wrongly translated in the common English." The title of this work sufficiently shews its design; and though Socinian writers chose to treat his theory as a mere idle dispute about words and grammatical niceties, it soon received the attention it deserved from sound and judicious scholars. Dr. Wordsworth, the late eminent Master of Trinity College, Cambridge, incontestably proved that *some* of the passages brought forward by Sharp were understood by the Greek Fathers in the very sense which he had attached to them (Wordsworth's Six Letters to Sharp, 1802). The whole question was soon afterwards re-examined by Bp. Middleton, who has so firmly established Sharp's leading principle, and so clearly and concisely pointed out its limitations and exceptions (Doctrine of the Greek Article, pp. 56—70, Rose's edition), that every objection which has since been alleged, either to the general theory, or to its application in the New Testament, may be removed at once on referring to the Bishop's work, where it will be found to have been fore-seen, and answered by anticipation.

Mr. Sharp's rule, then, (though in truth it was known to many divines long before the publication of his " Remarks"), is simply the following :—When two *personal* nouns of the same case are connected by a copulative conjunction, if both have the definitive article, they relate to different persons; if only the former has the article, they relate to the same person. Thus, for instance, we read in James iii, 9 εὐλογοῦμεν τὸν Θεὸν καὶ Πατέρα, which our Authorised version renders "We bless God, even the Father;" but which would be more accurately translated "We bless God the Father." Now in this passage, since both Θεὸν "God," and Πατέρα "Father" are personal nouns (or attributives, as Middleton terms them), and since the first Θεὸν has the definite article τὸν before it, while the second has not, it follows from Granville Sharp's rule, that they refer to one and the same Person; for if they related to different Persons, Πατέρα would be preceded by the article as well as Θεὸν. I have purposely chosen for our example a passage wherein no one ever doubted that the two nouns refer to the same Divine Person; but the reader must already see how important this principle becomes in such a case as Eph. v, 5 Βασιλείᾳ τοῦ Χριστοῦ καὶ Θεοῦ, whose *literal* rendering is "the kingdom of the Christ and God." Here the presence of the article before "Christ," and its absence before "God" amount (if Mr. Sharp's canon be correct) to an express and positive declaration on the part of St. Paul, that Christ and God are one and the same Being: a most weighty conformation of the doctrine maintained by the Church universal, respecting the godhead of our Lord Jesus Christ.

If we examine the renderings of such passages as these in our English Bible, we shall be led to conclude that its translators were not so much adverse to the grammatical rule here stated, as ignorant or forgetful of it. Confining ourselves for the present to those texts which do not involve an assertion of the Deity of Christ, we shall find that the very same form of expression in the Greek original is translated in the Authorised version with every possible variety of phrase. Thus in 1 Cor. xv, 24 τῷ Θεῷ καὶ Πατρὶ is rendered " To God, even the Father" (where even Tyndal has " to God the Father"): so also in Rom. xv, 6; 2 Cor. i, 3; James iii, 9. But in the following passages, besides some less notable variations, we read " God and the Father:"—2 Cor. xi, 31; Gal. i, 4; Eph. i, 3; v, 20; Col. i, 3; ii, 2; iii, 17; James i, 27; 1 Peter i, 3. From this inconsistency we may fairly infer, that if our translators were acquainted with the property of the Greek article so ably insisted on by Sharp and his followers, they at all events failed to perceive its direct bearing on the profoundest mysteries of our Faith.

The texts alleged by Mr. Sharp, as calculated, if rightly translated, to testify to the Divinity of our Saviour, are eight in number :—Acts xx, 28; Eph. v, 5; 2 Thess. i, 12; 1 Tim. v, 21; 2 Tim. iv, 1; Tit. ii, 13; 2 Pet. i, 1; Jude v. 4; each of which will be carefully investigated in its proper place. The result, I think, will be found to be, that while later researches have thrown more or less of doubt on the propriety of applying his principle to five out of the eight texts; the canon has been confirmed with respect to the other three (Eph. v, 5; Tit. ii, 13; 2 Pet. i, 1) to as high a degree of probability as is attainable in questions of this nature.

I ought not, however, to suppress that Mr. Green in his Grammar of the New Testament Dialect, has not adopted the precise view of this matter which Middleton advocated. In the course of a valuable disquisition on the use of a single article with several words connected by conjunctions, after assigning to the first class those instances where the description involved in each separate word extends to the whole (which form of expression exactly coincides with that in Sharp's rule, when the attributives are personal nouns); he admits a second class, where each of the words, *which are generally, though not always incompatible*, is descriptive of only part of a subject (Grammar p. 208). But it is clear, that if compatible appellatives can *ever* be thus used with a single article before them, and yet be respectively descriptive of only parts of a subject, that however probable may be the theological deduction from Tit. ii, 13, such an inference is not grammatically necessary; and thus the whole superstructure which Sharp had raised upon this property of the article, falls at once to the ground. Now Bp. Middleton unequivocally denies that the second article is ever omitted in such instances as are contemplated in Mr. Green's second class, unless indeed the attributives be in their nature absolutely incompatible; since in this last case the perspicuity of the passage does not require the rule to be accurately observed (Middleton p. 67, 3rd edition). This is a strong assertion, and one which can be disproved only by the production of examples to contradict it; a course which Mr. Green has not thought it necessary to adopt. One part of the Bishop's statement is certainly capable of modification. It is adviseable to explain that the " absolute incompatibility" of the attributives, is often an incompatibility *not* inherent in their own nature, but rather arising from the context in which they stand. Thus in Æschin. c. Timarch. c. 2 we read τὰ μὲν τῶν δημοκρατουμένων σώματα καὶ τὴν πολίτειαν οἱ νόμοι σώζουσι, τὰ δὲ τῶν τυράννων καὶ ὀλιγαρχικῶν [these seem to be the orator's words] ἀπιστία, καὶ ἡ μετὰ τῶν ὅπλων φρουρά. Now there is nothing very incompatible, at least to modern notions, in the ideas of tyranny and oligarchy; but the omission of the second article in this place is permissible from the circumstance that Æschines had just before drawn a pointed distinction between them : ὁμολογοῦνται γὰρ τρεῖς εἶναι πολίτειαι παρὰ πᾶσιν ἀνθρώποις, τυραννὶς καὶ ὀλιγαρχία καὶ δημοκρατία. A similar explanation may be given to the passage cited from the opening of Aristotle's Rhetoric by Rose (Prelim. Observ. to Middleton, p. xxvii).

But whatever be determined on the point thus raised by Mr. Green, our version must at all events be corrected in texts of this description, since it inevitably suggests to the English reader that another article is prefixed to the second appellative in order to distinguish it the more carefully from the first. Whereas, on the contrary, the circumstance of only one article being employed indicates, if not personal identity, at the very least an intimate connection between the two appellatives.*

We come at length to the errors of our common translation with respect to the tenses of verbs. No two languages precisely agree in their mode of expressing the time of an action; and the Greek in particular is furnished with so extensive an ap-

---

* Now that we are speaking of the formula ὁ Θεὸς καὶ πατὴρ I may be allowed to correct a slight inaccuracy of Bp. Middleton. He says (Doctrine of Article, p. 366, 3rd edition) that this expression is frequently, *but not always*, rendered in the Peshito by " God the Father," without καί. If we may trust Schmidt's Concordance, the term occurs in the New Testament 21 times. In 19 of these I find no copula in the Peshito; of the two remaining cases, in James iii, 9 the Syriac reads Κύριον, and has therefore nothing to do with the question. The other case is Rev. i, 6: but this book is no part of the Peshito, but is of a late and inferior version. Hence it appears, that the practice of the Peshito is uniform on this point.

paratus for this purpose, that it is often hopeless to render its rich and varied forms into English or any modern tongue (encumbered as they are with the awkward system of auxiliary verbs,) without entirely losing the concise energy of the original. Under these circumstances, our wisest course would seem to be, not to press too closely those minute peculiarities of the Greek, which, however they may add to the perfect comprehension of the writer's spirit, are by no means essential to his sense: and on this principle the translators of our English Bible have for the most part acted. Yet there are cases in which the omission to render fully the exact force of the Greek tense, has produced obscurity in the version, or even destroyed the meaning of the sentence. In such cases it is manifestly better to be verbose than unintelligible, and we must not hesitate to sacrifice brevity to perspicuity. Thus I have attempted to express the full signification of the imperfect in Matth. iii, 14; Luke v, 6; 1 Cor. x, 4; xi, 30; the aorist has been rendered as a Latin pluperfect in Matth. xxviii, 17; as a present in 1 Cor. v, 9; 11; Philem. v. 19, &c. The full sense of the perfect has been given in Luke xiii, 2; and of the pluperfect in Luke xvi, 20. In every chapter of the historical books the inspired authors have perpetually used the present tense in the narrative of past events; but though such a practice lends vigour and animation to the style, I have not thought it necessary to bring the corresponding past tenses of the English New Testament into strict conformity with the original: nor, on the other hand, to propose a change in those rarer instances, in which the English present is used for the Greek past (Matth. xvii, 26) or future (Luke xxiii, 46). In the similar case of the Greek present being used to intimate the certainty or near approach of some future event (Matth. xxvii, 63; Luke xiii, 32; Acts i, 6; 2 Pet. iii, 11), the future of our English version will be left untouched. It would be injudicious to propose a multitude of trifling alterations, for the purpose of forcing upon one language the idioms of another.

(II, c.) The third and last species of error committed by our translators with respect to the interpretation of the Greek text, arises from a mistaken distribution of the several parts of the same sentence or paragraph. One or more words may be joined to the wrong clause, and thus a material change will be produced in the sense (Luke vi, 9; Rom. i, 9; 10; viii, 20; 1 Cor. vii, 29; 34; 1 Thess. i, 4). Or if the construction be a little involved, it may become doubtful where the concluding member of the sentence, technically called the apodosis, begins (Luke xiii, 25; Acts x, 37; 2 Cor. iii, 13; Eph. iii, 1—14): a species of difficulty by no means uncommon in the best Classics. Or, since in certain phrases the apodosis is entirely suppressed, as being readily supplied in the reader's mind (e. g. Homer. Il. A, 136; Luke xiii, 9), it may happen that our version avails itself of its licence too freely (Matth. xv, 6; Mark vii, 11; and perhaps 1 Tim, i. 4), and thus misrepresents the meaning of the whole context. Again, in some books of the New Testament, more especially in St. Paul's Epistles, it is not always easy to trace the precise connection of one clause or period with another. So frequently does the Apostle digress from his main subject, to dwell upon some incidental fact or doctrine remotely connected with his argument; and so abruptly does he sometimes return to the topics which he had abruptly quitted:

that on no point have commentators been more divided, than in marking the limits of his parentheses, and in arranging the punctuation of his sentences. I may refer the reader to Rom. v, 12—19; or to Gal. ii, 2—10, if he wishes to form an idea of the perplexities which beset us in this branch of our enquiry.

With regard to the general subject of the punctuation of Scripture, I cheerfully accord with the sentiments expressed by Bp. Middleton (on Matth. xvi, 13), who after Wolf condemns the liberty assumed by Grotius and others, of introducing the most arbitrary changes in the stops, provided only that the *words* of the text remain unaltered. Even were we to grant that no such points were employed by the writers of the New Testament themselves, still the system of punctuation which long usage has established, is not to be disturbed on slight grounds. It has existed from time immemorial, and is doubtless the arrangement which those whose native tongue was Greek, judged most suitable to the order of the words, and the exigency of the sense. Hence it is that I look with much suspicion on the innovations in punctuation which have been proposed by Griesbach, and more recently by Lachmann. Though there are cases in which their adoption may possibly be the least of antagonist difficulties (e. g. 1 Cor. vi, 4; Hebr. vii, 18, 19; x, 2; James iv, 5), yet it is a resource to which we should betake ourselves only in the last extremity.*

---

* " If I give a man the liberty of punctuating for me, I resign him much of interpretation." English version of N. T. by a " Layman" 1840. Preface, p. xi, see above p. 15 note.

Chapters, verses and paragraphs. Closely connected with the punctuation of the sacred text is its division into chapters and verses. On this subject our Translators received positive instructions from King James: " The division of the chapters to be altered either not at all, or as little as may be, if necessity so require." (Instruction v). And when we consider the endless confusion which even then must inevitably have ensued from any change in their arrangement, we cannot but think that the authors of our version exercised a sound discretion in retaining them as they found them. It is not however difficult to perceive that the present is far from being the best distribution of chapters that might have been made. Bp. Terrot (Ernesti's Institutes, English translation, Vol. ii, p. 21) observes that Acts v should commence at chapter iv, 32; and that 1 Cor. v, 1—5 should be appended to ch. iv. In like manner Campbell would join Matth. xv, 39 to ch. xvi; ch. xix, 30 to ch. xx; Mark v, 1; ix, 1, to chapters iv and viii respectively. We may also remark that the first clause of Acts viii, 1, belongs to ch. vii; that Acts xxi concludes with striking abruptness; that Luke xxi, 1—4 ought to form part of ch. xx, in the same manner as the parallel passage of St. Mark is arranged; that Col. iv, 1 should be a part of ch. iii; and several other instances of the same kind. But even were these defects of more consequence than they are, a revision of the chapter-divisions would be an intolerable evil, for which no prospective advantages could adequately compensate.

Respecting the verses still less need be said. This hasty and incorrect notation was first inserted in the Genevan English Testament of 1557 from Robert Stephen's Genevan Greek Testament of 1551; and the facilities which it affords for reference are so great and visible, that it never will or can be dispensed with. Its faults as a guide to the sense, are too glaring to escape the merest tiro in Biblical criticism; and the merest tiro may regard them with indifference, since no respectable edition of the Greek Testament will hereafter be published, in which the figures indicating the chapters and verses are not banished to the margin.*

Since the distribution of the text into chapters and verses is thus useless as a help to the interpretation of Scripture, it is much to be regretted that more pains were not bestowed by our translators on the marks which denote the commencement of paragraphs or sections; inasmuch as these might in some measure have supplied the deficiency. But not to insist on the discrepancies in this particular between various modern editions of the Bible (for Dr. Blayney's attempts to preserve uniformity on this point have signally failed); it is impossible, I think, to comprehend the principle on which our translators acted with respect to the paragraph marks. They are distributed so unequally over the several parts of the New Testament, being introduced in some places where they break the thread of the discourse (Matt. xxviii, 19; Luke xviii, 22; 1 Cor. xv, 42); and sometimes, though less frequently, neglected where they are absolutely requisite; that I am bound to recommend to the reader the sections of Bengel, Knappe, Vater, or Bishop Lloyd (Nov. Test. Oxon. 1830), in preference

---

* The chief design of Wynne's English version of the New Testament, London, 1764, is to get rid of the division by chapters and verses, the latter of which he calls "a wild and undigested invention." In other respects his attempt is not deserving of much regard.

to the careless and capricious arrangement in the first edition of King James's Bible.

III. The third general division of my subject relates to those errors of our Authorised version, which arise from blemishes in the language of the English Translation itself. This class of inaccuracies also may be divided into three varieties.

(III, a.) The version may be faulty from a want of uniformity in rendering the same Greek word. On this topic our Translators speak out boldly in their Preface to the Reader. "We have not tied ourselves to an uniformity of phrasing or to an identity of words, as some peradventure would wish that we had done, because they observe that some learned men somewhere [is Hugh Broughton here glanced at?] have been as exact as they could that way. Truly, that we might not vary if the word signified the same thing in both places (for there be some words that be not of the same sense everywhere), we were especially careful, and made a conscience according to our duty. But, that we should express the same notion in the same particular word; as for example, if we should translate the Hebrew or Greek word once by "purpose," never to call it "intent;" if one where "journeying," never "travelling;" if one where "think," never "purpose;" if one where "pain," never "ache;" if one where "joy," never "gladness," &c. thus to mince the matter, we thought to savour more of curiosity than wisdom, and that rather it would breed scorn in the Atheists, than profit to the godly reader. For is the kingdom of God become words and syllables? why should we be in bondage to them, if we may be free as commodiously?" Now had our excellent Translators been content to abide by the principles they have just laid down, no rational objection could have been alleged against them in this matter. It will at once be admitted that such a compulsory uniformity as they here describe would have given an appearance of constraint to their version, without being attended with the slightest benefit. Had they really been "especially careful" not "to vary from the sense of that which they had rendered before," every candid critic would freely have granted to them the use of as large a collection of synonymous words, as they might judge conducive to variety and neatness of style. Thus we do not complain that the same word $μετοικεσία$ is rendered in three different ways in the very first chapter of St. Matthew (vv. 11, 12, 17); or that $μαρτυρία$ is translated "witness" in John i, 7, and "record" in v. 19; or that the verb $μαρτυρεῖν$ is not uniformly represented in vv. 7, 8, 15, 32, 34, of the same chapter. Since the sense is not in the least obscured by this variation in the words, it would be captious and idle to found an objection upon it. The case is somewhat altered in another passage, in which $μαρτυρία$ and $μαρτυρεῖν$ perpetually recur. Within the limits of nine verses (John v, 31—39) is comprised a train of close and connected reasoning on the evidences of our Lord's mission. Here he successively appeals to the testimony borne in His behalf by John the Baptist, the burning and shining light (vv. 33—35); by His own miraculous works (v. 36); by His Father at His baptism (v. 37); and by the prophetic Scriptures (v. 39). In this last instance we cannot hesitate to declare, that the force and cogency of the argument is not a little hid from the plain English reader, by a needless change in the rendering of the above-mentioned leading words: for we have "testimony" in v. 34; "testify" in v. 39;

"witness" and "bear witness" in the other places. From these examples I trust that my distinction between important and unimportant deviations from uniformity will be sufficiently understood. The latter occur, under every possible aspect, in almost every chapter of our version (e. g. Mark v, 10, 12, 17, 18, 23; Rev. iv, 4; xix, 15, 21), and will be suffered to pass unnoticed. The former, which are comparatively unfrequent, shall be diligently corrected; and I believe it will be found that several texts may receive valuable elucidation, by the simple process of translating the same Greek by the same English word, throughout the whole passage (e. g. John xix, 28, 30; Rom. v, 2, 3; 16, 18; 1 Cor. ii, 14, 15; 2 Cor. vii, 4, 14).

In one particular, however, our Translators seem to have considered themselves bound to neglect uniformity, in consequence of the directions drawn up for their guidance by King James. "The names of the prophets and the inspired writers, with the other names in the text, to be kept as near as may be, as they stand recommended at present by customary use." (Instructions to Translators, Rule 2). From a too rigid interpretation of this rule springs one of the most obvious imperfections of the Authorized version, which I here mention once for all. The precise mode of representing Hebrew Proper Names in English is a matter of very little moment; but it *is* important that the same forms (whatever they may be which are adopted) should be employed in every part of the Bible alike. Now in the common translation, the persons who are called in the Old Testament Elijah, Elisha, Isaiah, Hosea, &c. are introduced to us in the New as Elias, Eliseus, Esaias, Osee (Rom. ix, 25), &c. to the certain embarrassment of the unlearned reader, and for no better reason, as it would seem, than that the Vulgate and the preceding English versions had used the same forms before our Translators. The substitution of "Jesus" for "Joshua" in Acts vii, 45; Heb. iv, 8; is a much more serious fault; and since it was avoided by most of the earlier Translators into English, it cannot be accounted for on the same grounds as the other errors which relate to Proper Names.

(III, b.) It is now time to speak of the grammatical errors which have been imputed to our Authorised version. The public attention was first directed to this point by Bp. Lowth, in his excellent "Introduction to English Grammar;" a little work which, however slightly its author thought of it, may be regarded as the text book on the subject of which it treats: for we might truly apply to this accomplished Prelate what Bentley said of Bp. Pearson, that "the very dust of his writings is gold." Yet I cannot wholly approve of Lowth's management with respect to the Vulgar Translation of the Bible. He seems to regard it as an indisputable fact, that "it is the best standard of our language" (p. 110); but, notwithstanding this high encomium, he so perpetually quotes its inaccuracies in his notes, as to convey a notion of its general character which is neither favorable nor true. The real state of the case appears to be, that it was not before the middle of the eighteenth century that our language was finally settled, and the more recondite laws of grammar became generally acknowledged and observed. What English writer is more artless or elegant than Addison? Whose style is so pure and perspicuous as Swift's? Yet the bare inspection of Bp. Lowth's notes may convince us, that they are guilty of solecisms no less numerous and gross, than those which have been laid to the charge of King James's Bible. In all our earlier writers grammatical accuracy is but *comparative;* and tried by this test, the vernacular translation has nothing to fear. That Lowth did not dispute the general principle here insisted on, is clear from what he says respecting the interchange of "shall" and "will," "should" and "would," which occurs in every page of our older classics: for he appeals to the Authorised version to prove that " the distinction between them was not observed formerly" (Eng. Gram. p. 79). Had he extended this liberal concession to some other usages of the more antient dialect, we should not have had to complain of his sweeping condemnation of the employment of an adjective in the adverbial sense, (2 Tim. iii, 12; Tit. ii, 12; Jude, v. 15), as " not agreeable to the genius of the English language" (p. 159): nor would several minute deviations from modern practice (such as " either" for " or," Luke vi, 42; xv, 8 &c. " either" for " each," John xix, 18; Rev. xxii, 2; " chiefest" for " chief," Mark x, 44 &c.) have been positively rejected as " improper" and incorrect. At the same time I am bound to express my deep obligation to this learned Prelate, who has detected several important errors in the language of our translators, which will be more fully noticed in their proper places (e. g. Matth. xvi, 13; xviii, 12; Luke v, 10; vi, 2; 4; John xvi, 13; Acts i, 15; xxii, 30; Hebr. v, 8; ix, 13).

I have endeavored to maintain on this point a course analogous to that which I pursued with regard to uniformity of expression. I have proposed no change on slight grounds, but have always retained the words of our version, unless I could give satisfactory reasons for disapproving of them. Much allowance has been made for the looseness of construction, in which the best writers of the seventeenth century freely indulged; the utmost possible latitude has been given to those variations in idiom which our language must necessarily have undergone during the lapse of two centuries. In a word, I trust that I shall be found to have ventured on no grammatical alteration, to which our revered translators might not have assented, had it been suggested in their own age (e. g. Matth. ii, 8; Luke xxiii, 32; Eph. iii, 9; 1 John v, 15).

(III. c.) But the diction of our English version may be in complete accordance with grammatical propriety, and yet it may be obscure, ambiguous, or obsolete. It is not easy to define before hand the causes from which such effects may arise in each individual instance, and we should carefully guard on this point also against the hypercritical temper to which I have already adverted. Dr. Symonds, for example, having discovered that the Bible is usually read by a single chapter at a time, is anxious to meet the wants of the poor and ignorant, whom he fears may forget that our Blessed Lord is the Person, whose life and discourses form the subject of the Gospels. Accordingly, at the commencement of about half the chapters in the historical books of the New Testament, he considerately substitutes Proper Names for the Personal Pronouns of the Original. Thus, he renders the beginning of the fifth chapter of St. Mark in the following manner. "And *Jesus and his disciples* came over unto the other side of the sea, into the country of the Gadarenes; and when *Jesus* was come out of the ship".. ; and he recommends a similar interpolation in the opening sentences of no less than nine other chapters in the single Gospel of St. Mark. How much more commendable is the practice of our translators in this respect; who insert the name of the person in such rare cases only, as present some real difficulty (e. g. Luke xix, 1*), safely leaving it to be supplied, in the vast majority of passages, by the memory or common sense of the reader.

More than one of the critics who have undertaken to revise our translation, have formed large collections of obsolete, vulgar, or difficult words, which they met with in the Authorised Bible. Without any wish to disparage their labors unduly, I confess that I think their diligence misplaced. An assemblage of expressions torn from their context, and strung together in a list, leave a very different impression on the mind from that which they originally produced, when read in connection with the sentences to which they rightly appertain. The word " bewray" is perhaps one of the most obsolete which we find in our version of the New Testament; yet the most unlearned reader of Scripture is at no loss for its meaning in Matth. xxvi, 73. Let us beware of admitting such alterations into our venerable translation, as without materially adding to its value, might deprive it of that air of solemn antiquity, which would be ill exchanged for the more gaudy refinements of modern phraseology.

But at however low a rate I may estimate the great bulk of the changes which Campbell and Symonds have proposed with respect to this division of the

---

* The word " Jesus" is in types corresponding to italics, in the first edition of our public version, so that it cannot be thought that it was inserted in this place on the authority of the few manuscripts and versions in which it forms part of the text.

Introduction.

subject; I hope that I shall not fall into the opposite extreme of obstinately retaining what in point of sense or language is justly censurable (e. g. Matth. xx, 11; xxiii, 6; Acts xviii, 14; 2 Cor. viii, 1). Quaint and mean expressions should at all events be avoided in speaking of the awful realities which the Bible reveals to us: and the example of the sacred writers themselves may teach us, that perfect simplicity of manner is quite compatible with a rigid abstinence from every thing which can offend the purest and most delicate taste.

Such are the general divisions or classes into which my subject is distributed; and before every rendering of our common version which may be examined in the course of the present work, shall be placed the number of that class to which I refer it. Yet since it will sometimes be necessary to discuss alterations either in the Greek text or in the translation, which have been proposed by eminent scholars, but where, on the whole, I consider the English version correct, I shall distinguish these passages from the rest by prefixing this mark (°) to them.*

Before we proceed to investigate the character and value of each of the several versions cited throughout these pages, I wish to offer a few remarks respecting the marginal renderings, and the words printed in italics, which so often occur in the Authorised Translation.

The Marginal Renderings. It will soon be seen that our present version only follows the example of several of its predecessors, when it places in the mar-

---

* Thus in Matth. xvii, 5 °(I) denotes that a change in the Greek text has been proposed, to which I do not accede. See also Matth. xx, 12; Luke vii, 47; John v, 39; Rom. ix, 3 &c.

58   Introduction.

gin explanations of obscure or doubtful expressions. But these brief notes (for such in fact they are), are much more numerous in King James's Bible than in the earlier translations. In the New Testament alone we meet with 855 marginal annotations, whereof 724 are found in the first edition of 1611; the rest (including twenty explanations of coins, measures &c), having been subsequently added by various hands, chiefly by Dr. Blayney in the Oxford editions of 1769. Of the original marginal notes about eighteen point out various readings of the Greek text (Matth. i, 11; vii, 14; xxvi, 26; Mark ix, 16; Luke ii, 38; x, 22; xvii, 36; Acts xxv, 6; 1 Cor. xv, 31; Gal. iv, 17; Eph. vi, 9; James ii, 18; 1 Pet. 1, 4; ii, 21; 2 Pet. ii, 2; 11; 18; 2 John v. 8). Much the greater part present a different rendering of a single word, or propose a change in the construction of a clause; the sense given in the margin being often, though not I think for the most part, superior to that in the text. Some may be interesting to an English reader as affording specimens of Greek or Hebrew idioms (Luke xii, 20; Acts vii, 20; xviii, 11; Rom. vi, 13; Col. i, 13; Rev. xi, 13); while a few, no doubt, are sufficiently trifling (John xix, 25; 1 Cor. v, 8; 1 Thess. v, 11; Tit. iii, 6). Of the unauthorised additions to the margin of the New Testament I cannot speak quite so favorably. Here again several relate to various readings of the Greek (Matth. vi, 1; x, 10; Acts xiii, 18; Eph. ii, 5; Hebr. x, 2; 17; James iv, 2; 2 John v. 12; Rev. xv, 3; xxi, 7; xxii, 19*), and

---

* To these may be added the frivolous variation "Beelzebul" for "Beelzebub" thrice repeated, Matth. x, 25; xii, 24; Luke xi, 15.

so far may be deemed useful. The greater part, however, are either totally erroneous (Acts xv, 5; 1 Cor. iv, 9; 2 Pet. i, 1, 1st note); or very idle (Matth. xxi, 19; xxii, 26; Mark vii, 22; Acts viii, 13; xvi, 13; xxvi, 7; Gal. iv, 24; Eph. vi, 12 &c.); or explain peculiar phrases of the original with unnecessary minuteness (Matth. xiv, 6; Luke ii, 15; John xi, 33; 2 John v. 3). In some places, however, this later margin is undoubtedly correct (Matth. xxviii, 19; Luke, xviii, 2; Acts xiii, 34; xviii, 5; 28; Rom. v, 11; 2 Pet. i, 1, 2nd note); and in several others it should not be rejected without further enquiry (Mark xi, 17; Luke xxi, 8; Acts ii, 6; Hebr. i, 6; 7); though on the whole I do not conceive that the additional notes have much enhanced the value of our excellent translation. I need not dwell longer on this topic, since every marginal rendering, whether proceeding from the translators themselves, or from critical editors since their time, will be carefully examined in the body of this work, unless it shall appear too slight or unimportant to deserve our special attention.

The Italic character. On the subject of those words and clauses which in our Authorised Bibles are printed in the Italic character, I am not equally left to my own resources. The reader may remember that a pamphlet was published about twelve years ago, in the form of "Four Letters to the Bishop of London," arraigning in no measured terms the conduct of the privileged publishers of the English Bible, whom it accused of wilfully departing from the original edition of 1611, in numerous important instances. The author of this production soon afterwards obtained and made public the sanction of a Sub-committee of four dissenting ministers in London (more than one of them men of high and well-merited literary reputation) with regard to a portion of his charge; those gentlemen declaring in a formal minute their disapprobation of the great increase of italics in our modern Bibles, " as deteriorating the vernacular translation, discovering great want of critical taste, unnecessarily exposing the sacred text to the scoff of infidels, and throwing such stumbling blocks in the way of the unlearned, as are greatly calculated to perplex their minds, and unsettle their confidence in the text of Scripture." In reply to the individual with whom the controversy began a statement was drawn up by Dr. Cardwell (British Mag. Vol. iii. pp. 323—47), quite decisive as against his opponent, and in defence of the University of Oxford, but scarcely touching at all on the question of the italics, which had now become the heaviest article of the whole accusation. It is to this point exclusively that Dean Turton directs his attention in his "Text of the English Bible Considered," (2nd. edit. 1834): a work of permanent value, which will long outlive the occasion that called it forth. By a copious and close induction of particular passages he has proved (I presume to the satisfaction even of the Sub-committee) that the changes which have been introduced with respect to italics in the editions of Dr. Blayney and others, were absolutely needed, in order to carry out the principle of the translators themselves. The end proposed by the use of italics is thus explained in the Geneva edition of 1578: "Whereas the necessity of the sentence required anything to be added (for such is the grace and propriety of the Hebrew and Greek tongues, that it cannot but either by circumlocution, or by adding the verb, or some word, be understood of them that are not well-practised

Introduction. 61

therein), we have put it in the text with another kind of letter."* If this be the rule which the translators of our present version proposed to themselves (and we have every reason for believing that it was), it follows that such a rule should be carried out uniformly, and on all occasions. But the most superficial view of the original edition of 1611 will convince us, that consistency in this matter is not even attempted. To the numerous instances collected by Dr. Turton I shall add two or three which appear to me remarkable; and they may be greatly increased by any one who will take the trouble to investigate the subject. In Luke iii, 23—38 τοῦ Ἡλί κ.τ.λ. is thus rendered in the edition of 1611; "which was *the son* of Eli," &c. agreeably to which, in the corresponding expression ὁ τοῦ Ἀλφαίου we find "*the son* of Alpheus" in Mark iii, 18; whereas the same words are printed without italics in Matt. x, 3; Mark ii, 14; Luke vi, 15: in all which verses italics are very properly used in our modern editions. Again, in the Beatitudes, Matth. v, 3—11, the copula "are" is uniformly printed in italics, and rightly; since it is not expressed in the Greek: in the parallel passage Luke vi, 20, 21, the form of the original being precisely the same, the copula is found in

---

* The quotation given above is borrowed from Dean Turton; but perhaps it would be more satisfactory to cite the words of the *original* Geneva editors, from the Preface to their first edition of 1557. It is to the same purport, though not quite so explicit. " And because the Hebrew and Greek phrases, which are strange to render in other tongues, and also short, should not be too hard, I have sometimes interpreted them without any whit diminishing the grace of the sense, as our language doth use them, and sometimes have put to that word, which lacking made the sentence obscure, but have set it in such letters, as may easily be discerned from the common text." "To the Reader," p. 2.

ordinary characters in the edition of 1611; but in the later Bibles it is assimilated to the parallel text of St. Matthew. In Mark ix, 34 τίς μείζων; is rendered in the original edition "who *should be* the greatest?" in a like expression Matth. xxiii, 19 τί γάρ μεῖζον; the verb has been put in italics only by a recent hand. From these and a thousand similar instances it is abundantly clear, that so far as the use of italics is concerned, the first edition of our common version (to adopt the strong language of Dr. Turton), "cannot be depended upon in the least." We are now therefore in a condition to put one simple enquiry. Are the modern editors to be held guilty (I quote the words of the Sub-committee's Report) of a "wanton abandonment of the standard text;" or did they not rather act with reverence and discretion, when adhering closely to the spirit of the translators' design, they corrected what was anomalous in its execution, and supplied what they judged deficient? Or will any one pretend to reconcile the actual practice of the translators with reference to italics, either with itself, or with any intelligible principle that may be devised?

In the course of the present work, then, whenever mention is made of italics, I would be understood to refer to those of our modern Bibles, not to those of the editio princeps of 1611: unless indeed in a few cases (to be specified as occasion shall arise), in which the later editors have displayed needless refinement, or a mistaken judgment, in changing the common character of 1611 into italics. To the italicised words and phrases the same criticism will be applied, as to the other portions of the English text. It will, perhaps, be seen in the sequel that several expressions of this description are inserted from a false notion of the meaning of the passages

Introduction.

wherein they occur (e. g. Matth. xv, 6; xx, 23; Mark vii, 11; x, 40; Acts vii, 59); and that many of the rest, having nothing in the original to which they correspond, may be omitted altogether without detriment to the sense (Matth. xxv, 14; xxvii, 27; Mark xiii, 34; Luke xiii, 29; John vii, 36; Acts xxii, 3; Col. ii. 16; 1 Thess. v, 23; Rev. ii, 25).

I will now take a brief review of the several versions, which have been collated for every passage illustrated in this work; avoiding, as much as possible, such topics as have been exhausted by preceding writers; and limiting my observations, almost exclusively, to the internal condition and critical character of the translations themselves.

The Peshito Syriac Version. The age and merits of the Peshito version have been so often discussed, that it cannot be necessary for me to detain the reader by recapitulating arguments with which every Biblical student is presumed to be familiar. On few points are the learned so generally agreed, as in assigning a very high antiquity to this translation. Michaelis has fully stated his reasons for believing that it was made *not later* than the commencement of the second century. The most plausible objections yet alleged against so early a date are refuted by Dr. Wiseman, whose unfinished "Horæ Syriacæ" impress us with a melancholy sense of the loss sustained by Sacred literature, when their author was seduced from these peaceful studies, to become the champion of a mistaken and a hopeless cause. But the antiquity of the Peshito is not the chief ground on which it claims our attention. It is not only the oldest, it is one of the best of those many versions of Holy Writ, by which God's Providence has enriched and edified the Church. Composed in the purest style of an elegant and expressive, if not a very copious language, no version with which I am acquainted is so perfectly free from the constraint and stiffness, which are the usual faults of a literal translation. Yet while it is remarkable for its ease, the Peshito is by no means loose or paraphrastic. In numerous passages a few words are added to the original, in order to elucidate what would else be obscure (e. g. Luke ix, 34; xvi, 8; Acts i, 19; ii, 14; 24; v, 4; xii, 15; Rom. xii, 16), or to explain some involved construction, (Acts x, 38; Eph. iii, 1; 1 John i, 1); but seldom would the liberty it claims in this particular offend any but the most servile adherent to the letter of the Greek. Few persons, I believe, have long made this version their daily companion without assenting to the judgment of Michaelis; who, after thirty years study of its contents, declared that he could consult no translation with so much confidence in cases of difficulty and doubt.

But notwithstanding the value and venerable antiquity of the Peshito, little care has been taken by its editors to exhibit a correct text, such as came from the hands of the translator. In fact, a critical edition of the old Syriac version is one of the few great works in this department of study yet open to the enterprise of scholars. The first edition, that of Widmanstadt (Vienn. 1555), though a most beautiful specimen of typographical skill, was printed from a single manuscript, still preserved in the Imperial library. And although some of the later editors (as, for instance, Tremellius and the superintendents of the Antwerp press) had access to other copies, they seem to have contented themselves for the most part with reprinting the editio princeps, the vowel and diacritical points alone being varied according to their own taste or opinions. That such was Schaaf's practice he has expressly told us in his Preface; and we need but examine his laborious and accurate * collation of the twelve editions which preceded his own, to be convinced that the variations (where they do not concern the vowel points, or are mere errors of the press) are too few and insignificant to be the result of a careful and systematic use of manuscripts.

Yet materials for a complete revision of the Syriac text exist in abundance. Not to mention other uncollated documents which are known to be deposited in the chief libraries of Europe, Adler has described no less than fourteen (several of them being upwards of a thousand years old), which he discovered in the Vatican, at Florence, and other continental cities. Nor are our own libraries at all deficient in this respect. An interesting collation of Schaaf's text with two manuscripts of the Gospels preserved in the Bodleian, as well as with the citations in the "Horreum Mysteriorum" of the famous Jacobite Patriarch Gregory Bar-Hebræus, was published at Oxford in 1805 by Richard Jones. In 1806 Dr. Buchanan found among the Nestorian Christians of the Malabar coast, a very fine copy of the whole Syriac Bible, which is now the property of the University of Cambridge. Among the treasures of Oriental learning collected by Mr. Rich, and purchased for the

---

* I say *accurate*, for I have repeatedly collated the various readings in Schaaf's two editions (1709, 1717) with the editio princeps, with Plantin, Antwerp, 1575, 24°, and with Trost. Anhalt Coth. 1621, without discovering a single error worth notice.

British Museum in 1825, are six manuscripts of the Peshito version, five of which are most carefully written in the old Estrangelo character, and bear every appearance of great antiquity. Surely, it is not creditable to the learned that so plentiful a harvest has not ere this been gleaned by diligent and reverential hands.

I have hitherto refrained from mentioning Dr. Lee's edition of the Peshito New Testament (London, 1816), printed for the use of the Eastern Christians, at the expense of the British and Foreign Bible Society. In a work of this kind a critical apparatus of various readings would no doubt have been out of place; but the text of this edition so often differs from that of Schaaf and his predecessors, that some information respecting the sources whence it is drawn should manifestly have been afforded; at least in such copies as, having Latin title-pages, were destined for European circulation. No such intimation however was thought requisite, and it was not till Hug had expressed a very reasonable desire for further explanation, that Dr. Lee made known the authorities which had guided him in altering the text. They consist, he tells us, of Buchanan's Travancore manuscript which I have just alluded to; and of another in the Cambridge Public Library (Ff. 2, 15); of the previous collections of Jones and others; and (strange as the statement may seem) of *Greek* manuscripts of the original (See Dr. Lee's Letter in Hug's Introduction, Wait's translation, vol. i. p. 369 note). I do not share in Scholz's suspicion (Proleg. N. T. vol. i, p. 124) that the London edition derived its corrections of Schaaf's text from Griesbach's Greek Testament; indeed we need seek for no other confutation of this grave accusation than some of the passages he produces in its support (e. g.

Introduction.

Mark i, 29 ; ii, 3) : yet it must be confessed, that (however the practical purposes of a particular edition may be promoted by such a course), to correct a translation from manuscripts of the original, is a critical error of the first magnitude.

The reader is possibly aware of another opinion maintained by Scholz touching this version, and which cannot be read without some surprise. He informs us (Proleg. p. 133) that he has examined manuscripts of the Peshito both in the Paris and Medicean libraries, but discovered his labor to be vain: that on receiving a description and certain readings of the Rich MSS from the officers of the British Museum, he came to the conclusion that those documents are of little service, so very rarely do they differ from the printed text. Now we may readily believe that the variations to be found in these manuscripts are not so great as to change the character of the translation, or materially alter the sense, as represented in the early editions ; but they may not be on that account the less worthy of consideration. If Scholz had consulted Jones's collation of the two Bodleian MSS mentioned above (a volume of whose existence he seems to be ignorant), he would have seen for how many minute but not unimportant improvements the patient student may be indebted to codices which, in their general features, strongly resemble the common text. And when we consider that some of the documents which he treats so superciliously are at least a thousand years old; it might have occurred to Pr. Scholz that a proof of their agreement in the main with Schaaf's edition is of itself of no slight value; both as supplying another link in the great chain of evidence which assures us of the integrity of the text of Scripture ; and as giving a silent but decided answer to those critics, who have imagined that the union of the Maronite Syrians with the Church of Rome, has occasioned the corruption of the Peshito from the Latin Vulgate. The real value of the Paris and Florentine MSS I have no means of estimating: but that Scholz's notion of the Rich MSS is not confirmed by the judgment of persons somewhat better acquainted with them, may appear from the testimony of the late Professor Rosen, who was associated with Mr. Forshall in the task of arranging the whole collection. " Inter quos ante alios omnes memorabile est Novi Testamenti exemplar Nestorianum, numer. 7157 Rich., liber et antiquitate suâ, quum sæculo octavo scriptus est, et summâ scripturæ diligentiâ atque elegantiâ, inter omnia quotquot nobis innotuerunt Syriaca N. T. exemplaria, eximiâ laude dignus. Etenim remotioris etiam ætatis codices Syriacos extare comperimus quidem; sed de nullo nos vel audire vel legere meminimus, qui omnes quos Nestoriani agnoscunt N. T. libros amplecteretur. Si quis vir doctus, *id quod jamdudum desideratum est*, N. T. Syri textum curâ criticâ recognoscendum suscipere vellet, *magni interfuturum esse censemus hunc codicem*, textûs, quo Nestoriani sæculo octavo usi sunt, egregium testem, *quàm diligentissimè inspicere*. (Præf. Cat. MSS. Syr. Brit. Mus. 1838).

The Philoxenian Syriac version.   No one perhaps who is much acquainted with the Philoxenian Syriac version will be disposed to complain that I have so rarely cited its renderings. It is, in truth, nothing but the result of a close collation of the Peshito with two Greek manuscripts of about the fifth century. Whenever the old translation appeared to follow a different reading of the original from that which the two manuscripts presented, the Syriac text was altered in accordance with them. Hence arises the *critical* value of the Philoxenian version, inasmuch as it enables us to determine the readings of what were considered good manuscripts at the time it was composed (A. D. 508). As a guide to the *interpretation* of the New Testament it is nearly worthless. In addition to his design of correcting the text, its author Polycarp labored to force the bold and elegant style of the Peshito into rigorous conformity with the letter of the Greek, and hence produced a version which can be compared with nothing more fitly than with the " metaphrase" of Arias Montanus, so mercilessly condemned by Campbell (Prelim. Diss. x, Pt. 2).* If verbal exactness be the highest merit of a translation, then is the Philoxenian version an admirable representative of the original New Testament. The numerous idioms of the Greek are sedulously transfused into a language whose genius is widely dissimilar. The order, and in many instances, the very etymology of the words are superstitiously retained, to the sacrifice of all propriety, and sometimes in violation of the dictates of common sense. Indeed, to appreciate the Peshito as it deserves, it is worth while to compare a chapter taken from it with the corrected version of the Philoxenian. I choose Matth. xxviii merely on account of its moderate length. It appears then,

---

* Campbell however would probably have mitigated the severity of his strictures had he remembered that Arius Montanus never intended his Latin version to be separated from the original (vid. Leusden, Præf. N. T. 1698). Correctly speaking it pretends to no higher character than that of an interlinear translation, for the aid of persons imperfectly acquainted with the sacred languages. This apology cannot be pleaded in behalf of the Philoxenian Syriac.

that though the old translation is evidently the basis of the later, yet there are about 76 variations from it in the twenty verses which comprise this chapter. Of these not more than two can be considered as various readings of the Greek (vv. 2 ; 18), and one seems to be a subsequent addition made by Thomas of Harkel (Ναζαρηνόν, v. 5). In six places the order of the Syriac words is brought closer to that of the Greek ; and in about five instances words or phrases then in common use are substituted for others, which in the lapse of four centuries may have grown obsolete. But the great mass of the alterations are of the most frivolous description. The definite state of nouns is perpetually placed for the absolute, and *vice versa ;* the Greek article is always represented by the Syriac pronoun ; the inseparable pronominal affixes, which characterise the Shemitic languages, and in the Aramæan dialects prove the sources of such graceful redundancy, are retrenched and as much as possible discarded ; while the most unmeaning changes are made in the tenses of the verbs, and in the lesser particles. Since the same result appears on a similar analysis of any other portion of the Philoxenian version, I cannot avoid the conclusion, that inasmuch as neither the age nor the judgment of Polycarp give him a strong claim to our deference, it is not expedient to make very frequent appeals to his authority.

The Latin Vulgate. The merits and defects of the Latin Vulgate version have been so carefully examined by Campbell (Prel. Diss. x, Pt. iii), that I will simply refer to his work, which is, or ought to be, in the hands of every theologian. If Campbell errs at all in his estimate of this translation, it certainly is not on the side of excessive indulgence.

All its blemishes, whether in style or matter, are prominently displayed in the course of his review, while what he alleges in its favour is of too general a nature to weigh, as it deserves, in the opposite scale. If I am not deceived, the reader will find, in the following pages, many examples of concise yet accurate interpretation, in which the Vulgate will suffer no disparagement by a comparison with any other version antient or modern.

Perhaps I may be forgiven if I digress from my subject for a moment, to express an earnest wish that some competent critic would undertake a renewed investigation of the history and sources of the Vulgate New Testament. After the labors of Blanchini and Sabatier we cannot expect, nor indeed do we require, a large accession of fresh materials. Assuming the existence of a single common version, called the Italic, prior to the fourth century (a fact which really ought never to have been questioned), the contrast in point of style between Jerome's own translation from the Hebrew in the Vulgate Old Testament, and the mixed version which is exhibited in the New, will indicate at once what portions of the Italic have been retained in the present Vulgate, and also what old Latin documents now extant approach nearest to that primitive version. I am not ignorant of the difficulties which beset such an enquiry (see Ernesti Instit. Pt. iii, ch. iv, 16); but if it be pursued with prudence and caution, I am persuaded they will not be found insuperable. The causes of all past failures are by this time sufficiently ascertained; and few enquiries would contribute more powerfully to the advancement both of the criticism and the right interpretation of the New Testament (See above p. 26).

Modern Latin translations of Beza and Castalio.

Of the later Latin versions I have chiefly used Castalio's (1550, 1573), and Beza's (1st edition, 1556), though I have not thought it necessary to cite them, as I have cited the Vulgate, for every text which I have reviewed. Campbell's critique on these translations is so admirable and exact (Prel. Diss. x, Pts. iv, v), that it would be worse than useless were I to attempt to imitate or revise what he has accomplished so well. I am sorry that I cannot rebut that which Campbell has advanced to prove the gross partiality of Beza; though it is but equitable for us to bear in mind, that the principles of sacred criticism were so little settled in his age, that a strong theological bias might very possibly be allowed to influence his translation of Scripture, without any serious imputation on his moral honesty.

Boisii Collatio.

The "Collatio Veteris Interpretis cum Bezâ, &c" written at the request of Bp. Andrews by John Bois, Canon of Ely (London 1655), is a work of some celebrity, which I consulted with the greater interest, as his plan appeared to have some affinity to my own. I must candidly admit, that on the whole I was a little disappointed. Adopting the Vulgate Latin as his standard, he compares it with the revisions of Erasmus, Piscator, Beza, and occasionally of one or two others (he never once names Castalio), throughout the Four Gospels and the Acts. As we might expect from the man and his connections, Beza is the chief, I might almost say, the sole object of Bois's attack, though I am not sure that his animadversions are much calculated to injure that translator in the estimation of impartial judges. The great end of the "Collatio" is to vindicate the rendering of the old version, wherever it cannot be proved absolutely false. At the end of a long note on Matth. xv, 6, he says " Mihi, in locis hoc genus perplexis et obscuris, pro optimis interpretibus sunt, qui verbis usquequâque adhærent, nec tam ponderant ea, quam numerant :"—as if a heavier charge could be brought against any version, than that it does not even endeavor to be intelligible. But in every case of difficulty or obscurity, his panacea is a marginal rendering :—" quòd si quid addendum videbitur," he goes on to remark, " juvandi lectoris causâ, quanto rectiùs id in Scholia, aut marginales annotationes, quam in contextum ipsum conjiciatur." And this irrational desire of maintaining the integrity of the version against the sense of the original, disfigures every page of his book, and leads him to reject, as needless or presumptuous, several indubitable improvements of the later translators (e. g. Matth. v, 29; Mark vii, 3; ix, 18; John iii, 10; Acts, i, 8). It might readily be supposed that with such a resolution to find fault, Beza's real errors are not allowed to escape. Yet Bois scarcely condemns as it deserves his scandalous perversion of Acts i, 14; and actually approves of his interpretation of Matth. v, 21; xx, 23: but several less important failings are carefully rectified (Mark xiv, 3; Luke i, 78; Acts ix, 7; xiii, 34). When I add that Chrysostom and Theophylact among the Fathers, and the great Casaubon of the moderns, are Bois's favorite authors, some idea may be formed of the spirit of a work which has become extremely scarce; and which, however useful and instructive, is not sufficiently comprehensive, either in design or execution, to regain the place it once held in the public estimation.

Early English Versions. But it is full time to speak of those early English versions, which have been mentioned above as the basis of our present Translalation (See p. 2), and which I have diligently collated in every passage which is discussed in the progress of my work. They consist of Wickliffe's Bible, translated about A. D. 1380; Tyndal's first edition of the New Testament, published in 1526; his last edition, of 1534; Coverdale's Bible, of 1535; Cranmer's or the Great Bible, of 1539; the Geneva New Testament, of 1557; the Geneva whole Bible, of 1560; the Bishops' Bible of 1568, 1572; and lastly, the New Testament printed at the Popish Seminary at Rheims, 1582. Besides these versions which I have perpetually consulted, many references are made to Sir John Cheke's translation of St. Matthew, and a few to Taverner's Bible, 1539, and some other less important editions; as also to Laurence Tonson's New Testament, 1576; which usually, though not always, is a mere translation of Beza's Latin version.

The external history of these several versions has been so copiously described by popular authors, that it is quite superfluous for me to enter upon the topic. Anthony Johnson's Historical Account, reprinted among Watson's Theological Tracts, is short and lively, though rather superficial. Lewis's History is valuable, and descends much into details. Its inaccuracies are of no great moment, and were almost inevitable in the imperfect state of bibliographical knowledge a century since. It is now ascertained that he derived considerable aid from the eminently learned Dr. Waterland, two hundred pages of whose collected works are covered with letters which he addressed to Lewis on this single subject (Waterland's Works, Van Mildert's edn. Vol. x, pp. 195—401).* The portion of Archbishop Newcome's "Historical View of English Biblical Translations" which relates to this point is little more than an abstract of Lewis's book; and Dr. Cotton's elaborate "List of editions of the Bible," is rather (as its title intimates) a chronological catalogue of reprints of the whole Scriptures and various portions of them, than a history of particular versions. The most recent and the best account of the elder translations is found in the Introduction to Bagster's Hexapla, 1841; wherein all that need be known respecting them and their authors is presented in a pleasing form, though with a visible leaning towards the Puritan party.

But in all these works the external history of the translations is almost exclusively attended to. Their respective critical characters, and mutual relations to each other are considered but slightly and incidentally. In the hope of supplying in some degree the omissions of others in this particular, I hazard the following observations, which have occurred to my mind in the prosecution of my present design.

Wickliffe's Bible, 1380. Respecting John Wickliffe's version of the Bible, executed about A.D. 1380, I need say but a few words. It is chiefly important

---

* In Crutwell's Preface to Bp. Wilson's Bible 1785, a succinct account is given of all the English versions of the Bible, but it is chiefly borrowed from Lewis. The value of this edition is much enhanced by a collation of our common translation with those that preceded it, contained in Mr. Crutwell's notes. For though that collation is very imperfect, even in places where we should most have expected information, yet until the publication of Bagster's excellent reprints, it was the only means by which the general reader could obtain a notion, however inadequate, of the contents of those scarce and precious volumes.

as being the first *complete* translation of the Scriptures into English; but since it was soon proscribed by the authorities of the Church, its circulation was comparatively limited, and its influence on succeeding versions is barely perceptible.* The universal ignorance of Greek, which prevailed in Wickliffe's age, compelled him to translate the New Testament from the Latin Vulgate; a circumstance which, while it renders his work almost useless to the Biblical interpreter, gives it a certain critical value, as it enables us to determine how far the Latin manuscripts then in most repute, differed from the present, or Clementine text (See Matth. viii, 15; xvi, 20; xxi, 17; 1 Cor. x, 17; Hebr. v, 11, &c). I hardly know on what grounds it has been conjectured, that Wickliffe is " the real original of Chaucer's celebrated picture of the village Priest." (Lebas, Life of Wickliffe, p. 212). The courtly and licentious poet surely had little in common with our Reformer, save the patronage of John of Gaunt. But if Tyrwhitt's calculations be correct, the " Canterbury Tales" must have been composed about the time of Wickliffe's death (Introd. Discourse to Canterb. Tales, p. clxi). Hence it becomes interesting to compare the style of his version with that portion of his contemporary's masterpiece which most resembles it in subject: the " Persone's Tale," or Sermon. Now Chaucer's diction (I wish to say nothing of his matter), is clear, terse, and

---

* I have used the edition of Wickliffe's N. T. which is printed in Bagster's Hexapla, because it seems somewhat more accurate than that published by Lewis and Baber. Several manuscripts of Wickliffe's Translation are interpolated or corrupted from other versions of portions of Scripture made by various hands. Of these latter an account may be seen in the Introduction to Baber's edition of Wickliffe's N. T. or in that prefixed to Bagster's Hexapla.

spirited; so little antiquated by the lapse of 460 years, that a reader of ordinary intelligence may peruse his prose with fluency, without consulting the glossary once in a page.* The style of Wickliffe's controversial writings is pronounced by Sharon Turner to be involved and obscure; a defect which may also be noticed in his version of Scripture. It is so close a translation from the Vulgate, that the harshest Latinisms are often retained (e. g. Matth. iv, 10; Acts v, 7; 1 Cor. v, 1; 5; Tit. iii, 5, &c); but this is not the sole, nor indeed the chief cause of that want of perspicuity which pervades his great work. Familiar though we be with the diction of the New Testament, his version is much more difficult to a modern ear than Chaucer's Parson's Discourse. The obsolete words and phrases are more numerous, and the construction of the sentences is by no means so simple. Yet let us not disparage his immortal labors by ungenerous criticism. Taken as a whole, his venerable translation is no unfaithful image of the sacred original; and during the dreary period which separated his age from the dawn of the Reformation, many a humble saint slaked his thirst in secret at the living fountain which, by John Wickliffe's means, God had mercifully opened for the refreshing of his people.

Since both Wickliffe's and the Rhemish Testament (which will be described hereafter) are but secondary translations, it would be fallacious to cite their evidence as that of independent witnesses. I

---

* The "Persone" seems to be his own translator from the Vulgate. At least it is evident that he does not use Wickliffe's version. See his renderings of Matth. v, 34—37; Luke xxiii, 42, 43; Acts iv, 12; 1 John iii, 15 &c

shall therefore appeal to their renderings of Scripture in those cases only, where some happy expression or striking peculiarity claims our especial notice.

Tyndal's N.T. 1526, 1534. Almost a century and a half after Wickliffe's death, in the year 1526, William Tyndal, once an Observant Fiiar of Greenwich, but then an exile for religion, had the honor of publishing the first printed edition of the New Testament, a distinction which the proudest scholars in the realm might well have coveted. In spite of his own positive declaration to the contrary, in the title-page to his third edition (1534), it has been asserted by some who might have known better, that Tyndal's version was in a great measure derived from the Latin Vulgate, and Luther's German Testament (1st edition, 1522). Now it would be a severe reflection upon Tyndal's modesty and discretion to suppose that he neglected to consult these excellent translations; and even after we have made due allowance for over statement and casual mistakes, enough will remain in Bp. Marsh's arguments to shew that Luther's authority had considerable weight with our countryman (Compare Bp. Marsh's Lectures, Appendix to edition of 1838, with Mr. Walter's second letter to him, 1828). But we have a decisive proof that Tyndal was fully competent to translate from the original, without slavishly depending on Luther's or any other version. In his "Memoirs of Tyndal" (pp. 8, 9) Mr. Offor has recently brought to light a few manuscript translations of various parts of the New Testament, bearing the signature of "W. T." and the date of 1502, just twenty years before the publication of any portion of Luther's Bible. From these most curious fragments it appears, that Tyndal's version of Scripture was no hasty compilation to serve an emergency, but the matured fruit of careful practice and patient study, continued through the course of four and twenty years. The passage which Mr. Offor quotes at length (Luke vii, 36—50), nearly agrees with his first printed edition; and is so admirable a specimen of his skill as an interpreter, that its language is retained, with very slight alterations, in our present Authorised translation. That it is not rendered from the Vulgate is perfectly clear, since within the compass of fifteen verses it conforms in seven places to the Greek against the Vulgate (vv. 37; 38 twice; 42 twice; 44; 49); whereas it accords with the Vulgate but three times in opposition to the present Greek text (39; 47 twice).* From a close examination of Tyndal's printed editions, the same conclusion may be drawn: namely, that his New Testament is, in all essential points, a primary version, made immediately from the Greek original. The Vulgate had no greater influence with him than may reasonably be accounted for, both from the effects of early habit on the translator's mind; and from the circumstance that the Latin version was the only aid to the right interpretation of Scripture, which was available to students at the opening of the sixteenth century.

Of the intrinsic merits of Tyndal's translation Biblical critics have spoken in the highest terms. Dr. Geddes has declared that " in point of perspicuity and noble simplicity, propriety of idiom and purity of style, no English version has yet surpassed it."

---

* See also Bagster's Hexapla, Introd. p. 41, where ἄνωθεν (John iii, 3) is said to be translated in these fragments " from above." The Vulgate has " denuo."

And though the opinion of this Romanist writer is probably biassed by his hostility to King James's Bible, I am not disposed to dispute its accuracy. It is no mean evidence of Tyndal's general worth, that his New Testament is the virtual groundwork of every subsequent revision. Page after page of his translation of the Gospels, in language and phraseology; in the arrangement of the words, and turn of the constructions; bears so strong a resemblance to our common version as to be scarcely distinguishable from it. The variations that do occur are often so minute as easily to escape observation; and the changes that have been introduced are not always for the better. Mr. Hallam's information respecting the English versions is rather loose and meagre;* but there is much justice in his remark, that if the style of our Authorised Bible be the perfection of the English language; " in consequence of the principle of adherence to the original versions which had been kept up ever since the time of Henry VIII, it is not the language of the reign of King James." (Literat. of Europe, Vol. iii, p. 134).

In the Epistles, as might be expected, the similarity, though still great, is not so striking. The earlier version partakes more of the character of a paraphrase than that now in use (See Rom. xiv, 1; 2 Cor. iii, 10; 1 Thess. ii, 3; James i, 17; 1 Pet. v, 9). Ellipses are perpetually supplied by Tyndal with a boldness which his more wary successors

---

* For example, what edition can he possibly mean by " the English translation of Tyndal and Coverdale, published in 1535 or 1536;" which, he tells us, is " avowedly taken" from the Latin Vulgate, and Luther's German Testament (Literat. of Europe, Vol. i, p. 526)? Of course Mr. Hallam may fairly plead that " operi longo fas est obrepere somnum," but *his* oversights are very likely to grow into other people's authorities.

Introduction.

feared to imitate; sometimes indeed to the manifest improvement of the sense (1 Cor. vii, 19; Eph. vi, 2; Hebr. vii, 20; 1 Pet. iv, 11); but occasionally on grounds too doubtful for a cautious interpreter to approve (Rom. viii, 23; xiv, 20; Eph. ii, 15; iii, 1; Hebr. vi, 1). Yet I conceive that on the whole, an unlearned reader will find Tyndal's version at least as intelligible as our own; and few indeed are the places in which he materially misrepresents the meaning of the sacred writers. His most prominent defect is a disregard of the Greek particles, even where they are most needed to indicate the logical connection between the several members of a sentence. And notwithstanding the laudable care of some of the later editors on the point, this negligence of the first translator continues to exercise a pernicious influence on our present Bible.

In his address to the reader, appended to the first edition of 1526, Tyndal besought " them that are learned Christianly, forasmuch as I am sure, and my conscience beareth me record, that of a pure intent, singly and faithfully I have interpreted it, as far forth as God gave me the gift of knowledge and understanding: that the rudeness of the work, now at the first time offend them not; but that they consider how that I had no man to counterfeit, neither was holpen with English of any that had interpreted the same, or such like things in the Scripture before time." In these words he seems positively to disclaim the use of Wickliffe's New Testament; and accordingly, on comparing the two translations, I can trace no other marks of affinity between them, than might arise from accident, or some faint recollection of the expressions of the older version, still lingering in Tyndal's mind. He concludes his address with a promise, that this first attempt, which is "a thing begun rather than finished," shall hereafter undergo a thorough revision, desiring "them that are learned and able, to remember their duty, and to help thereunto."

It was not before 1534 that Tyndal was enabled to redeem the pledge he had thus given. In that year he published his third and last edition, which, as he informs us in his Prologue, he had "looked over (now at the last) with all diligence, and compared it unto the Greek; and weeded out of it many faults, which lack of help at the beginning, and oversight did sow therein." On this last edition his reputation as a translator of Scripture is chiefly founded. Although the character of the two editions is in the main the same, yet several variations occur in every chapter; and it cannot be questioned that Tyndal's second thoughts were usually the best. Many obsolete words and undignified phrases are removed; the more obvious inaccuracies are for the most part corrected (e. g. 2 Cor. vi, 12; Phil. ii, 4; Hebr. ix, 1; xi, 21); and I believe it may be added that the critical readings of the Vulgate have less weight than in the first edition (e. g. Matth. vi, 13; xxv, 21). On the other hand, some of the most singular renderings of the first edition remain unaltered in the third. Thus in Eph. iv, 27 διάβολος is translated "backbiter:" in 1 Tim. iii, 2 a bishop must be κόσμιον "honestly apparelled:" the κλῆροι of 1 Pet. v, 3 are "parishes:" and the strange expression "but and if" (which is not quite banished from our present Bibles),* is very frequently used. Tyndal

---

* See our Authorised version, Matth. xxiv, 48; 1 Pet. iii, 14. "And" is similarly used after "but" in other phrases by Tyndal. Thus "but and thou," Matth. xix, 17; edition of 1526.

so far complied with the representations of others as to substitute the technical word "elders" in the book of 1534 in the room of "seniors" (πρεσβύ-τεροι); but in both editions ἐκκλησία is translated "congregation," not "Church;"* ἀγαπή "love," not "charity;" and very often χάρις "favor," not "grace." It would not be difficult also to point out instances in which a change has been introduced into the later edition decidedly for the worse. I have noticed no less than fifty-four such cases (many of them, doubtless, of little consequence), in the Gospel of St. Matthew alone (See particularly ch. v, 24; vi, 34; ix, 1; 2; xix, 28; xxiii, 18; xxv, 28; xxvi, 31).

A conviction of the great intrinsic merit of Tyndal's New Testament of 1526, no less than the interest attached to it, as being the first English version made immediately from the Greek, has induced me to distinguish by a separate notation, all its variations from the later and more perfect edition, which I may meet with in the progress of my present work.

Coverdale's Bible, 1535. To Miles Coverdale, sometime Bishop of Exeter, we owe the first English version of the whole Bible, including the Apocryphal books (1535). Although for prudential reasons his work is called in the Prologue "a special translation," the slightest collation will shew that, at least in the New Testament, he has made a freer use of the labors of Tyndal, than the circumstances of the times would permit him to acknowledge. Many paragraphs may be found in Coverdale, which corres-

---

* In Matth. xvi, 18 " congregation" is retained after Tyndal in all our versions before King James's, whose third Instruction to the Translators proscribed its use.

pond to the letter with the version of his predecessor; and still more wherein he contents himself with a few verbal alterations. Yet in such texts as present any difficulty he must be considered an independent translator, since in them he often departs widely from the renderings of Tyndal. In his beautiful prologue he says, " to help me, I have had sundry translations, not only in Latin, but also of the Dutch interpreters; whom .... I have been the more glad to follow, for the most part, according as I was required." And in his dedication to King Henry he mentions "*five* sundry interpreters," out of whom he had " with a clear conscience purely and faithfully translated." I cite these words the rather, because they have been held to prove that Coverdale's is but a secondary translation, and not the result of a comparison with the Greek. Since it seems impossible to discover the precise versions to which he here alludes,* or even to determine with certainty whether each of them contained the whole or only a portion of Scripture; we cannot hope to arrive at any positive conclusion in this matter. It would appear, however, that though he makes no direct mention of the Greek text, it is tacitly referred to throughout his Prologue. If his Bible be after all but a selection from previous translations, if Coverdale really did nothing more than " purely and faithfully follow his interpreters," it is hard to understand what advantage he could expect to accrue from it to " the congregation of God;" or how he could state, with an immediate view to his own undertaking, that " there cometh

---

* For some vague conjectures on this subject (they are really nothing more) see Mr. Walter's First Letter to Bp Marsh, p. 98; and Introd. to Bagster's Hexapla, p. 72.

more knowledge and understanding of Scripture by sundry translations, than by all the glosses of our sophistical doctors." On the other hand it must be confessed, that we possess not the same proof of Coverdale's learning that we have of Tyndal's; and certainly the history of this good man's subsequent career, would not lead us to think highly of his judgment and consistency.

Bishop Coverdale's Translation is spoken of in very favorable terms by Kennicott (Diss. Gen. ad Vet. Test. § 89 note), who, besides several passages of the Old Testament, quotes Luke xxiii, 32; John, xviii, 37, as instances where his interpretation is preferable to that of our present Bibles. Kennicott should have stated that Tyndal's, and indeed most of the other English versions, have avoided the gross error of King James's Translators in the former of these texts; and I fear that we must not assent to the lavish praise he has bestowed on Coverdale's labors. The services rendered by that prelate to Biblical science are chiefly confined to the Old Testament, a large proportion of which had not been translated by any Englishman since the days of Wickliffe. His version of the New Testament is very unequal, and betrays so many marks of precipitancy, as almost to lend credibility to the conjecture, that he began and ended his translation of the whole Scriptures within a year! (Introd. to Bagster's Hexapla, p. 73) Yet no competent judge will deem his work destitute of merit. The style is vigorous; the renderings of difficult texts are very perspicuous, though they are often questionable and diffuse; while an air of freshness and novelty pervades the volume, since no one of our translators has ventured on such bold interpretations as Coverdale, and but little of his peculiar diction was adopted by those who followed him.

In Coverdale's Bible we may trace the rise of marginal notes, as they are still retained in the Authorised version. The first edition of Tyndal's New Testament, in 8vo. 1526, contains the bare text; but his 4to. edition, published later in the same year, as also his third edition of 1534, exhibit glosses in the margin: but they are brief annotations on the subject matter of Scripture, and not various renderings of the words. Coverdale appears to have first used the margin for this latter purpose; though his notes are so few that I have counted but eighteen in the whole New Testament, whereof five are explanatory remarks; and only three occur in all the Epistles;—another proof of his haste as he approached the end of his task. On an analysis of the remaining thirteen cases, the rendering of Tyndal appears in the text, and that of the Vulgate in the margin, in Matth. xxiii, 25; Mark i, 11; Acts xv, 3 where Tyndal's first edition agrees with Coverdale's). The Vulgate reading is in the text, that of Tyndal in the margin of Matth. xvi, 13; Acts ix, 40. A less literal version is in the margin of Matth. xi, 11; xx, 25: one more literal in Mark iii, 21. The notes on Rom. iii, 28; x, 17, seem mere idle glosses, resting on no proper authority; while those on Matth. i, 18; xxvi, 17 ("some read, a glass with precious water"); Mark xiii, 9, are so forced, that I hardly know how to account for them. I have been thus minute in my description of these marginal notes, as they promise to afford us a tolerable index of the sources and character of the version which contains them.

Introduction.

Cranmer's or the Great Bible 1539. The "Great Bible" of 1539, published under the auspices of Archbishop Cranmer, was used as the Authorised version of our Church for many years. Its translation of the Psalms is still retained in our Prayer Book, and the Epistles and Gospels were taken from it until the last review in 1661. In the title page to this edition we are informed that it is "truly translated after the verity of the Hebrew and Greek texts, by the diligent study of divers excellent learned men, expert in the foresaid tongues;" and it has been conjectured by some that John Rogers the Martyr was the person chiefly employed under Cranmer's own eye. That it is the version which was prepared, with King Henry's sanction, by Gardiner and several other prelates, is a supposition irreconcileable with the fact, that the prohibited New Testament of Tyndal is manifestly the groundwork of that portion of the Great Bible. One thing however is certain, that no one of our earlier versions contributed so little as this to the formation of a perfect translation. The publication of this edition was doubtless hurried forward by the pressing necessity of providing a Bible fit to be set up and read in Churches. Hence, although slight variations and minute corrections of Tyndal's style may be found in almost every verse, it is useless to expect that the "Great Bible" will throw much light on difficult passages, or explain the more involved constructions. In such cases it mostly copies verbatim from the older translation. No primary version, either before or after it, allowed so great weight to the readings of the Vulgate. Cranmer's New Testament is full of interpolations (distinguished however from the rest of the text by a difference in the character) which depend mainly or even exclusively, on the authority of the ancient Latin version. I subjoin a few instances, selected from a much larger number, in all which the additions of the " Great Bible " have been rejected by subsequent English translators. Matth. xxvi, 53; xxvii, 8; Mark ii, 23; Luke xvi, 21; xxiv, 36; Acts xv, 34; 41; Rom. i, 32; v, 2; 8; xii, 17; 1 Cor. iv, 16; xiv, 33; 2 Cor. xi, 21; Col. i, 6; James v, 3; 1 Pet. v, 2; 3; 2 Pet. i, 10; ii, 4. In the following texts it agrees with Latin manuscripts, against the present printed text, both Latin and Greek. Matth. xix, 21; John vii, 29; Acts xiv, 7; 1 Cor. x, 17; 2 Cor. viii, 20. The interpolated clause in the last five instances is also found in Wickliffe. In 1 Cor. xv, 47 Coverdale follows the Vulgate reading, while the Great Bible annexes it to that of the Greek, which had been adopted by Tyndal. On the other hand, this edition very properly inserts from the Complutensian Polyglott or the Vulgate, the latter part of James iv, 6; which not being found in the manuscript chiefly used by Erasmus (2 of Wetstein), had not yet been admitted into the received text. Another addition, derived from the same source, is Luke xvii, 36; the authenticity of which is not so well established.

Sir John Cheke's Translation of St. Matthew, about 1550. A curious fragment of a translation of the New Testament, by Sir John Cheke (that illustrious scholar, the pride of his age, who " taught Cambridge and King Edward Greek"), was published by Mr. Goodwin in 1843, from one of the Parker manuscripts deposited in Corpus Christi College Library. Though this version was apparently unknown to all succeeding translators, and consequently is not comprehended within the strict limits of my design, a slight account of its character and scope will scarcely be condemned as an impertinent digression. The manuscript which contains it being without date or signature, Sir John Cheke is discovered to be its author chiefly by its close resemblance to his beautiful and peculiar handwriting. Mr. Goodwin conjectures, on no very sufficient data, that the translation was executed about A.D. 1550; it should certainly be placed between the publication of Cranmer's and of the first Geneva version. In 1539 Cheke was but twenty-five years old; in 1557 he went down to the tomb, a penitent and heart-broken man. Unfortunately this fragment comprises only the Gospel of St. Matthew, and the first twenty verses of St. Mark; two leaves have been lost, the one containing Matth. xvi, 25—xviii, 8; and the other the last eleven verses of ch. xxviii. There is no reason to think that any farther progress was ever made in the prosecution of the work.

Although there are abundant proofs in every page that the earlier translations were much used in forming that now under review, none of the older versions so little resembles our present Authorised Bible; none is so free from all restraint, so loose and paraphrastic as Sir John Cheke's. Like some modern interpreters, he feels himself at liberty to remodel the whole form and arrangement of the original, in order to round a period or render a construction more regular. Thus Matth. xxiv, 45, 46 runs as follows in his version: "The servant therefore who is a faithful and a wise servant, whom his Lord hath set over his meini to give them meat in convenient time, and his Lord findeth him doing so at his coming, is happy." He represents the discourses held by our Lord with his disciples and other enquirers, in the degrading idiom of familiar dialogue. "They have no need, said Christ to them, to go away. Give you them some meat. 'We have nothing here, said they, but five loaves, and two fishes. Bring them hither to me, saith he" (ch. xiv, 16—18). Nay even in that awful description of the solemnities of the Great Judgment-day, we are offended by expressions such as these, " Then shall the righteous answer, Sir, shall they say . . ." (ch. xxv, 37). Every obscurity, whether in the language or the sense, is unhesitatingly removed by the boldest expedients. Thus in Matth. i, 18 we read " it was perceived she was with child, and it was indeed by the Holy Ghost." In ch. xxv, 21 we find " go you in thither, where your Master delighteth to be." It would appear then that nothing was more foreign to our learned translator's intention, than to emulate the verbal accuracy, and scrupulous fidelity to the original, which honorably distinguish the public versions of those times.

The diction of this little book is perfectly unique. It was manifestly Cheke's desire to banish from our language every word, however simple or well-known, which was derived from a Latin root. Of this rather pedantic and whimsical attempt Mr. Goodwin gives us several instances (Introduction, p. 15): I will add a few more for the reader's edification. Where the English versions use " mount," Cheke employs " hill ;" for " diligently" he substitutes " busily ;" for " people" or " multitude," " throng" or " resort ;" for " scribe," " learned man" (but not in ch. ii, 4; vii, 29); for " endure," " abide ;" for " similitude," " by-word" (but " parable," ch. xiii, 34); for " verily," " truly ;" for " tribulation," " wretched time," &c. He also sought to force upon our native tongue a profusion of strange compounds, invented after the analogy of the German; not merely comparatively obvious forms like " cursedness" for " abomination" (ch. xxiv, 15); " unstaidness" for " excess ;" unlawfulness" for iniquity ;" " soulish" for " natural" (Ψυχικὸς 1 Cor. ii, 14); &c. but uncouth monsters such as " gain-birth" for " regeneration ;" " onwriting" for " superscription ;" "small-faithed" for " of little-faith ;" " gainrising" for " resurrection ;" words which never could have been generally received without altering the genius of our language, and throwing it back full two hundred years. In the same spirit he sedulously employs the English possessive case to an extent seldom met with elsewhere; and strives to rescue from oblivion many words which at that period had become nearly obsolete. Of this kind is Chaucer's and Wickliffe's " meini" for " household ;" Wickliffe's " tollboth" for " receipt of custom ;" " shire" for " kindred" or " tribe," &c. His motive for retaining " margarites" for " pearls" (ch. vii, 6, &c) ; " phantasm" for " apparition"(ch. xiv, 26) ; " acrids" in Matth. iii, 4, for which he has " locusts" in Mark i, 6, I do not pretend to explain.

But while I cannot speak very favorably of Sir John Cheke's taste and judgment in the particulars to which I have referred, it would be unjust to deny that Mr. Goodwin has done good service to sacred literature by the publication of this version. In addition to the interest attached to it both on account of its author and his times, it displays much intrinsic worth, and has afforded me many valuable hints in the course of the present volume. See especially Matth. iv, 5 ; 23 ; v, 21 ; vi, 22 ; ix, 2 ; xv, 6 ; xx, 23 ; xxiv, 12 ; 31 ; xxv, 14 ; xxvi, 2. The translator's notes, if not very deep, are sensible and instructive; but the inaccurate state of the whole manuscript may tempt us to suspect, that we are in possession of little more than his first rough outline, which he would doubtless have retouched and completed, had peace and leisure been granted to his later years.

<small>Geneva New Testament, 1st ed. 1557.</small> Very superior to the "Great Bible" is the English Translation made at Geneva by a few Marian exiles, and first published in that city in 1557. I know not whether King James's words at the Hampton Court Conference are truly reported, that though he had not yet seen a good English version of the Scriptures, the Geneva was the worst of them all; but unless he had reference solely to the marginal annotations, I fear that I cannot agree with the royal critic. Each of the previous versions seems to have been executed by one man; every portion of the Geneva New Testament is said to have been revised by several of the ripest scholars of the age, whose devotion to this noble work beguiled the hours of banishment and deep affliction. They appear to have paid little attention to Coverdale and the "Great Bible;" but taking Tyndal for their model, they subjected his version to a searching examination, retaining his renderings where they deemed them satisfactory, and never deserting his text without some adequate motive. The Geneva editors bestowed much care on the Greek particles; for although Cranmer's version had already supplied some of Tyndal's deficiencies on this head, numerous important omissions were still left for its successors to detect. Another considerable improvement was their representing in a separate character the words they found it necessary to insert, in order to complete the sense

of their translation. This admirable expedient is supposed to have originated with Sebastian Munster (Biblia Latina, 1534), but it was first used in English for the Geneva New Testament. In the " Great Bible" the same variation in the type had been applied to a widely different purpose. The practice of the Geneva in this respect was followed in due time by the Bishops' and King James's Bibles, in which last italics were soon substituted for the small Roman letters of the earliest editions. The brief annotations which crowd the margin of the New Testament of 1557, will find favor with none save the admirers of the theological school then predominant at Geneva. A few, and but a few of them, relate to the interpretation of the text (e. g. Matth. xxii, 24 ; xxvi, 49; Luke, i, 28; Acts ii, 13 ; xx, 9 ; xxviii, 15 ; Rom. xvi, 23 ; Col. i, 24 ; Hebr. ix, 7 ; 9, &c), and so far resemble those in Coverdale's Bible, described above (p. 86). In general, they comprise a sort of running commentary on the sacred writers, strongly impregnated with the peculiar views of Calvin and Beza, which are set forth in a tone as positive and uncompromising as can well be imagined. When we reflect that the Geneva version was the Family Bible of the middle classes in England for two full generations after its first appearance, we may conceive how powerful an engine these notes became in the hands of that party, which in the next century laid the throne and altar in the dust. The piety and unaffected earnestness of their authors only served to render the poison thus disseminated doubly noxious. But the feeling that we are treading hostile ground must not make us blind to the merits of these excellent men. They were intimately versed in the Scriptures,

94 *Introduction.*

and profoundly imbued with their spirit. It is not too much to say, that their version is the best in the English Language, with the single exception of our present Authorised Bible. And even King James's revisers sometimes retain the renderings of the Bishops' Bible, where they are decidedly inferior to that of the Geneva New Testament (e. g. Matth. v, 29; xii, 14; xiii, 45; xvi, 1 &c.). With the edition of 1557, however, commenced that unhappy deference to Beza's Latin version, published only the year before (see the Geneva renderings of Matth. i, 11; Luke ii, 22; Gal. iv, 17; Hebr. x, 38), which has in some instances warped the judgment of our own translators also.

It is proper to state, that the version of the New Testament given in the Geneva *Bible* of 1560, varies considerably from that in the first edition of 1557. The alterations can scarcely have proceeded from the original translators; and, considered as a whole, are inferior to the interpretations which they displace. Wherever the edition of 1560 is not expressly quoted, I have used the earlier New Testament of 1557.

The Bishops' Bible, 1568, 1572. The Bishops' Bible is a revision of Cranmer's or the " Great Bible," executed by several Bishops and other eminent divines, under the superintendence of Archbp. Parker, who wrote the eloquent and instructive Preface. It was first published in 1568, but the second edition of 1572, which is esteemed the more correct, has been chiefly consulted for the present work. This Bible became the Authorised version of our Church, in the room of the " Great Bible," until it was superseded in its turn by King James's translation of 1611; but the Geneva translation retained its footing in private families, during the whole reign of Elizabeth. To the spirit of rivalry thus engendered must be ascribed the terms of unfair depreciation, in which some writers have spoken of the Bishops' Bible; as though it derived its sole worth or interest from the accidental circumstance of its being the basis of our present Translation. I certainly do not prefer it to the Geneva version; but it little deserves the contemptuous neglect it has often experienced. Its most obvious blemish is a closer adherence to the letter of the Greek than our language requires, or indeed admits. Thus the Bishops' Bible is the first which renders $\pi\alpha\iota\delta\iota\text{o}\nu$ in Matth. ii, "young child" (see p. 34); and the following expressions sound very harshly in English: Matth. ix, 38 "that he will thrust forth ($\dot{\epsilon}\kappa\beta\acute{\alpha}\lambda\eta$) laborers into his harvest;" xxi, 19 "one fig-tree;" xxviii, 14 "make you careless;" Luke ii, 15 "the men the shepherds;" Acts xxiii, 27 (still retained in our present version) "came I with an army;" 1 Thess. iv, 17 "we which live which remain;" Hebr. ii, 16 "he taketh not on him the angels." But though these instances may convict the translators of a lack of critical discernment, they spring from an honest anxiety to approach as near as possible to the precise words of the original. A more serious fault is their extravagant multiplication of the smaller characters within brackets, the use of which they borrowed from the earlier versions (see p. 92). With the legitimate design of this notation the reader is familiar (see p. 60); but it is a mischievous practice to insert in the body of Scripture words or clauses intended to limit or explain the subject matter of the text. Thus in Luke i, 56 this edition reads " and [afterward] returned to her own house;" the term within brackets being added by the translators on their own unsupported authority. Several instances of this kind had been found in the Geneva version, and the fault is retained (e. g. Mark xiv, 62; Eph. ii, 5), or even increased (1 Cor. x, 30) in the Bishops'. The interpolations from the Vulgate in Cranmer's Bible (see p. 88) are for the most part rejected in Parker's. In some places, however, they are retained (e. g. Luke xvi, 21; John xii, 19; Rom. xii, 17); and though the Geneva New Testament may not have had any great influence with its successors, they adopt its rendering in at least one important passage, where it is undoubtedly wrong (Luke ii, 22). Only a few of the marginal notes in this edition relate to the interpretation of the text of Scripture; they are, however, rather expository than doctrinal, and consequently are not liable to the same objection as those of the Geneva version. It was reserved for the wisdom of our own translators to reject every marginal note that savoured of the nature of a comment. Neither in this, nor in other respects, can the Bishops' Bible stand in competition with King James's. But, at the very lowest estimate, it is the careful production of conscientious and learned men; and supplies us with the means of determining how far the idioms of Hellenistic Greek can safely be transfused into our native tongue.

Laurence's Critique. While this Bible was in preparation, Archbishop Parker consulted one Laurence, an eminent Scriptural critic of that age, respecting the plan and details of the revision then in progress. Laurence's brief critique on the earlier versions is preserved in Strype's Life of Parker (Appendix lxxxv, pp. 139—142; see also Townley's Biblic. Literat. vol. iii, p. 180), and possesses some value as being the only document of the kind now extant. If it be anything more than a hasty sketch, it will by no means raise our estimate of the scholarship of that period: for though his remarks are apposite, and for the most part true, yet they are superficial and sometimes even trifling (as that on Matth. xxviii, 14). Although he examines but twenty-nine texts (all of them, except Col. ii, 13, from the first three Gospels), he distributes his observations into no less than six distinct heads. Either the passage is " not aptly translated ;" or " words and pieces of sentences are omitted ;" or " words are superfluous ;" or "the sentence changed ;" or there is " an error in doctrine ;" or " the moods and tenses are changed." He moreover notes one or two texts as "not well considered by Beza and Erasmus." On his suggestion the last clause of Mark xv, 3 was admitted into the text, and the words found in the margin of our present Bibles at Luke x, 22 would have been inserted in the Bishops' Bible had his opinion been adopted. Yet in some instances he blames Cranmer's version for too easily receiving doubtful clauses on the authority of the Vulgate. He considers it an error in doctrine that ἵνα in Luke ix, 45 was not rendered τελικῶς, "that they should not understand it." On the whole therefore, notwithstanding the laudatory terms in which Laurence is usually referred to, I cannot think that the arrangement of his materials is the best that could be devised ; nor are his criticisms of that worth or importance which several writers have attached to them.

Rhemish New Testament, 1582. The Anglo-Romish version of the New Testament, published at Rheims in 1582, is a very literal translation from the Latin Vulgate, which the crooked policy of the Roman

Catholic Church had recently raised to that paramount authority, which rightfully belongs only to the original text. Among the many excellencies of the Vulgate itself, perspicuity will scarcely be thought the most prominent; and the Rhemish translators adhered so servilely to its idioms, and even to the very order of its words, that they produced a version which is neither English nor Latin, but composed in an obscure and perplexing dialect of their own; such as always must have been (as perhaps it was designed to be), in a great measure unintelligible to all who were unable to read the Vulgate for themselves. On no other supposition can I account for their perpetual employment of barbarous words, which no one ever did, or would wish to meet with elsewhere. Such are "sindon," Mark xv, 46; "zealators," Acts xxi, 20; "præfinition," Eph. iii, 11; "contristate," iv, 30; "agnition," Philem. v. 6; "repropiciate," Heb. ii, 17; and a host of others of the same stamp, that remind us of nothing so forcibly, as of Gardiner's famous list of untranslateable expressions, which amuses the student of the History of the Reformation (Burnet, Hist. Reform. Pt. I, Bk. iii).* Yet in justice it must be observed, that no case of wilful perversion of Scripture has ever been brought home to the Rhemish translators. Wherever the Vulgate rendering is erroneous or insufficient, its followers of course are equally defective. To tread in its steps was all they aimed at, and this poor object of their ambition they have not failed to attain. Wickliffe's Bible, I think, they never saw; but with all their

---

* "Gardiner, though wanting power to keep the light of the Word from shining, sought out of policy to put it into a dark lantern." Fuller, Church History, Bk. v, Sect. iv, 35.

contempt for our vernacular translations, they have not scrupled to use some of the earlier versions as the basis of their own. Nor should I suppress the fact, that the Rhemish divines may occasionally do us good service, by furnishing some happy phrase or form of expression, which had eluded the diligence of their more reputable predecessors.

If then it be asked on what grounds the Rhemish New Testament has always been so severely condemned by Protestant writers, I confidently reply, chiefly on account of its notes; which present to us a mass of bigotry, sophistry, and unfairness, of which the world has seen but few examples. We are indebted to Dr. Fulke, sometime Master of Pembroke College, Cambridge, for an acute and unanswerable though rather angry refutation of this production of the "traiterous seminarie" at Rheims; in which he traces his hapless victims through every paragraph of their Preface and Annotations, and prints the version of the Bishops' Bible (which was then the Authorised Translation of the English Church) in parallel columns with the Rhemish text. I can best convey a notion of the truly jesuitical character of the Popish notes, by submitting to the reader a few choice extracts from their comment on the sacred volume. Thus on Luke xvii, 14 we find the following edifying remarks. "A man may sometimes be so contrite and penitent, that his sin is forgiven before he come to the priest; but then also he must notwithstanding go to the priest, as these lepers did: specially whereas we are never sure how contrite we are, and because there is no true contrition but with desire also of the sacrament in time and place." Now without disputing that this precious note contains what Dr. Fulke calls in his homely phrase "a beggarly petition of two principles," I would rather draw attention to the editors' insinuation of what they have not the courage to say plainly; namely, that our Lord sent the lepers to the priest, that they might receive "the sacrament" of absolution. The Rhemish rendering of Heb. xi, 21 is well known, "and adored the top of his rod," an error which was derived from the Vulgate. In their note the editors, after indulging in a sneer at the Hebrew verity, draw from these words the modest conclusion, "that adoration may be done to creatures, or to God at and before a creature." On Acts xvii, 34, after telling the idle story of Dionysius the Areopagite, and identifying him with St. Denys of France, they condescend to inform us that some persons deny the authenticity of "his notable and divine works on the Sacrament, &c. . . by an old sleight of heretics, but most proper to these of all others. Who, seeing all antiquity against them, are forced to be more bold, or rather impudent than others on that point."

But it were endless to enumerate every violation of common sense, or common decency (1 Cor. vii, 5), with which the Rhemish notes on the New Testament overflow. I will content myself with one more instance, which is in itself enough to justify the strongest censures that have at any time been passed on this miserable farrago of impertinence and falsehood. On John v, 39 they say: "Christ reprehendeth the Jews, that daily reading the Scriptures, and acknowledging that in them they should find light and salvation, they yet looked over them so superficially, that they could not find therein Him to be Christ, their king, Lord, life and Saviour. For the special masters and scribes of the Jews were like unto our heretics now, who be ever talking and turning and shuffling the Scriptures, but are of all men the most ignorant in the deep knowledge thereof. And therefore our Master referreth them not to the reading only or learning them without book, or having the sentences thereof gloriously painted or written in their Temples, houses or coats: but to the deep search of the meaning and mysteries of the Scriptures; which are not so easily to be seen in the letter." How grave and seemly is Fulke's rebuke of this flippant insolence. "We confess that the Scriptures are not only to be read, written, or painted on walls, but diligently to be searched, and deeply to be studied, in which we know eternal life is to be found, without all addition of Popish doctrine, which is not to be found in Holy Scripture." Thus far of the Rhemish New Testament.

King James's Bible, 1611. Of the Authorised, or King James's version of the Bible, first published in 1611, it seems adviseable to say little in this place, since the examination of its excellencies and defects forms the subject of the present work. I hardly need observe that it has received the highest panegyrics from Biblical scholars of every shade of theological sentiment, from the date of its publication to the present time. For more than a century after its completion almost the only person of respectable acquirements and station who wrote against it was Dr. Robert Gell, a London clergyman, whose twenty Discourses or Sermons on this subject (London, 1659, folio) I have not been able to meet with.* Judging from Lewis's description of the book, my loss has not been great. Gell had taken up a foolish and very unfounded notion

---

* They are not in the British Museum, nor in Sion College Library.

that the Calvinistic bias of some of the translators had a prejudicial effect on the version: but Gal. v, 6 is the only text I can discover to which he objects on this ground. The New Testament he thought to be worse rendered than the Old, and he complains that the order of the words in the original is wholly neglected (Heb. x, 34). Lewis also mentions Matth. xx, 23; 1 John iii, 20, as passages which Dr. Gell thought capable of improvement; but if he gives us any approaching to a fair analysis of the contents of these Sermons, they never could have endangered the reputation of the translation which they assailed.

Having thus endeavored to prepare the reader for what he may look for in our earlier versions, I pass on to a brief consideration of the principal revised translations of the New Testament, which have appeared in this country since the publication of King James's Bible.

And not to revive the memory of the disgraceful travestie of 1729, or of Dr. Harwood's "liberal translation" into polite English; or of several other attempts long since forgotten (see p. 49 note); we will first speak of the "Family Expositor" of Dr. Doddridge, a learned and most estimable man, who made it the sole business of his life to consecrate his moderate abilities to the service of Him that gave them.* The common version being recommended by Doddridge for the purpose of family worship, it is exhibited in a column parallel with his own paraphrase, in the body

Doddridge's Family Expositor, 1739—1756.

---

* Were not Mr. Borrow a very good-humored person, I should suspect a little malice in his manner of associating the name of our worthy nonconformist Divine with that of Fielding, his uncongenial neighbour in the English burial-ground at Lisbon. I will not quote the passage I allude to, for who has not read the " Bible in Spain?"

of which a new translation is contained whose text is distinguished from the comment merely by being printed in italics. Since the style of this author's paraphrase is rather florid and verbose, the translation which is so intimately incorporated with it must unavoidably partake of the same character: a defect however which those readers will scarcely censure who regard the paraphrase and the text (as in truth they ought to be regarded) as but parts of an inseparable whole. It is evident, therefore, that some wrong was done to Dr. Doddridge by an injudicious admirer, who after his death extracted the scattered portions of his version from the paraphrase, and published the collected fragments as a continuous translation of the New Testament. Tried by so unfair a test the modern phraseology and affected elegance which sometimes deform Dr. Doddridge's writings will appear very offensive: and we may well believe that several bold interpretations which are not much out of place in a commentary, would never have been admitted into the text of Scripture by this humble-minded and pious divine (e. g. Luke vii, 47; Acts xvi, 12; Rom. i, 17; 1 Cor. xv, 29; 1 Pet. iii, 7). But if we are content to use his work as Dr. Doddridge intended it to be used, we may derive from it much edification, and perhaps more knowledge than we should be inclined to confess. To his version I shall often have cause to refer in favorable terms; it is faithful, perspicuous and agreeable. The notes and paraphrase contain much information, not always very exact or profound, but amply sufficient for practical purposes. On the tone and spirit of his devotional " Improvements " it is needless to enlarge. They have received too many proofs of the public approbation to require praise from me.

Towards the close of the last century much the

greater part of the New Testament was translated by two ministers of the Scottish kirk; by Campbell in his work on the Four Gospels, and by Macknight in that on the Apostolical Epistles. Of these authors Dr. Campbell most deserves our attention. For though he had not a particle of that modesty and unaffected gentleness which in Macknight conciliate respect even where they fail to convince; yet he possessed in a high degree several qualities which are essential to a good interpreter of Scripture: great acuteness of intellect, unwearied industry, competent learning, and independence of mind. Indeed, the last-named feature of his character is rather amusingly displayed in the contrast presented by his ardent professions of candor and impartiality, with the hard measure he deals to established prejudices. His Preliminary Dissertations will reward the most careful study; so richly do they abound in the development of correct principles, and in just and elegant, though severe criticism.

<small>Campbell on the Gospels, 1788.</small>

Of his translation itself it is not easy to speak with commendation. That it ordinarily conveys the sense of the original may be true; since many inaccuracies of our common Bibles are amended by Dr. Campbell; but nothing can be more repugnant to good taste than the perpetual striving after petty ornament, which disfigures every page and every line of his version. Instead of the simple sentences and parallel clauses which so strongly mark the style of the Gospels, and distinguish them from all other writings, we are constantly disgusted by those involved constructions and balanced periods which properly belong only to regular and artificial composition. As some of my readers may not happen to have Campbell's book at hand, I will extract a few passages at random, to explain my meaning. Mark vi, 19, 20. "This roused Herodias' resentment, who would have killed John, but could not, because Herod respected him, and, knowing him to be a just and holy man, protected him, and did many things recommended by him, and heard him with pleasure." Luke xvi, 11, 12. "If therefore ye have not been honest in the deceitful, who will intrust you with the true riches? And if ye have been unfaithful managers for another, who will give you any thing to manage for yourselves?" John ii, 10. "When the director of the feast had tasted the wine made of water, not knowing whence it was (but the servants who drew the water knew), he said, addressing the bridegroom, Every body presenteth the best wine first, and worse wine afterwards when the guests have drunk largely; but thou hast reserved the best until now." How infinitely is this gaudy verbiage surpassed in dignity and real beauty, by the plain old version, which our Scotch critic sought to supersede.

To this strange and incongruous translation Campbell has annexed a body of notes in every respect superior to it. Occasionally, indeed, he falls into distressing errors, by venturing to discuss topics of which he knows little;* and more often, when he is in the right, his dogmatic tone excites an involuntary prepossession against his decisions (See his notes on Matth. v, 21; Luke xxiii, 15). But these are the exceptions. Considered as a whole, we may truly

---

* For instance, he often speaks of the Peshito Syriac with an air of confidence. Yet when on John v, 39 he tells us that in the Syriac language the word $\dot{\epsilon}\rho\epsilon\nu\nu\tilde{a}\tau\epsilon$ has the same ambiguity as in Greek and Latin, he proves his ignorance of the very elements of Aramæan Grammar.

say, that the student will seldom consult Campbell's annotations, without deriving from them a high degree of pleasure and instruction.

Macknight on the Epistles, 1795. Macknight's New Translation and Commentary on the Apostolical Epistles has been received so favorably even by first-rate scholars, that it must necessarily be considered a useful and excellent work. Its chief merit (and that confessedly is no slight one), consists in tracing the connection between the several parts of the Apostles' reasoning, and in unfolding those less obvious links of their discourse which are apt to escape an inexperienced eye. Sometimes indeed this difficult investigation is pushed beyond all reasonable bounds. I dare assert that Dr. Macknight is the only reader of the First Epistle to the Thessalonians, who ever thought he had discovered in it a formal and regular argument on the evidences of Christianity. In general his remarks are characterised by good sense, patient reflection, and a sincere love of truth for its own sake. His main defect is an ignorance of the Greek language so gross, as to be perfectly astonishing in a professed translator of the New Testament. In the course of the thirty years which he devoted to his great work, it never seems to have occurred to him that a tolerable acquaintance with the original tongues is indispensable to the Biblical critic. I conceive that no one will deny the truth of my statement, who has read Macknight's fourth Preliminary Essay "On translating the Greek language used by the writers of the New Testament." We are there told that ἴδετε (Phil. i, 30) and φάγεται (James v, 3) are present tenses, that ἑαυτὸς is often used for ἄλληλυς, that ὁ γὰρ "for he who" and ὁ δὲ "but he who" (Rom. vi, 10. The common text has ὁ) are analogous to ὁ δὲ σπαρεὶς in Matth. xiii, 20; and much more *ejusdem farinæ*, with which I am ashamed to trouble my readers. In tracing the various senses of the particles (a matter of the utmost importance in the Epistles), he has no idea of first fixing the primary sense of each, and then deducing all others from it. His account of the preposition εἰς, for example, is a sad medley of blunder and confusion. Hence it follows, that in questions of mere philology and grammar the judgment of this diligent and good man is worth absolutely nothing. It is painful to speak thus of the labors of a virtuous and most exemplary person; but were a foreigner to test our advancement in critical science by the lasting popularity of Macknight's Translation among us, his estimate would certainly not be flattering, and I may add it would be very unjust.

One fanciful opinion held by Macknight my subject compels me to notice. With scarcely any other knowledge of the earlier versions than may be gleaned from Johnson or Lewis, he has chosen to pronounce that Tyndal and Coverdale formed their translations from the Latin Vulgate: and that all the rest (our present Authorised version included) "are not different translations, but different editions of Tyndal and Coverdale's translation." From these premises the inference is direct, that "the first English Translators, having made their versions from the Vulgate, the subsequent translators, by copying them, have retained a number of the errors of that antient version." (General Preface, Sect. II).

It cannot be required of me in this place to unravel the tissue of misapprehensions which led Macknight to conclusions so remote from the truth. It is sufficient to aver that no one could believe Tyndal's translation to be made from the Vulgate, who had taken the trouble of glancing at a few chapters of the version in question.* Since Macknight has alleged no passages in support of his assumption, I need only refer the reader to the materials brought together in the present work. If he shall find in them (as I am persuaded he will not find) any proof that Tyndal systematically deserted the Greek text for the Latin Vulgate, or made any other use of the latter than that which I have already mentioned (see p. 79), then he may be allowed to believe with Macknight, that "as Greek was very little studied in those days, it may be doubted whether Tyndal understood it so well as to be able to translate the New Testament from the Greek;" and that "in translating the more difficult texts which he did not understand, he implicitly followed the Vulgate."

Archbishop Newcome's Translation, 1796, &c.

The station and high character of Primate Newcome render it difficult to speak of his Translations with freedom. His critical taste had been formed in the school of Lowth and Kennicott, men never to be named without respect and gratitude, but who delighted to wander in the slippery tracks of plausible conjecture. From this spirit proceeds the constant tampering with the Hebrew text, which grieves us in the Archbishop's version of the Minor Prophets. To such an excess is this vicious practice carried, that in the short book of Hosea alone he proposes no less than fifty-

---

* On the sources of Coverdale's Bible of 1535 I have spoken above, p. 84. Much of Macknight's fallacious reasoning arises from his confounding this version with one published in 1538 by Coverdale, under the feigned name of Hollybushe, and which was a *professed* translation from the Vulgate.

one emendations, on authorities so insufficient that Bp. Horsley (himself no very cautious interpreter) enumerates only to condemn them. To a mind thoroughly imbued with such principles Griesbach's theory of recensions, bold and ingenious as it is, must have appeared a self-evident truth; and Newcome's first object in preparing his Translation of the New Testament, was to impart to the English reader the results of that editor's investigations. So devoted indeed is he to his new master, that in one remarkable passage (1 Cor. x, 9) he has even outstripped him in the march of innovation, and brought upon himself a sharp rebuke from no unfriendly pen. (Magee on the Atonement, Vol. iii, p. 203). Yet in an earlier work, his "Historical View of English Biblical Translations," the Primate had given evidence of so correct a judgment, and a knowledge of his subject so accurate, that he would have been esteemed equal to a revision of our Authorised version, had he never attempted it. Within the limits to which he confines himself, nothing can be more exact and complete than his twenty-one Rules for the guidance of a reviser; few failures are more signal than his own application of them: so much less difficult is theory than practice. The fate of Archbp. Newcome's literary character has been singularly hard. After a life devoted to studies which adorned his sacred profession, a posthumous and perhaps an ill-considered production, marred the honorable reputation which it had been the first object of this able and industrious scholar's ambition to acquire. By his imprudent liberality and excessive thirst for novelty he rendered himself a fit tool in the hands of mischievous and unprincipled men; and must now go down to posterity as one on whose foundations the authors of the "Improved Version" were glad to build, when they endeavored to expunge from the New Testament the blessed doctrine of our Lord's Divinity.

Dr. Boothroyd's Bible, 1823, 1836.
Among the admirers of the Archbishop's Translation the first place may be assigned to Dr. Boothroyd; who in his valuable "Family Bible" (3 vol. 4to. 1823), as also in his later and more condensed edition (1 vol. 1836), has exhibited a version of his own, differing widely in many particulars from that in common use. In those parts of Newcome's work which are open to the gravest objection, he is not followed by Dr. Boothroyd; who has however adopted the Primate's renderings in certain passages, where sound discretion might have prompted him to abide by the Authorised Translation (Acts xvii, 22; xxv, 25; 1 Cor. vii, 8; Rev. xxii, 2). In the Preface to his last edition Dr. Boothroyd informs us that his chief reason for altering the English text was a conviction that "the common version is too verbal and literal to be in all instances faithful and *perspicuous.*" Since he produces no instances of this want of perspicuity, we are compelled to gather his precise meaning from the materials his own work affords us. Thus in the corrected text of his Bible, we frequently meet with such renderings as the following: Matth. xviii, 32. "O thou wicked servant, I *released thee and so far* forgave thee all that debt." Acts xxi, 4. "That he should not go up to Jerusalem, *if he regarded his own liberty.*" 2 Cor. iii, 17. "Now the Lord is *he who imparteth* the Spirit." Now even admitting for the moment that the clauses here printed in italics, and of which there is no vestige in the original, assist in bringing out the full meaning of the sacred writers, it will hardly be disputed that they are not so much translations of

Introduction. 111

the words in the Greek text, as rather loose paraphrases upon them.* But since Scripture is the word of God, it becomes those on whom a gift so precious has been bestowed, to be very jealous in preserving it separate from the uninspired comments of men: we must neither add thereto, nor diminish from it. And though the difference of idiom often renders it impossible to translate the Greek Testament into a modern language, without supplying a few words to complete the sense or the construction, yet should this necessary liberty be restricted within the narrowest bounds. It is on no account to be allowed, unless the words which are added are so certainly implied by the holy penmen, that they would have been expressed had the genius of the Greek language permitted or required them. Disapproving, therefore, as I do of Dr. Boothroyd's first principle of translation, it is superfluous for me to dwell on that less important error of judgment, which led him to banish from his version, as far as possible, those peculiar Hebrew phrases, so venerable and full of meaning, which strongly characterise our common Bibles; and which, without perplexing the ignorant, or justly offending the most refined, are stored up in our memories in happy association with the most solemn and affecting truths of Religion.

Holy Bible with 20,000 emendations, 1841.   Some interest was excited about three years ago by the publication of an edition of the Holy Bible, which professes to contain no less than twenty thousand emendations of the Authorised version, and is, I believe, the

---

* A somewhat similar misuse of the Italic character (or rather of the type which corresponds to it), though not carried to the same extent, was noticed in the Bishops' Bible, see p. 95.

avowed production of an eminent London physician. It is possible that Biblical learning may not have gained very much by so laudable an employment of this gentleman's leisure hours for thirty years; and the examples of Mead and Mason Good might have warned him, that theology is a profession no less exclusive than his own, since it demands and repays the devotion of the whole mind. Still it is cheering to see a pious and intelligent man, in the midst of pursuits which are commonly deemed unfavourable to spiritual improvement, dedicating a portion of his time to the critical study of God's word. The fundamental error of his plan is that his edition contains the bare text of Scripture, without a single note to intimate his reasons for the changes he has introduced, or the authorities by which they are sanctioned:* nor has he devised any means of shewing in what places his interpretation differs from that of King James's version, or where he agrees with it. In common with all competent judges our physician speaks highly of the Authorised Translation, which he has taken as the groundwork of his own, and has followed in several cases where it is usually considered faulty (e. g. Matth. i, 25; xxviii, 17; 1 Cor. xv, 1, 2, &c.): but he has no marginal ren-

---

* It may be proper to state that in the Preface we find a list of about 300 authors, from whom, either mediately or immediately, he has derived his materials. But it is clear that such a list can be of no practical service, and the extraordinary order in which the names are arranged can scarcely fail to provoke a smile. I quote the first line which meets my eye. " Bush, Pagninus, Geierus, Valckenæar, Herodotus, Bennett, Dobree, Clarke, Johnson." The name of Watson occurs twice: if Bp. Richard Watson and Richard Watson of the Methodist connection are meant, it would be as well to say so. And are not Dathe and Dathius the same person?

derings, and does not use italics. Limiting my remarks to the New Testament, I conceive his attempt to be respectable, and even useful. He admits some of the best corrections of modern scholars (Matth. xx, 23; John viii, 44; Acts xxii, 9; 2 Cor. iii, 18; Tit. ii, 13; 1 John v, 16 &c.); he arranges the hymns in Luke i, ii, and all the poetical portions of the Old Testament, in parallel lines; and adopts the great improvement of assimilating the forms of Proper Names throughout both Testaments. There are, however, a few difficult texts in which he has ventured on a doubtful paraphrase (e. g. Luke iii, 23; Rom. ix, 3); more often he has erred by resigning himself to the guidance of Newcome, or some other unsafe authority: and with one petition in the Lord's Prayer he has most rashly tampered, on no grounds either critical or philological that I can discover, but wholly induced by what he presumes to consider the exigency of the sense. "And leave us not in temptation," Matth. vi, 13.

Dr. Symonds's Observations, 1789—1794. The "Observations" of Dr. Symonds of Cambridge "On the expediency of revising our Authorised version" are for the most part confined to the language of the English Translation itself, which forms the subject of my third general head. His work gives evidence of much sagacity and research, but the bitterness of the temper in which it is written renders it a wearisome task to read it throughout: indeed so wearisome that nothing but a sense of duty prevented my closing the book after looking over a few pages. His absurd and passionate prejudices are too much for the patience of one of the mildest of critics, Dean Turton, who says of him, "Dr. Symonds had taken such a dislike to everything connected with our

Authorised version, that he scarcely ever permitted his judgment to interfere, in that matter, with his determination to find fault." King James's Bible is pronounced by this person perpetually "ambiguous and incorrect, even in matters of the highest importance." The adoption also by our Translators of so much of Tyndal's phraseology and diction was, it seems, a most fortunate circumstance, inasmuch as "their original compositions were deficient in point of elegance and style." (Pref. to Observ. on Epistles). Since Dr. Symonds's opinion is somewhat novel, we are obliged to him for informing us which of their original compositions he had specially in view. He alludes to the " pedantic and uncouth " Preface of the Translators to the Reader, a production which less enlightened students are content to regard as a treasure of wisdom and sacred eloquence.*

Symonds's mode of dividing his matter appears rational and convenient. He considers first the ambiguities of our translation: whether they arise from the obscure reference of the relative to the antecedent (a defect to some extent unavoidable in a language whose relatives are indeclinable); or from the use of equivocal words or phrases; or from the indeterminate sense of the prepositions. From these ambiguities he passes on to the grammatical errors of our version, after sneering unmercifully at the " brisk manner " of the translators, " who seemed to think grammatical accuracy beneath them." Many of his corrections are utterly frivolous; many are delivered

---

* In spite of this angry critic's denunciation it is much to be wished that all the larger editions of our Bibles contained the admirable Preface. Can any thing in language be more beautiful than the concluding paragraph?

Introduction. 115

in the hypercritical tone which Bishop Lowth had but too much countenanced (See p. 53, 55); but no small portion of the rest has been adopted in the present work: His next topic is the obsolete or harsh, and (such is his gentle appellation) the "mean and vulgar" expressions of our version. If the reader will turn to Matth. xxviii, 4; 14; Luke ii, 6; xxi, 16; Acts vii, 26; xxvi, 21; Eph. v, 5 &c. he may find some honest English words and phrases, which Dr. Symonds holds to be " low." He concludes with a sensible discussion of the question, " how far a version of the Bible should be literal ;" and justly determines that a translation of Scripture should always retain the peculiarities of the original, excepting where by such a course it would become unintelligible.

I have entered into this detail respecting a performance which is now little remembered, not only that my readers may be enabled to compare Dr. Symonds's plan (so far as it extends) with my own; but because it cannot be uninstructive to observe how good mental endowments, both natural and acquired, may serve only to make their possessor ridiculous, if they be not regulated by a temperate, kind and candid spirit.

Pr. Scholefield's Hints, 1836, 2nd ed. Widely removed from this arrogant and supercilious bearing is Professor Scholefield, in his " Hints for an Improved Translation of the New Testament," a work to which I owe much that I have suggested in the following pages. His scheme in one respect differs from my own, since he anticipates with complacency a public revision of our common version, and offers his " Hints" as a contribution to the existing stock of materials for executing that revision satisfactorily. But it is obvious that had he filled up his own outline in a manner worthy of his subject and himself, such a work as mine need never have been projected. For all practical purposes it will matter little, whether a series of critiques on particular passages be designed as a "Supplement" to the present version, or as "Hints" towards a revision of it. But the fact is, that this book (like too many others which proceed from the same learned pen), is but a slight and imperfect sketch; a collection of notes accidentally brought together in the course of private study: tolerably full in the Apostolical Epistles (though even in them passing over many obscure texts), but extremely meagre in the Historical books. On those points where as Greek Professor at Cambridge he might have spoken with the greatest weight, we are often disappointed by his total silence: yet when we meet with so much that is admirable, it seems ungrateful to complain that we have not more. His most elaborate notes are those on Acts x, 36—38; Rom. v, 7; 1 Cor. ix, 23; xv, 1, 2; 24; 2 Cor. iii, 17; 18; Gal. ii, 2—9; Phil. iv, 3; 1 Thess. iii, 5; Hebr. ix, 15—17; James iv, 5; each of which will be considered in its place. In the perplexing sentence Eph. iv, 16, he is not, I think, equally successful. Those of his emendations which at first sight may appear frivolous or unmeaning (e. g. Rom. xvi, 9; 1 Pet. v, 13) must be vindicated by recollecting the end he had in view; namely, to provide means for a thorough correction of the Authorised version: an undertaking concerning which I have already delivered my sentiments (See p. 1), but which has been too often recommended by great and virtuous men, for its advocacy to be imputed as a fault to any one.

Introduction.

Principles of Interpretation.
It may be fit to apprise the reader, that the principles of interpretation which I have adopted, are those established by the researches of eminent continental scholars, among whom Planck and Winer hold the chief place. They have been recently brought before the English public by Mr. Green, in his valuable " Grammar of the New Testament Dialect" (1842). We may now regard the relation which the Greek of the New Testament bears to that of the Classics as precisely ascertained: and the conclusion is that, so far as grammar is concerned, there is no broader distinction between them than must always exist between a written language in its most perfect state, and the spoken dialect of a later and declining age. Hence it follows that we may securely apply to the interpretation of the New Testament even the more refined laws of Greek syntax which are observed by the best Attic writers; since both reason and analogy teach us that the difference between the written style and that of ordinary speech in reference to those idiomatic niceties, is merely a difference in the frequency of their employment; for where such forms occur at all in common conversation, they are *unconsciously* used in strict accordance with grammatical propriety and the practice of standard authors. The importance of arriving at settled principles on this point will be duly estimated by those whose minds have been bewildered by the vague hermeneutics of the Hebraizing school of critics; men who by a dexterous use of the Septuagint and the Hebrew Concordance contrive to assign to the words of the sacred text (the unfortunate particles more especially) almost any sense which happens to suit their own preconceived opinions. Of course I would not be understood to deny that the

Introduction.

New Testament abounds with Hebraisms, which must be illustrated and explained by perpetual reference to the Septuagint and other Hellenistic sources: but I believe it will be found that this foreign influence never affects the *grammatical construction* of the Greek, except in such obvious and simple cases as can create no practical difficulty.*

I can scarcely hope that this view of the subject will prove satisfactory to Mr. Grinfield, whose enthusiastic veneration of the Alexandrine version is so warmly expressed in the eloquent Preface to his Hellenistic edition of the New Testament (1843). As it cannot be doubted that an intimate knowledge of that Translation is indispensable to the sound interpretation both of the Old and New Testament, his learned and laborious work entitles him to the gratitude of students of the Bible, whose necessary toil it greatly relieves. But it must be confessed that Mr. Grinfield's zeal for his favorite pursuit has in some measure biassed his judgment with respect to the utility of the Classics, as auxiliaries to the full understanding of the New Testament. "The way through Jerusalem and Mount Sion" he tells us " is open, plain and straight; that through Rome or Athens devious, and often perilous" (Præf. p. viii): forgetting, it would seem, that Alexandria is not Jerusalem, and that the " brooks which wash Mount Sion's hallowed feet" do not discharge themselves into the muddy channel of the Nile. At the risk, therefore, of incurring the imputation of " polluting

---

* As for example, the pleonastic use of the pronoun αὐτός, and of καὶ *in apodosi* (See note on Matth. ch. xv, 5, 6): or the construction of prepositions after certain veibs: e. g. φοβεῖσθαι, Matth. x, 28; ὁμολογεῖν, ibid. v. 32 &c.

Jordan's streams with the slime of the Tiber, or Arethusa, or Alpheus" (ibid. p. x), I shall endeavour to elucidate the inspired writings by a sparing use of such pertinent quotations from the Greek classics as the diligence of others, or my own slender store shall supply: bearing always in mind that Mr. Grinfield's complaints, though possibly over-earnest in tone and a little exaggerated in statement, are far from being entirely groundless. For there are critics, and those of high name and real genius, whose annotations on Scripture may not unjustly be described as " omnigena et pæne Babylonica barbaries, e scriniis Oratorum, Historicorum, Comicorum, Tragicorum, Eroticorum, omniumque fere scriptorum dicendi genere, frustatim et minutatim compilata." (ibid. p. ix).

Jebb's Sacred Literature, 1820.

I may reasonably be expected to deliver my sentiments with regard to the theory developed in Bp. Jebb's Sacred Literature, a volume which enjoys the good fortune of being highly esteemed by many, who cannot be suspected of any predilection for the theological tenets of its author.* His great object, as is well known, is the application to the New Testament of those principles of Hebrew poetry, the truth of which Bp. Lowth had irrefragably demonstrated in the case of

---

* I lately heard a Wesleyan preacher express his gratification at the light thrown on a portion of the Lord's Prayer by Bp. Jebb's simple arrangement.

   Thy name be hallowed:
   Thy kingdom come:
   Thy will be done:
   As in heaven, so upon the earth.

Thus referring " As in heaven &c." to each of the three petitions, not exclusively to the last.

the metrical books of the Old Testament: an hypothesis which at first sight is rather startling, but which he has established by such an overwhelming mass of evidence, that his general conclusions cannot be shaken. To a superficial reader, indeed, Bp. Jebb's work may appear loose and excursive: so frequently is he drawn aside from his subject into some delightful episode of criticism, or philology, or moral reflection. But on a closer examination it will be seen, that though he often strays from the direct road to dwell on a lovely prospect that may chance to arrest his attention; yet amidst all his roamings the end of his course is kept steadily in view. This seeming capriciousness is but a charm in the hand of a wizard, to beguile the tedium of abstract discussions, on a topic in itself perhaps rather dry and repulsive.

While we admit, however, that in the New Testament, and more particularly in our Lord's discourses as recorded in the Gospels, numerous passages occur which are constructed on the principles of Hebrew parallelism, we are by no means bound to acquiesce in all the details which Bp. Jebb alleges in illustration of his theory. Thus, his arrangement of the Hymn of Zacharias into two distinct parts, designed to be sung alternately by two semi-choruses, each carrying on a construction and sense of its own, independent of the other, has always seemed to me extremely arbitrary. That it accounts for the grammatical difficulties of this noble poem can prove but little, since Bp. Jebb distributed the Hymn into members for that very purpose. Nor will the analogy of several of the Psalms, which Bps. Lowth and Horsley divide in a similar manner, entirely remove our doubts. The Psalms were composed by the inspired penmen with a direct view to their use in the public worship of the Temple; such could not have been the design of the father of the Baptist.

An objection might also be raised to Jebb's occasional alterations of the text, when the received reading is not quite in accordance with the equilibrium of parallel clauses. Thus he would reject τοῦ προφήτου in Luke xi, 29 on testimony much weaker than that which he condemns Griesbach for relying on in 1 Cor. i, 22, 23. And this tendency in our author is the more to be regretted, as he confesses that his acquaintance with the subject of various readings was far from considerable (Letter liii. in vol. ii. of his Life, by Forster).

Such are the slight imperfections of a production which is an honor to the country that gave it birth: a production which would be eminent for elegant taste, profound scholarship, and manly piety, were not the lustre of these qualities dimmed by the original thought and severe logic which comprise its most striking features. On the value of Jebb's Sacred Literature as a help to the interpretation of Scripture it is needless to enlarge. The reflecting reader will easily perceive that a correct knowledge of the principles of composition adopted by the sacred writers cannot fail to be a key to their meaning in numberless doubtful cases, and to expand fresh beauties of conception or language even where the sense is sufficiently clear. Of the many texts which have derived new light from Bp. Jebb's investigations, I would particularise the examples of Epanodos in Matth. vii, 6; Philem. v. 5; his analysis of St. Paul's mixed quotation, Rom. xi, 33—35; and the sublime hymn of triumph over mystical Babylon, Rev. xviii, 1—xix, 3.

The Greek Commentators, Chrysostom, Theophylact &c.

I trust that I shall incur no censure for the frequency of my appeals to the Greek commentators, to Chrysostom and Theophylact more especially. Were it only that these venerable men were so happy as to read the Greek Testament in their native language, and made that one volume the study of their lives to an extent that the change of times and circumstances forbids to us, it were surely worth our while to consult them; the rather as they no doubt preserve many expositions of Scripture, which were current among generations anterior to their own. But in truth John Chrysostom, their Coryphæus, would have been conspicuous in any age or clime as the mightiest master of pulpit eloquence the Christian Church has hitherto beheld. Even now as we hang over the dead pages, and contemplate his passionate earnestness, his boldness in rebuking sin, and his all-absorbing zeal for the salvation of souls, a spark of that flame is kindled within us, which once glowed in the breasts of his enraptured hearers at Antioch or Constantinople. By some he has been compared to our English Barrow, and between their respective *styles* much similarity exists. Each of them is full of vigour; each of them tasks the resources of language to the utmost, by the copiousness, I might say the exuberance of his expressions. But here the parallel must end. Isaac Barrow was as little capable of emulating the delicate pathos and affectionate warmth of Chrysostom, as the Eastern Patriarch of brooking his calm, and patient, and exhaustive ratiocination.

For the purposes of the interpreter, however, Theophylact will be found more convenient than Chrysostom, since the work of the former is a perpetual commentary in the strictest sense of the term, unbroken by those practical exhortations which must and ought to form a large portion of every public homily. Presenting to us nearly all that is valuable in Chrysostom's explanations of Scripture (usually in the very words of his author, though in an abridged form), like his great model he is clear, rational, and orthodox. Nor have we any right to regard him as a mere compiler. He abounds in passages, some of them of great merit, which we have good reason for thinking original (see his note on John xvi, 8—11); and he occasionally cites the opinion of Chrysostom with a modest but decided intimation of dissent. It is not hard to point out errors both of doctrine and of fact in the writings of Theophylact (see his notes on Matth. xxiii, 35; xxvi, 26); but the student who observes how little that is really satisfactory has been added to our knowledge of the New Testament since his day, will scarcely deem the eleventh century a period of such dismal ignorance as it has pleased certain historians to imagine.

From Theodoret, the Ecclesiastical historian, we have a short exposition of St. Paul's Epistles, very inferior in value to those above mentioned. It contains little that may not be found in his preceptor Chrysostom, though for some motive which it is not easy to understand, his language seems studiously varied from that of his predecessor.*

---

* I have used the following editions. Theodoreti Opera, Schulze et Nosselt, Hal. 1771, Tom. iii. Theophylacti Opera, Venet. 1754, 4 tom. Chrysostomi Opera, Par. 1834, which is but a slight improvement on Montfaucon's edition of 1728. But the best edition of any portion of Chrysostom is the Homilies on St. Matthew by Field, Cambridge, 1839, 3 tom: for which more than twelve manuscripts and the Armenian version were consulted. Why will not Mr. Field continue his labors through the Homilies on John, the Acts, and Pauline Epistles?

A principal cause of the neglect into which the Greek Fathers have fallen in modern times, is the disagreement of their sentiments respecting Predestination and Free-will, with the doctrine which has prevailed on those points in the Western Church from Augustin downwards. And it must be admitted that their opinions are rather unseasonably insisted on in their Comments upon texts, which certainly appear to favor the antagonist view of the question (See, for instance, Chrysostom or Theodoret on Rom. ix, 22). If any are inclined on such grounds to discourage the study of their writings, I would venture to suggest, that let our own convictions on these mysterious topics be what they may (and every thinking being will have arrived at some conclusions regarding them), we knowingly and of necessity exclude half the truth from our minds. Being utterly unable to reconcile God's foreknowledge with man's responsibility, we are driven to lose sight of the one or the other, in order to relieve ourselves from suspense and doubt. Let this consideration, then, teach us moderation. Far be it from us to scan the hidden counsel of the Almighty: it is our wisdom to believe and to obey. One thing, however, may safely be asserted, that the staunchest adherent of the Augustinian scheme will find much in Chrysostom not only to inform his judgment, but to probe his conscience, and to quicken his spiritual affections. So correct, at least in this particular, is the fine remark of Archbishop Newcome, that " the volumes of sacred criticism may be compared to an antient and ample treasure-house, containing numerous offerings of different value. Men are frequently warped in their appreciation of these gifts, but God will graciously accept

Introduction.   125

all those, which are presented with a sincere desire to promote His glory."

Modern Commentators. Kuinöel.

Among the several modern commentators consulted for the purposes of this work, it may possibly be asked why I have so seldom referred to Kuinöel's Annotations on the Historical Books of the New Testament; a compilation which, in spite of Rose's earnest protest (German Protestantism, Supplement p. xlii, 2nd edition), appears to retain a degree of popularity in this country which it ill deserves. I will not say that I think meanly of Kuinöel as a critic, because this is far from being my principal objection to the use of his book in England. It is enough surely to render it unfit for a place in the library of a Christian, that its pages are largely devoted to the collecting and preserving, for the corruption of another generation, those irrational and wicked speculations on various passages of the Gospel history, which were the bane and disgrace of Germany fifty years ago: —would that they were not so still. This is a serious charge, and one which I would not willingly bring against any one on insufficient grounds. But (to confine my strictures to his remarks on a single chapter), it is impossible that those who speak favorably of Kuinöel can have even glanced at his commentary on the 27th chapter of St. Matthew. He there abuses his reader's patience by discussing deliberately and at leisure (see his note on v. 50) the shocking blasphemy of "the most learned Paulus," who tells us that the Saviour's death upon the cross for our redemption was in reality nothing more than a syncope, or fainting-fit, from which he recovered in the tomb; Paulus himself being a shade less impious than some others who conjectured—it makes one shudder to repeat it—that our Lord's syncope might be *feigned*. But Kuinöel's own explanations of Scriptural "myths," though more harmless, are equally daring. The Apostle's narrative respecting the bodies of the saints that slept, is thus illustrated by his commentator. " On the day of Jesu's death an earthquake (v. 51) broke open the sepulchres of several persons who had lately died, and who had been entombed, after the custom of the Jews, in the rocky caves which abound near Jerusalem. Their bodies being crushed in the ruins, or devoured by the jackals (shakal), could not be found by their pious relatives; who, however, were consoled after Christ's resurrection by dreams or visions, wherein their departed friends appeared unto them and declared that they had returned to life. Matthew by no means vouches for the truth of this report, but simply tells us in passing what 'many' believed, to show how strong a hold the circumstances of Jesu's death had taken on men's imaginations." I cannot doubt that such delectable specimens will prove to others no less than to myself, that neither pleasure nor profit need be looked for in the volumes of this liberal " Professor of Theology."*

Conclusion. I have now explained, at some length, my design in the present work, and have offered a short account of the materials used in

---

* One other instance of this wretched man's extravagance I cannot refrain from mentioning. The Evangelists, being rude and illiterate men, put together loose memoirs of our Redeemer's words and actions, but shrank from the task of composing a regular Life of Christ, lest their writings should be drawn into an unequal comparison with those of the Greek and Roman historians. Prolegom. p. v. It is quite necessary to add the reference.

executing it. In a production of this nature, composed as it is of numerous isolated details, I must unavoidably have fallen into many errors. I only presume to hope that they are not errors of rashness, or dogmatism, or wilful ignorance. A formal critique on King James's version it is not my province to attempt. It is enough if I have afforded to others the means of forming a more exact estimate of its worth, than can be gathered from the vague encomiums of our popular writers. Yet I should be acting wrongfully both to my theme and to myself, were I to suppress the conviction which the devotion of several years to this employment has fixed on my mind : that if faithfulness and perspicuity ; if energy of tone and simplicity of language be the true tests of merit in a translation of Holy Scripture ; our Authorised Bible is in no wise inferior to the most excellent of the other versions with which I am acquainted :— that it will be the pride and blessing of England, so long as she values her privileges as a nation professing godliness.

NOTES

ON THE AUTHORISED ENGLISH VERSION OF

THE NEW TESTAMENT.

ADVERTISEMENT.

The reader is requested to bear in mind the general heads to which all critiques on our Authorised version are referred in the following pages.

I. Errors of Criticism, arising from following false readings of the Greek text (Introd. p. 5).

II. Errors of Interpretation,
   a. in the signification of single words (p. 32).
   b. in the grammatical construction of one or more words in the same clause (p. 36).
   c. in the dependence of clauses on each other, including punctuation (p. 46).

III. Errors of Expression in the language of the English version, arising
   a. from a want of uniformity in rendering the same Greek by the same English word (p. 50).
   b. from grammatical inaccuracies (p. 53).
   c. from ambiguous, obscure, and obsolete expressions (p. 55).

N. B. If the note on any passage be distinguished by this mark (°), it indicates that no change in the common translation of that passage is recommended (p. 57).

ABBREVIATIONS.

The following abbreviations are used throughout this work :—

Syr. The Peshito Syriac version.
Vulg. The Latin Vulgate.
Tynd. 1. Tyndal's first edition of 1526.
Tynd. 2. Tyndal's last edition of 1534.
Tynd. Where Tynd. 1. and Tynd. 2. agree.
Cov. Coverdale's version of 1535.
Cran. Cranmer's, or the Great Bible, 1539.
Gen. The Geneva New Testament, 1557.
Bish. The Bishops' Bible, 1572.
Auth. King James's or the Authorised version, 1611.

Eng. denotes *all* the above-mentioned *English* versions.

The English rendering which immediately follows the Greek text of each passage, is that proposed to be adopted: e. g. Matth. x, 29, (III, c). ἓν ἐξ αὐτῶν οὐ πεσεῖται " not one of them shall fall"]. Here the words " not one of them shall fall" comprise the amended translation.

NOTES
ON THE AUTHORISED VERSION OF THE NEW TESTAMENT.

The Gospel according to St. Matthew.

CHAPTER I.

(I)°. v.11. THE margin of Auth. informs us that "some read *Josias begat Jakim, and Jakim begat Jechonias.*" The same note occurs in the margin of Bish., and the words are found in the text of Gen., which deferred in this matter to the judgment of Beza (see Introd. p. 94). Mill (Proleg. N.T. p. 130) censures Beza for admitting τὸν 'Ιακείμ, 'Ιακείμ δὲ ἐγέννησε into the earlier editions of his Greek Testament. Mill might have added that he afterwards became sensible of his error, and retracted it in the edition of 1582. The words proposed to be inserted are certainly supported by some authority. Besides Codex ιδ´ of Stephens (Griesbach's 120 of the Gospels), and Colinæi N. T. 1534 (which misled Castalio and Beza), nine other manuscripts have been cited in their favor by Scholz. The same clause (with the variation of Ἰωακεὶμ for Ἰακεὶμ), is found in about twenty-five other manuscripts, including several of respectable antiquity; as well as in the margin of the Philoxenian Syriac, and some copies of the Jerusalem Syriac version. In all other translations the words are omitted, and this is a case in which the testimony of versions manifestly deserves to have considerable weight.* The addition is unknown to all the Fathers except Irenæus, whose precise meaning is very doubtful, and Epiphanius, who has a reading peculiar to himself. Hilary, on the contrary, points out the deficiency in the number of generations between the captivity and our Lord's birth; Porphyry cavils at it; and Chrysostom resorts to the forced apology, ἐμοὶ γὰρ ἐνταῦθα δοκεῖ τὸν χρόνον τῆς αἰχμαλωσίας ἐν τάξει γενεᾶς τιθέναι. Thus the arguments for the spuriousness of the clause decidedly preponderate. It probably originated in a marginal gloss made by some person who adopted Jerome's explanation of the passage: namely, that by Jechonias in v. 11 we ought to understand Jehoiakim, the son of Josiah; and in v. 12 Jehoiachin, the son of Jehoiakim; a view of the subject approved by Whitby; whether correctly or otherwise it is not for me to enquire. Syr. Vulg. Tynd. Cov. Cran. here resemble the received Greek text.

(III, c). v. 18. μνηστευθείσης γὰρ τῆς μητρὸς αὐτοῦ Μαρίας "When his mother Mary was betrothed"]. So Tynd. 2. Gen. Bish. "married," Tynd. 1. Cov.†

---

* "Multarum gentium linguis Scriptura ante translata, docet *falsa esse, quæ addita sunt,*" is the well-known rule of Jerome on this point.

† Coverdale's margin here has "Some read, before they sat at home together," (συνελθεῖν).

Cran. and Matthew's Bible, which conveys a totally false idea. "ensured," Cheke. "espoused," Wickliffe, Taverner, the Rhemish version and Auth. But "to espouse" is nearly obsolete in the sense of betrothing; and in a matter of so great importance, the utmost perspicuity is desirable. It is difficult, if not impossible, to render γὰρ satisfactorily in English ("when as" Bish. Auth.); but its exact force is excellently explained by Krebs, "*Observationes in N. T. e Flavio Josepho.*"

(II, b). v. 20. ἄγγελος Κυρίου "an angel of the Lord"]. Thus all Eng. render the words in ch. ii, 19; although both here and in ch. ii, 13; xxviii, 2 they implicitly follow Tynd. in prefixing the definite article, without the least shew of reason for doing so; ὁ ἄγγελος Κυρίου in v. 24 being evidently a case of renewed mention. Doddridge in this place corrects the common version, but is himself wrong in ch. ii, 13. Campbell translates "a messenger" in all the four verses.

ibid. γεννηθὲν is rendered "begotten" by the margin of the editions of Auth. subsequent to that of 1611 (see Introd. p. 58): but this is unnecessary. Gal. iv, 23, 24 refutes Parkhurst's notion that γεννᾷν when applied to women is always synonymous with τίκτειν.

(II, b). v. 23. ἡ παρθένος "The Virgin"]. So Campbell and Bp. Middleton. "La Vierge," Martin's French version. "Virgo illa," Beza. "that maid," Gen. was an improvement on "a maid," of Tynd. Cov. Cran. "a virgin," Cheke, Bish. Auth. The words are, as Middleton remarks, a close translation of the Hebrew text of Isaiah vii, 14; and so essential to the sense is the retaining of the article, that even Aquila and Symmachus render הָעַלְמָה by ἡ νεᾶνις, however perverse their interpretation may be in other respects. Dr. Lee (Hebrew Grammar § 180, 14) says that ה the Hebrew article, is used " to mark the noun to which it is prefixed, as already known and definite, either from the context, or from general consent." Since the former alternative is out of the question in the present instance, we cannot doubt that "The Virgin" was a person familiar to the meditations of pious Israelites in the prophet's age, as the future mother of Him, who was to bruise the serpent's head (Gen. iii, 15).

ibid. " his name shall be called " of the margin of Auth. is a trifling variation of expression in the loose style of Castalio, who renders " qui nominabitur."

(II, c). v. 25. καὶ ἐκάλεσε τὸ ὄνομα αὐτοῦ Ἰησοῦν "and called his name Jesus"]. This is the rendering of all Eng. previous to Auth. of Cheke, and Syr. (ܐܝܗ). The Vulgate is ambiguous, although Wickliffe and the Rhemish translation (as indeed we might expect) make Mary the nominative to ἐκάλεσε. From an opposite bias Castalio and Beza refer the verb to Joseph, in which they are followed by Auth. and most of the modern English versions. It will probably be admitted that ἐκάλεσε ought to have the same nominative as ἔτεκε which stands just before it, unless some good reason can be alleged to justify the insertion of "he" in the latter clause, when there exists no trace of it in the Greek. Now Grotius assigns two causes for his preference of the rendering of Auth.: first, that it is the sense adopted by the Syriac; and secondly, that it is necessary, in order to reconcile the narrative with the angel's direction in v. 21. On the first point he is undoubtedly mistaken. Every extant edition and manuscript of the Peshito represents the feminine verb; and though in the *Philoxenian* Syriac the verb is masculine, that version could scarcely have been known to Grotius, nor is its testimony worthy of much consideration (see Introd. p. 70). His second argument is much stronger, and would be almost decisive of the controversy, had not the same command been given to *Mary* in Luke i, 31; a sufficient proof that Matth. i, 21 must not be pressed too literally. The view of Grotius, however, is fully borne out by the Greek Fathers. Chrysostom, for example, thus paraphrases v. 21, εἰ γὰρ καὶ εἰς τὴν γέννησιν οὐδὲν συντελεῖς ... ὅμως ὅπερ ἐστὶ πατρὸς ἴδιον ... τοῦτό σοι δίδωμι, τὸ ὄνομα ἐπιθεῖναι τῷ τικτομένῳ· σὺ γὰρ αὐτὸν καλέσεις. Εἰ γὰρ καὶ μὴ σὸς ὁ γόνος, ἀλλὰ τὰ πατρὸς ἐπιδείξῃ περὶ αὐτόν (Hom. in Matth. iv, p. 49, ed. Field). Theophylact also on v. 25 bids us remark τὴν εὐπείθειαν τοῦ Ἰωσήφ, ὅτι ὅσα εἶπεν αὐτῷ ὁ ἄγγελος, ἐποίησε. I must confess too that the passage quoted from the Septuagint by Mr. Grinfield (2 Sam. xii, 24) is identical in form with the present, while the gender of the Hebrew verb removes all ambiguity as to its sense. Having therefore laid the whole question before the reader, I must leave him to take his choice between the two interpretations.

CHAPTER II.

(III, c). v. 4. ἐπυνθάνετο " asked"]. So Tynd. 2. Cov. Cheke, Gen. " inquired," Wickliffe, Rhemish version, Doddridge. Either of these is preferable to " demanded," the rendering of Tynd. 1. Cran. Bish. Auth.

(III, c). v. 6. ποιμανεῖ " shall feed"]. So Syr. Beza, Cheke, the Geneva Bible of 1560, and the margin of Auth. Since the word indicates the pastoral nature of Messiah's rule, this rendering is more proper than " shall govern," as in Tynd. Cov. Cran. Gen. Bish.; or "shall rule," as in Vulg. Castalio and Auth. The reader who desires to see St. Matthew's citation concisely, yet satisfactorily, reconciled with the prophecy in Micah v, 2, should refer to Bp. Jebb's Sacred Literature, pp. 98—100.

(III, b). v. 8. κἀγὼ ἐλθὼν "I also may go"]. A similar confusion in the use of the verbs " to go" and " come" may be seen in v. 23 ; where however all Eng., except Bish. and Auth., are perfectly accurate. In the present passage they are all wrong alike. Dr. Symonds (Observations Pt. I, ch. vi, 2) points out the ungrammatical position of " also" in Auth. " I may come and worship him also;" and quotes ch. xvii, 12; Mark xi, 25; Luke vi, 13; Acts xi, 18; xiii, 9 as similar instances. If the student should deem these remarks minute and over-refined, I trust he will not think that I lay much stress upon them. With Dr. Symonds indeed they are important matters, and provoke him to many a hard speech against our venerable translators. (See also note on ch. x, 32).

On the use of παιδίον in this chapter I have spoken already (Introduction pp. 34, 95). It is invariably rendered " child" throughout vv. 8, 9, 11, 13, 14, 20, 21 by Tynd. Cov. Cran.; and by Cheke in all places except v. 8, where he has " this young child." From Beza's " puerulus" came "babe" in Gen. vv. 8, 13. Bish. Auth. uniformly translate " young child." Diminutives occur very frequently in the New Testament, as in the later Greek in general. Upwards of thirty nouns of this form are used by the sacred writers, many of which it is difficult to distinguish, in respect to their sense, from the simple words whence they are derived.* If we take the context for our guide, we shall probably conclude, that though in the present case, it was not *necessary* to express the force of the diminutive, yet since it is expressed by Auth., it will be our wisest course to retain it.

(I)° v. 11. εἶδον " they saw"]. So Syr. Cheke, Bish. Auth. and all the critical editors. Εὗρον, the reading found in the received text and in Beza,† rests almost entirely on the authority of the old Italic manuscripts and Vulg. Having been inserted by some corrector in the copy of the Gospels most used by Erasmus (Codex 2 of Wetstein), it was adopted by him, and after his example by Tynd. Cov. Cran. Castalio: being no doubt favored by those who wished to avoid what appeared to them an inelegant repetition of εἶδον from vv. 9, 10. It is an evidence of great care in Bish., that it departed so judiciously from the common editions in this particular, and followed the reading of the Complutensian Polyglott. Compare Introduction, p. 8.

(III, c). *ibid.* προσήνεγκαν " they offered"]. So Tynd. Cov. Cran. Cheke, Gen. and the margin of Auth. after Syr. Vulg. This is much better than " they presented," of Bish. Auth. since it more fully implies a religious service or oblation.

(II, b). *ibid.* δῶρα " as presents"]. In apposition with χρυσόν, &c. So Campbell, Middleton.

(II, a). v. 16. τοὺς παῖδας " the male children"] *only*. So Gen. Doddridge, Campbell.

---

* In Matth. xxv, 33 ἐρίφια are unquestionably identical with ἔριφοι in the preceding verse.

† Yet Beza admits that " in omnibus vetustis exemplaribus legimus *venerunt.*"

(III, γ).° v. 18. ὅτι οὐκ εἰσί " because they are not"]. So Auth. Vulg. Beza and Bp. Jebb. " were not," Tynd. Cov. Cran. Gen. Bish. " were gone," Cheke. But it is advisable to preserve the Greek idiom in this passage, both as being more poetical, and as the exact translation of כִּי־אֵינֶנּוּ Jeremiah xxxi, 15. Instances of this Hellenistic euphemism are produced by Krebs from Josephus, and by his imitator Loësner from Philo. So also Herod. vii, 205.

(II, a). v. 21. ἦλθεν εἰς γῆν Ἰσραὴλ " went to the land of Israel"]. On " went" see note on v. 8. All Eng. interpret εἰς by " into:" but since it appears from v. 22 that Joseph did not enter Judæa, which is the part of the land of Israel nearest to Egypt, it seems best to translate εἰς " to," which is safer than Wakefield's rendering " towards." Joseph had intended to go to Judæa, but on learning the state of affairs in that country, he turned aside to the regions eastward of the Dead Sea, and reached Galilee by crossing the Jordan. A use of εἰς precisely similar occurs in John iv, 5 (compare v. 8), where even Auth. has " to."

CHAPTER III.

(I) v. 8. καρπὸν ἄξιον]. There is little doubt that the singular form, and not the plural, was here employed by St. Matthew. Syr. is the chief support of the received reading; but it is opposed by the vast majority of manuscripts of all ages and families, and was probably derived from Luke iii, 8. Origen goes so far as to assign a reason, though of course a very fanciful one, why St. Matthew preferred the singular; the Italic and Vulgate read it, and it has been adopted by every critic from Mill down to Lachmann.

ibid. Here Gen. and the margin of Auth. " fruits answerable (" belonging," Gen.) to amendment of life," are certainly clearer than " meet for repentance," of Bish. Auth. We find " fruits belonging to repentance," in Tynd. Cran. But Cov. closely follows Vulg. "due fruits of penance." The general meaning of the words is plain enough: οὐ μόνον δεῖ φεύγειν τὸ κακόν, says Theophylact, ἀλλὰ καὶ καρποὺς ἀρετῆς ποιεῖν. Compare Acts xxvi, 20. The rendering of Cheke and Doddridge " fruits worthy (of) repentance," is perhaps as neat as any. See also Raphel on Polybius, *ad. loc.*,

(III, c)°. v. 9. μὴ δόξητε λέγειν " think not to say"]. Auth. is quite tolerably, though " presume not," of Gen. may be somewhat better. " Seem not," Cheke. None of the versions countenance the idle notion that δόξητε is pleonastic here. Indeed it would not be easy to point out passages in which that verb is really superfluous, though it may not always be possible to preserve its force in a translation (e. g. Hebr. iv, 1). In the present instance no difficulty can arise. Οὐ κωλύων αὐτοὺς λέγειν ἐξ ἐκείνων εἶναι τῶν ἁγίων, ἀλλὰ κωλύων μὴ τούτῳ θαρρεῖν, is Chrysostom's simple comment. In truth δοκεῖν, as is often the case, is here the most emphatic word in the clause. Thus Æschyl. Agam. 814. εἴδωλον σκιᾶς, δοκοῦντας εἶναι κάρτα πρευμενεῖς ἐμοί. Plato, Euthyphro (I, i. p. 358 ed. Bekker), ὁ Μέλιτος οὗτος σὲ μὲν οὐδὲ δοκεῖ ὁρᾶν, ἐμὲ δὲ οὕτως ὀξέως ἀτεχνῶς καὶ ῥᾳδίως κατεῖδεν, ὥστε ἀσεβείας ἐγράψατο.

(II, a).° v. 12. τὴν ἅλωνα αὐτοῦ " his floor"]. So

Syr. Vulg. Eng. Campbell, however, adopts the opinion of Fischer, Schleusner &c. that ἄλων here signifies " grain ;" " corn after threshing mixed with chaff." This metonymy seems to take place in Job xxxix, 12, where גָּרְנֶךָ is rendered ἄλων in the LXX. The other texts quoted by Schleusner make nothing for his purpose, nor must we hastily transfer a highly poetical figure like that in Job, to the simple, though metaphorical, style of the Baptist.

(II, b. see Introd. p. 45). v. 14. διεκώλυεν " would have hindered"]. So Doddridge. " forbad," Auth. It is remarkable that none of our early translators understood this use of the imperfect tense, which is duly expressed by Syr. Vulg., and cannot be suppressed without detriment to the sense.

(III, c). v. 15. πᾶσαν δικαιοσύνην "every ordinance"]. " every institution," Campbell. " all righteousness," Eng. I propose this change, because the word " righteousness," in the present passage, seems liable to be misconceived. On the meaning of δικαιοσύνη in this context, all interpreters are agreed. Δικαιοσύνη γάρ ἐστιν ἡ τῶν ἐντολῶν ἐκπλήρωσις ... πρέπον ἐστιν ἐμοὶ πληρῶσαι τὸν νόμον ἅπαντα, is Chrysostom's paraphrase. Consult Suicer's Thesaur. Ecclesiast. δικαιοσύνη I § 6 : and Wolf's Curæ Philolog. *ad loc.*

(II, a). v. 16. ἀπὸ τοῦ ὕδατος " from the water"]. " de," Vulg. " ab," Castalio. But " ex," Beza ; " out of," Eng. Syr. (ܡܢ) will admit of either sense. " There can be no doubt whatever," a living prelate has observed, " that the expression implies only that they ascended from the hollow through which the river ran." See my note on Acts viii, 38, 39. Kennaway on Baptism, p. 8. Without being anxious to dispute that our Lord was baptized by immersion, we should take care that such a text as the present be not pressed into the service of those who consider that form essential to the validity of the rite.

ibid. Before εἶδε Castalio, Tynd. 2. Cov. Gen. Bish. supply the nominative " John," which is very properly omitted by Tynd. 1. Cran. Cheke, Auth. Dr. Symonds blames Auth. for thus " stumbling on the threshold" by leaving out the antecedent. He was possibly not aware that some critics have thought our Lord to be the person alluded to in αὐτῷ. I am not prepared to defend their opinion (see John i, 32 —34); but we have no right to corrupt the text of Scripture by interpolating words whereof no trace can be found in the original, and which unnecessarily restrict the sense.

CHAPTER IV.

(II, a). v. 1. ἀνήχθη " was led away"]. So Tynd. Cov. Cran. Cheke. " led aside," Gen. " led up," Bish. Auth. But removal, not ascent, is here implied. This is one of the many cases in which Schleusner represents the preposition to be otiose. Because St. Luke uses ἤγετο (ch. iv, 1), and Syr. (which has no compound verbs) employs the same word (ܐܶܒܪ,) in both places, he concludes that ἀνά might as well be omitted altogether. I have already stated my reasons for thinking such a principle of interpretation both uncritical and untrue (see Introd. p. 34).

(II, b). v. 5. τὸ πτερύγιον " the pinnacle"]. So Cheke. " les creneaux," Martin. It is useless to re-open the discussion respecting the precise meaning of πτερύγιον here and in Luke iv, 9. All Eng. have " a pinnacle." Yet the very obscurity of the passage should make us careful to express the article of the original, as it may serve to shew the futility of several conjectures which have been hazarded on this subject. Perhaps no view is encumbered with so few difficulties as that which supposes τὸ πτερύγιον to be the ridge of the high roof of the great Eastern Porch. See Middleton.

(III, c). v. 6. ἐπὶ χειρῶν " on their hands"]. I presume that both here and elsewhere " in" is used by our version for " on" (See ch. vi, 10; xxviii, 18). ἐπὶ τῆς γῆς is rendered " on earth" in Auth. ch. xviii, 18, 19. In this place Tynd. Cov. Cran. Gen. Bish. have " with." " in their arms," Cheke.

(I)° v. 10. After ὕπαγε the words ὀπίσω μου are added by Griesbach, Vater, Scholz and Lachmann. The external evidence in favor of this reading is rather strong, though it very slightly (if at all) preponderates over that for the received text. Ὀπίσω μου is not found in the Vatican (B of Wetstein) and many other manuscripts, nor is it rendered by Syr. Vulg. or the Italic versions. It bears every appearance of a gloss, derived not so much from v. 19, as from the parallel texts Matth. xvi, 23; Mark viii, 33; Luke iv, 8.

(III, c). v. 12. παρεδόθη " was delivered up "]. So Bish. and margin of Auth. This is somewhat better, because it is more literal, than " was cast into prison" of Bish.'s margin and Auth. " was taken," Tynd. Cov. Cran. Gen. " was put in prison," Cheke.

(I) v. 18. ὁ Ἰησοῦς at the beginning of this verse should be removed from the text. All the best editors reject it, and it is found in very few manuscripts. There are no traces of it in Syr., and though it is read in the *printed* editions of Vulg., the oldest copies of that version do not contain the words. Hence they are omitted by Lachmann, in his revised Latin translation (see p. 26). The fact is, that v. 18 is the commencement of one of the περικοπαὶ or lessons, used in the public services of the Greek Church. Since a large proportion of our extant manuscripts was written for ecclesiastical purposes, it was judged necessary to insert in them various Proper Names, in order to make the several portions of Scripture read in the congregation more intelligible to the hearer. Thus even in our English Prayer Book the name of Jesus is interpolated in the Gospels for the 14th, 16th, 17th, and 18th Sundays after Trinity; and whole clauses are introduced into the Gospels for the 3rd and 4th Sundays after Easter, and the 6th and 24th after Trinity; without ever subjecting the compilers of our Liturgy to the imputation of fraud, or of a want of respect for the integrity of the Sacred Text. See note on ch. viii, 5.

(II, b). v. 21. ἐν τῷ πλοίῳ " in the ship"]. So Tynd. Cov. Cran. Bish. "a boat," Cheke. "a ship," Gen. Auth. for what possible reason it is hard to imagine. They might have translated " in their ship," as τὰ δίκτυα "their nets" in v. 20. In ch. iii, 12 Cheke rightly renders τὴν ἀποθήκην "his garner," as indeed do Tynd. Cov. Gen. By "the ship" in the Gospels is to be understood that particularized in Mark iii, 9. See Middleton's note on Matth. xiii, 2.

(III, c). v. 23. κηρύσσων τὸ εὐαγγέλιον τῆς βασιλείας "proclaiming the glad tidings of the kingdom," or "reign"] viz. of God, Mark i, 14. Campbell justly censures the Authorised rendering "preaching the Gospel of the kingdom," as almost unintelligible in itself, and calculated to conceal from the reader's mind that tacit reference to the Prophetic Scriptures of the Old Testament, which the words contain (Prel.

Diss. V, ii, 11—13). All our English versions however resemble Auth. both here and in ch. ix, 35; xxiv, 14; Mark i, 14; only that Tynd. 2. Cran. Gen. have "glad tidings" in ch. ix, 35; and Tynd. 2. Gen. in ch. xxiv, 14.

(II, a). *ibid.* μαλακία " infirmity "]. So the Rhemish N. T. both here, and in the only other places where the word occurs, ch. ix, 35; x, 1. Cheke has "feebleness" here and in ch. x, 1; "weakness," in ch. ix, 35. "infirmitas," Vulg. "languor," Castalio, Beza. All Eng. have "disease," and like Syr., appear to confound μαλακία with νόσος. Yet there is an evident distinction between them; the latter referring chiefly to pressing and acute disease; the former to the languor consequent upon lingering sickness. See Schleusner.

v. 24. δαιμονιζομένους. In rendering δαίμων, δαιμόνιον &c. it is now customary to speak of "demons," not "devils." The subject is discussed by Campbell (Prel. Diss. VI, Pt. i), with even more than his usual ability. There are, on the whole, two passages in the New Testament (Acts xvii, 18; 1 Cor. x, 20, 21) in which this version, or something equivalent to it, is imperatively called for. But in texts like the present, which relate to demoniacal possession, I do not see that much will be gained by the change. That these δαιμόνια were instruments in Satan's hands (Matth. xii, 26, 27; Mark iii, 22—26) for the torment and *ruin* of mankind (Matth. xii, 43—45), is too plain to be called in question by any honest reader of Scripture. Whether we name them "demons" or "devils" is a very little matter; except indeed that "demon" is pretty unintelligible to the ignorant, and may suggest to the learned a false analogy between these servants of the Evil One, and the δαίμονες of Classical Antiquity.

CHAPTER V.

(II, b). v. 1. εἰς τὸ ὄρος " into the mountain country"]. i. e. " the mountains embosoming the lake of Galilee; a form of expression most natural to persons familiar with the country, but strictly correct on their part only in addressing others who were so too. Compare ch. iv, 18—v, 1; with Mark iii, 7—13." Green, Grammar of N.T.Dialect, p. 158. This explanation of the force of the article is rather more simple than that of Bp. Middleton, with which Pr. Scholefield was not entirely satisfied. All Eng. read "a mountain," but Cheke, somewhat more accurately, "the hill."

(III, b). *ibid.* καθίσαντος αὐτοῦ "when he had sat"]. All Eng. and even Cheke (so closely did he copy Tynd. &c.) have " was set." I notice this slight inaccuracy in deference to Bp. Lowth (English Gram. p. 97), who cites similar errors from Auth. in ch. xxvii, 19; Luke xxii, 55; John xiii, 12; Hebr. viii, 1; xii, 2; Rev. iii, 21, and adds " *set* can be no part of the verb *to sit*. If it belong to the verb *to set*, the translation in these passages is wrong: for *to set*, signifies *to place*, but without any designation of the posture of the person placed; which is a circumstance of importance expressed in the original."

v. 11. ψευδόμενοι. The trifling variation of "lying" for "falsely" in the margin of Auth. is from the text of Bish.

(III, b). v. 13. μωρανθῇ ." become unsavory"]. So Bish. " be once unsavory," Tynd. 1. " be unsavory," Cheke. " have lost her saltness," Tynd. 2.

"his saltness," Cov. "the saltness," Cran. "his savour," Gen. Auth: a tolerable variety of renderings for so simple an expression. The same license with respect to genders in old English may be seen in ch. xii, 33; xxiv, 32; xxvi, 52; Mark ix, 50; Luke vi, 44; xiv, 34; John xv, 19 &c. All Eng. except Bish. Auth. have misunderstood the clause ἐν τίνι ἁλισθήσεται; "what can be salted therewith?" Tynd. Cov. So Cran. Gen. nearly; and even Cheke has "wherewith shall things be salted?" as if the verb were used impersonally: "wherewith ("wherein," Bish.) shall it be salted," Bish. Auth. Campbell's paraphrase "how shall its saltness be restored?" gives the true sense. To the same effect are Syr. Vulg. Castalio, Beza and Bp. Jebb.

(II, b). v. 15. τὸν μόδιον, τὴν λυχνίαν "the corn-measure," "the candlestick," or "lamp-stand"]. All Eng., the French versions, and even Campbell (who knew better) use the indefinite article in this place. Yet these are evidently *monadic* nouns, denoting ordinary articles of furniture, whereof only one of each kind was usually found in an apartment; as we say "*the* table," "*the* bed." See Middleton. The *later* editions of Auth. put in the margin the exact capacity of a modius; describing it as "a measure containing about a pint less than a peck." But it is obvious that no specific measure is here designated by our Lord.

(III, a). vv. 15, 16. καὶ λάμπει πᾶσι τοῖς κ. τ. λ. "and it shineth to all in the house. So let your light shine before men"...]. Thus Bp. Jebb. I am no advocate for rigorous uniformity in the rendering of the same Greek word (see Introd. p. 51), but it is plain how much the force of the present passage is increased by translating λάμπει in the same manner in both verses. This course is recommended by Archbp. Newcome ("Historical View," Rule viii), and carried into effect by Syr. Vulg. All Eng. (even Cheke) here resemble Auth. " it giveth light unto all....So let your light shine"...

(II, b). v. 21. ἐρρέθη τοῖς ἀρχαίοις " it was said to them of old time"]. So Syr. (ℵ). Vulg. Castalio, Wickliffe, Tynd. Cov. Cran. Cheke ("unto old men"), Gen. Bish. the Rhemish version, and the margin of Auth. " qu'il a été dit aux anciens," Martin, and Ostervald's revised Geneva version. Thus also Doddridge, Wynne, Campbell, Newcome, Boothroyd, Jebb; and of the Commentators Grotius, Whitby, and many others. To the same effect Chrysostom observes, ὁ καὶ ἐκεῖνα [ῥήματα] δούς, αὐτός ἐστιν· and, after Chrysostom, Theophylact accounts as follows for the impersonal form of the clause: εἰ γὰρ εἶπεν ὅτι, ὁ μὲν πατήρ μου εἶπε τοῖς ἀρχαίοις, ἐγὼ δὲ λέγω ὑμῖν, ἔδοξεν ἂν ἀντινομοθετεῖν τῷ πατρί· ἀορίστως οὖν λέγει, ὅτι ....κ.τ.λ. manifestly never dreaming of the possibility of another mode of interpretation. *This* it was reserved for the daring genius of Beza to devise, who renders the words by " dictum fuisse a veteribus;" and has been followed by our Authorised version, by Bois (see Introd. p. 73), Raphel, Kypke, Krebs, and Kuinöel. The Geneva French also, previously to Martin's revision, had " par les anciens." Beza honestly gives us his reasons for this violent change. He does not think it likely that some of the injunctions mentioned in this chapter were actually delivered by God to the Jewish Church in the wilderness; but that they were rather the inventions of later scribes and doctors of the synagogue, " qui solebant patrum et majorum nomina suis falsis interpretationibus prætexere." But if there were any weight in this objection, it would be the duty of an expositor to endeavor to remove the difficulty, and not of a translator to conceal it, by misrepresenting the meaning of the sacred penman. With respect to the grammatical branch of the question, when we observe the pointed antithesis between ἐρρέθη τοῖς ἀρχαίοις in v. 21, and ἐγὼ δὲ λέγω ὑμῖν in v. 22; and when we find the same opposition subsisting in the corresponding clauses vv. 27 and 28; vv. 31 and 32; vv. 33 and 34; vv. 38 and 39; vv. 43 and 44; it is hard to believe that the construction of ἀρχαίοις after ἐρρέθη is totally unlike that of ὑμῖν after λέγω. Yet we cannot deny, that considered in itself, without reference to the context, there is nothing repugnant to the Greek idiom in Beza's opinion, that τοῖς ἀρχαίοις is equivalent to ὑπὸ τῶν ἀρχαίων. The utmost we can fairly say is, that such a form of expression is not generally employed with ἐρέω in the New Testament (see Rom. ix, 12; 26; Gal. iii, 16; Rev. vi, 11; ix, 4). This verb occurs no less than thirty times in St. Matthew's Gospel; and in every instance where it is not used absolutely, is joined with the dative of the person addressed, or with the genitive of the person speaking, governed by ὑπὸ or διά. Both constructions are united in ch. xxii, 31. To this tide of adverse examples (which may readily be verified by means of the Concordance), relating to the single word ἐρέω in the Gospel of St. Matthew alone, it is vain to oppose the occasional practice of profane authors (e. g. Herod. vii, 143, τῷ θεῷ εἰρῆσθαι τὸ χρηστήριον), or a few passages scattered throughout the Septuagint and the New Testament, in which *some other* verb than ἐρέω may seem to be followed by a dative of the instrument (Gen. xxxi, 15; Isai. lxv, 1; Matth. xxiii, 5; Acts ii, 3).

In v. 22 Cheke retains the Greek word "ῥαχα" (sic), as if he had not yet made up his mind how to render it. (See Introd. p. 92). The marginal note " vain fellow," is not in the *first* edition of Auth.

(II, a). v. 24. διαλλάγηθι τῷ ἀδελφῷ σου " reconcile thyself to thy brother"]. So Tynd. 1. Cov. after Syr. which employs the reciprocal conjugation Ethpaal (ܐܬܪܥܝ). " te reconcilier," Martin, Ostervald. This rendering is much better than " be reconciled" of Tynd. 2. Cran. Gen. Bish. Auth. and the Latin versions: "be agreed," Cheke. The passage before us is examined by Archp. Magee in his great work on the Atonement (Vol. i, pp. 200—203, 5th edition). He observes after Leclerc and Hammond that διαλλάττεσθαι has here a reciprocal sense, like the Hebrew Hithpahel, " to reconcile oneself to another ;" " to appease or obtain the favor of one whom we have offended." " In the present instance," he says, " the words must necessarily signify *take care that thy brother be reconciled to thee;* since that which goes before is not that he hath done thee injury, but thou him." Magee compares the LXX in 1 Sam. xxix, 4; 1 Esdras iv, 31, for similar uses of διαλλάσσομαι: as also for καταλλάσσομαι Rom. v, 10; 1 Cor. vii, 11; 2 Cor. v, 20. We may add Eurip. Helen. 1235 (ed. Matthiæ), σπονδὰς τέμωμεν καὶ διαλλάχθητί μοι. Demosth. Ep. 3 (p. 1478 Reiske), μηδὲ πρὸς τελευτήσαντας διαλλαγήσονται. Even Auth. translates ταπεινώθητε " humble yourselves" in James iv, 10; 1 Pet. v, 6. I ought however to state that Tittmann draws a distinction between the sense of διαλλάσσομαι (which occurs no where else in the New Testament), and that of καταλλάσσομαι: making the former to denote the causing a *mutual* enmity to cease ; the latter to have reference to one party only. But

Störr and Tholuck (in his commentary on the "Sermon on the Mount") demur to the truth of this opinion; and Tholuck severely remarks that "Tittman in his book on the Synonyms is in the habit of seizing on particular examples, while he passes over in silence much that is against him." In the case of διαλλάσσομαι he is supported by nothing but the etymology of the word.

(I). v. 27. τοῖς ἀρχαίοις " by them of old time" is omitted in this verse by Griesbach, Scholz and Lachmann; on the authority of many good manuscripts of both families, of Syr. and most of the Italic and other versions. Although the words are found in Irenæus and Vulg., they should probably be rejected, as they are more likely to have been inserted from vv. 21, 33, than overlooked by the negligence of copyists.

(II, a. See Introd. p. 33). vv. 29, 30. σκανδαλίζει σε " cause thee to offend"]. So Gen. Beza, the margin of Auth. and Syr. which uses the causative conjugation Aphel (ܐܟܫܠ). But Tynd. Cov. Bish. Auth. have " offend," Cran. Cheke " hinder :" "scandalizat," Vulg. " insnare," Campbell. That the margin of Auth. is here preferable to the text cannot be doubted. Aquila and Symmachus employ ἐσκανδαλίσατε for the Hiphil conjugation of כָּשַׁל in Malachi ii, 8. Dr. Symonds is pleased to observe that our translators always felt at liberty to put nonsense in the text, providing that they " foisted" the true rendering into the margin. See my notes on ch. xvii, 27 ; xviii, 6 ; 8 ; 9.

(II, a)°. v. 32. παρεκτὸς λόγου πορνείας " save for the cause of fornication"]. So Auth. correctly, after Syr. Vulg. Beza and Castalio. Thus also Cheke, though with his usual quaint idiom " for fornication's cause" (see Introd. p. 91). Tynd. Cov. Cran. Gen. Bish. have "except it be for fornication." But there is no reason to think λόγος pleonastic here, or indeed in any other passage of the New Testament. The Hebrew phrase עַל־דְּבַר אֲשֶׁר does not appear to be imitated here, for it is rendered ἐπὶ λόγου οὗ by the LXX in 2 Sam. xiii, 22. The expression εἰς φέρνης λόγον in 2 Macc. i, 14 is good Greek. In the present text we may, with Fritzsche, regard λόγος as equivalent to " crimen."

(I)°. v. 47. In the room of οἱ τελῶναι οὕτω "the publicans so," Lachmann reads οἱ ἐθνικοὶ τὸ αὐτό "the Gentiles the same." This change is supported by the uncial manuscripts B D Z, and by a small number of cursive MSS, nearly all of them Alexandrian. It is also found in the Vulg. and in most of the Italic documents, and is cited by Chrysostom *in the body of his commentary*, where there is less ground for suspecting that his text has been altered by transcribers. Syr. reads οἱ τελῶναι τὸ αὐτό, and of the two, the variation τὸ αὐτό for οὕτω is better sustained than ἐθνικοὶ for τελῶναι. Yet Griesbach, with an inconsistency for which I cannot account, adopts οἱ ἐθνικοί, and banishes τὸ αὐτό to the inner margin.*
Bp. Jebb approves of Griesbach's reading, and by a beautiful but perhaps over-refined application of his theory of parallelisms, labors to shew that the received text will not adequately express our Lord's meaning. " According to the common reading," he observes, "the fourth line would be merely tautologous; while, on the contrary, this alteration gives a

---

* Possibly Griesbach was misled by his erroneous information that this is the reading of B. But if Buttmann, Lachmann's fellow-laborer, may be depended on, that MS has οἱ ἐθνικοὶ τὸ αὐτό.

lively progress to the argument. Degraded as publicans were, they might still be Jews, and they frequently were so: but the Gentiles were objects of unequivocal and national hatred: the publican might be despised; the Gentile was detested" (Sacr. Liter. p. 207).* In spite of this ingenious reasoning, I must think with Wetstein and Scholz, that οἱ ἐθνικοὶ rests on too weak authority to be received as genuine; and Mill's conjecture is sufficiently probable (Proleg. N. T. p. 85), that it originated with some corrector, who was displeased with the repetition of τελῶναι v. 46; as certain of his brethren had been with εἶδον in ch. ii, 11 (see note *ad loc*).

CHAPTER VI.

(I) °. v. 1. The marginal note " or *righteousness*" in the *later* editions of Auth. (see Introd. p. 58) directs our attention to the various reading δικαιοσύνην instead of ἐλεημοσύνην "alms." This change is supported by five Greek manuscripts (including B, D and 1, or Basil. γ), and by a scholium annexed to two other MSS. It is the reading of Vulg. and the Italic

---

* Still more subtle is Bp. Jebb's defence of οὕτω in preference to τὸ αὐτό, in this same verse. " All who loved their lovers only, were actuated by one and the same principle of selfishness (v. 46): not so with respect to all who confined their courtesy exclusively to their own countrymen. The Jews did this from religious bigotry, the Gentiles from national pride. And, as principles determine the character of actions, the Gentiles in this particular could not be said to act in *the same*, but in *a like manner*, with the Jews." How instructive is every idea which emanates from this prelate's elegant and thoughtful mind; yet it is hard to believe that such metaphysical precision ought to be looked for in our Saviour's popular discourses.

versions, and has been approved by Mill, Griesbach, Vater and Lachmann. Syr. is of necessity neutral, since ܙܕܩ would very well answer to either Greek word. Internal probabilities plead strongly in favour of δικαιοσύνην, which is a familiar Hellenistic term, nearly synonymous with ἐλεημοσύνην: and it must be confessed that the latter has the appearance of a gloss, borrowed either from vv. 2, 3, 4; or from Luke xi, 41; xii, 33. Agreeable to this view is Jerome's exposition, "justitiam, hoc est, eleemosynam." See Lightfoot, Hor. Hebr. *ad loc*. But all such considerations must yield, where external testimonies are so decidedly adverse as in the present case. If we once give the reins to plausible conjecture, and set up ingenious arguments in opposition to established facts, it is impossible to foresee where the course of innovation will end. When the received reading is palpably absurd (if indeed it ever be so), or conflicting authorities are pretty evenly balanced (see Introd. p. 29), there is fair scope for internal evidence: but if we permit it to overstep its proper bounds, I do not see what security the text of Scripture will find against the wildest guesses of visionaries or unbelievers. In this instance the sense happens to be just the same, whichever of the two readings we adopt. But we shall soon come to an important passage, which has been most improperly expunged by a host of critics, on internal grounds far less weighty than those in the present verse, and in the face of documentary proofs which might well have been thought irresistible (See note on v. 13).

ibid. The margin of Auth. after Cran. has "with" (παρά). All other Eng. "of." I do not wish to overlook *any* marginal notes (see Introd. p. 59), but are trifles like this worth our notice?

(II, a)°. v. 2. μὴ σαλπίσῃς ἔμπροσθέν σου "do not sound a trumpet before thee"]. This rendering of Auth. is confirmed by Syr. Vulg. Castalio, Cheke, Bish. and Bp. Jebb. " Do not cause (or " make") a trumpet to be sounded" is found in Tynd. Cov. Cran. Gen. the margin of Auth. Beza, and his imitator Martin (" ne fais point sonner"); and approved by Schleusner and Kuinöel. In behalf of this latter interpretation it may be alleged, that a person can hardly be said to sound a trumpet *before* himself. Perhaps also the analogy of the causative verb σκανδαλίζω (ch. v, 29, 30) may have had some weight. The example cited by Schleusner from Isai. xliv, 23, in which the Hiphil form הָרִיעוּ is translated σαλπίσατε by the LXX, is nothing to the purpose; since that Hebrew verb being defective in its simple or Kal conjugation, Hiphil is here used merely in the signification of Kal. On the whole I agree with Mr. Rose, in his edition of Parkhurst, that there is little occasion for altering Auth. Since the expression is figurative (as Chrysostom remarked long ago), we need not press ἔμπροσθέν σου too literally; it is enough if our Lord be understood to mean, that the Pharisees distributed alms ostentatiously and in public. Besides, the verb σαλπίζω occurs in eleven other passages of the New Testament (1 Cor. xv, 52, and ten times in the Apocalypse); in all which it bears its ordinary classical sense " I sound a trumpet." See Elsner's Observ. *ad loc.*

(II, b). v. 13. ἀπὸ τοῦ πονηροῦ " from the evil one"]. So Doddridge and Bp. Jebb. " du malin," Ostervald. Middleton has clearly shewn that Syr. understood the words to refer to a person, both here and in ch. v, 37. Even in ch. v, 39 Syr. employs the masculine gender, although in that place Satan cannot be alluded to, but " the wrong-doer" generally. The

Latin versions in this verse are, of course, ambiguous. All Eng. have "from evil." Cheke translates "from the evil" here and in ch. v, 37; but "evil" simply in ch. v, 39: since the devil is called by him "the wicked" in ch. xiii, 19; 38, it is probable that the same being is meant in the present text. That we pray to be delivered from the power of Satan in this petition, was the constant persuasion of the Greek Fathers. Chrysostom expressly states that πονηρὸν ἐνταῦθα τὸν διάβολον καλεῖ. Theophylact observes, οὐκ εἶπεν ἀπὸ πονηρῶν ἀνθρώπων, οὐ γὰρ ἐκεῖνοι ἀδικοῦσιν ἡμᾶς, ἀλλ' ὁ πονηρός. Cyril of Jerusalem, in his exposition of the Lord's Prayer, calls πονηρός, ὁ ἀντικείμενος δαίμων, ἀφ' οὗ ῥυσθῆναι εὐχόμεθα. Other passages equally decisive, from Gregory Nyssen, Tertullian, &c. may be seen in Suicer's Thesaur. Ecclesiast. Indeed this conclusion might easily be drawn from the language of the New Testament itself. If the reader will turn to Matth. xiii, 19; 38; John xvii, 15; Eph. vi, 16; 2 Thess. iii, 3; 1 John ii, 13; 14; iii, 12; v, 18; 19; he will find that in most of these texts ὁ πονηρὸς and its oblique cases undoubtedly indicate our great spiritual enemy; while this is the fullest and most satisfactory interpretation in them all.

(I).° *ibid.* (See Introd. p. 23). The doxology which closes the Lord's Prayer (ὅτι σοῦ ἐστιν ἡ βασιλεία κ.τ.λ. .... [ἀμήν].) is rejected as spurious by Wetstein, Griesbach, Vater, Scholz, Tischendorf and Lachmann on the continent; in England by Mill, and recently by Dr. Bloomfield and Professor Davidson. In fact I am not aware that it is retained by any editor of note except Matthæi, whose exclusive adherence to his own Moscow manuscripts renders his judgment on such a point of as little weight, as that of an acute and profound scholar well can be. I cannot help feeling how perilous it is to dispute the verdict of this formidable array of Biblical critics; but we may reasonably demand something more than the bare authority of high names, before we consent to abandon a clause, which we have all regarded from our infancy as an integral part of the most solemn form of words ever delivered to man.

The sixth chapter of St. Matthew is contained in about five hundred Greek manuscripts of various kinds: the doxology is omitted in only *eight*. It is preserved in the venerable Peshito Syriac version, and (with some slight abridgment) in the Sahidic, which ranks next to the Peshito on the score of antiquity. It is also found in the Æthiopic, Armenian, Gothic, Sclavonic and Georgian versions; in the Philoxenian and Jerusalem Syriac; and in the Persic version of Walton's Polyglott, which is demonstrably a secondary translation, made from the Peshito Syriac (see Walton, Proleg. xvi, §. 9, and Pr. Lee's Excursus in Wrangham's edition). On the other hand the clause is omitted in most copies of the Coptic; in the Arabic (the least valuable, for *critical* purposes, of all the versions); in the Italic and Vulgate; and is consequently unknown to a long train of Latin Fathers, who did not understand, or seldom consulted the Greek original. Among the Greeks the doxology is first met with in the Pseudo-Apostolical Constitutions, a work of about the fourth century; and in Chrysostom, who comments upon the disputed words without shewing the least consciousness that their authenticity is doubtful. After Chrysostom's time the clause seems to have been implicitly received in the Eastern Church. The silence of earlier writers, such as Origen and Cyril of Jerusalem, who do not notice it in their expositions of the Lord's Prayer, may be accounted for by the supposition that they regarded the doxology not so much a portion of the Prayer itself, as a hymn of praise annexed to it by our Blessed Redeemer. But in truth, every person versed in these studies is aware, that however trustworthy may be the positive testimony of the Fathers, the argument derived from their silence is of all others the most precarious. Throughout every class of their writings, they perpetually overlook the most obvious citations from Scripture, with which, as we learn from other sources, they were perfectly familiar. Yet this slender presumption is suffered to outweigh the direct evidence of a vast majority of the Greek manuscripts and versions.

I wish not to disparage the character of the manuscripts which omit the doxology (B D Z. 1. 17. 118. 130. 209). The Vatican MS. (B) is probably the oldest now extant which contains this chapter; its rival the Codex Alexandrinus (A) being unfortunately mutilated from the beginning of St. Matthew down to ch. xxv, 6. The Dublin palimpsest (Z) is an important document, but it too closely resembles the Vatican MS to claim all the consideration due to an independent witness. Of the Codex Bezæ (D) I must speak much less favorably. Its warmest advocates will confess that it is much oftener wrong than right. The glosses that deform its text amount to several hundreds (see, for instance, its readings in Matth. xx, 28; xxi, 29; xxii, 13; xxiv, 31; 41; xxv, 1, &c.); and its notorious connection with the Italic versions detracts still further from its value. Respecting the five cursive manuscripts I need only remark, that they all with the exception of 17 (a MS. of the 15th or 16th century), belong to the Alexandrine family. The best of them is 1 (Basil. γ), which is about 800 years old, and in the Gospels constantly follows the Latin translations. Neither of the other three is earlier than the 13th century; a circumstance which I name, not because I deem the age of a manuscript a sure criterion of its worth, but because such is the doctrine of Lachmann (see Introd. p. 26), and to some extent of Griesbach also. We must not forget to state, that the doxology is omitted in the Complutensian Polyglott, no doubt through deference to the authority of the Vulgate (see note on 1 John v, 7); and that scholia, or notes by uncertain hands, are written in the margins of many manuscripts which contain the clause, importing that it is deficient in certain copies. Finally, it is found in all the English versions except Tynd. 1, which was probably misled by the Complutensian edition. Such then is a faithful summary of the external arguments both for and against the clause. Ought we to hesitate for a moment to pronounce our judgment in favour of its authenticity?

Among the versions the Peshito Syriac holds the foremost place. Yet it is superfluous for Dr. Bloomfield to remind us that "its solitary testimony is not decisive of the question" (Greek Test. *ad loc.*); since, in the present case, so far from standing alone, it is supported by full forty-nine fiftieths of the Greek manuscripts. But Dr. Bloomfield goes on to urge, that "there are passages in the Peshito which are admitted to be interpolated, probably from the later Syriac versions." Now it is perfectly true that the occasional conformity of the Peshito to the Latin versions has given rise to a suspicion (I will not say an unfounded one), that its text has been corrupted in accordance with the Vulgate; either at the period of the submission of the Maronite Syrians to the Church of Rome in the twelfth century (see Introd. p. 68), or by the persons who superintended the Vienna editio princeps in 1555. Even if this surmise be well-grounded, it can have no place in an instance like that now before us, where the Syriac reading *differs* from that of the Latin versions. That these " admitted interpolations " were introduced from the Philoxenian Syriac, never has been, and I believe never will be proved. The existence of the doxology in the early Persic translation affords us no slight evidence that it was already contained in the Peshito, when that secondary version was formed from it.

But it is on *internal* marks of its spuriousness that the objectors to this clause chiefly insist. " It is more likely," they say, " that the doxology should have been inserted in the text of St. Matthew from the Greek liturgies, than that the copyists should have rejected it in St. Matthew, because it is wanting in St. Luke (ch. xi, 4)." I have already protested against the admission of arguments of this kind, where the direct proofs are strong and cogent (see note on v. 1); and I have little inclination to adjust the balance between the conflicting possibilities mentioned above. Yet it were easy to reply, that a passage which has been received as genuine by the translators of the Peshito and the Sahidic in the second and third centuries, and by Chrysostom in the fourth, must have become a part of the text at a very early period. With all our veneration for the Primitive Liturgies, what right have we to assume, that *they* have continued unaltered, in their actual state, ever since the Apostolic age? Still more readily may we dispose of Scholz's remark, that the doxology interrupts the logical connection between the 12th and 14th verses.* If this plea were of any force, it would compel us to cancel the whole of v. 13, and not merely its last clause.

I trust that the reader will pardon the length of my present note; but the great importance of the subject made me anxious to explain fully the grounds of my conviction, that the doxology is a genuine portion of the Lord's Prayer.

(I). v. 18. ἐν τῷ φανερῷ "openly" is found in all Eng. in Beza and Castalio; but is omitted by Syr. Vulg. and Campbell, I fear correctly. A few authorities reject the words in vv. 4, 6, but there is no good reason for following them. Bp. Jebb defends the received reading because it best accords with the system of parallel lines, into which he considers the whole sermon on the Mount to be distributed. He also endeavors to shew that ἐν τῷ φανερῷ in this place is required by the sense. "The act of the individual not merely shews the absence of anxiety for display, but is studiously designed for concealment (ὅπως μὴ φανῇς). Does not the generosity of God's dealings indicate, and one might almost say, demand, that the reward of such an act should be of the most public nature?" (Sacr. Liter. p. 166). Every one, I think, must be sensible of the awkwardness which ensues from the rejection of these words in v. 18, if they be retained (as beyond a doubt they should be retained) in vv. 4, 6; but I cannot safely resist the evidence which Scholz has produced against them. They are not read in a very considerable majority of manuscripts of all ages and of both families. Nearly

---

* The same thing had been said, though much less positively, by Wetstein. But that eminent critic was necessarily ignorant of a large proportion of the evidence in favor of the doxology.

all Matthæi's MSS omit them, and Griesbach, Vater, Scholz and Lachmann remove them from the text. In fact they are found only in the Italic, Æthiopic, and Arabic versions, and in some late Byzantine manuscripts. They seem to be so much needed by the context, that there is more cause for surprise that they have been inserted in so few copies, than that they are found in those which actually contain them.

(III, c). v. 22. ἁπλοῦς "clear"]. So Gen. Doddridge. "clean," Cheke. "sound," Campbell. "single," Auth. (and in Luke xi, 34) after Tynd. Cov. Cran. Bish., a rendering which is not very perspicuous, even if it be taken in a moral rather than a physical sense. Syr. ܦܫܝܛܐ, as Vulg. "simplex." "sain," Ostervald. Chrysostom thus paraphrases the passage: τὴν ὑγίειαν τὴν τούτων [τῶν ὀφθαλμῶν] ἁπάσης τῆς τοιαύτης περιουσίας ποθεινοτέραν εἶναι νομίζεις. It would not be easy to cite apposite examples of this use of ἁπλοῦς from other writers; but it is too slight a deviation from the ordinary signification of the word to be attended with any difficulty. Πονηρός in v. 23 should be rendered "distempered," with Doddridge and Dr. Symonds. "wicked," Tyn. Cov. Cran. Gen. Bish. "not well," Cheke.* "evil," Auth.

(III, c). v. 25. πλεῖον "of more worth"]. "more worth," or "of more value," Tynd. Cov. Cran. Cheke, Gen. Bish. "pluris," Castalio, correctly. But "plus,"

---

* In the margin Cheke explains ἁπλοῦς by "clean, unmixt, as clean wheat, clean barley that hath no other thing mixed withal;" and says that "πονηρὸν here is that hath some foul disease or impediment in it."

Vulg. Beza, whence "more," Auth. See ch. xii, 41; 42.

(II, a). vv. 25, 27, 28, 31, 34. μεριμνᾷν " to be anxious"]. So Boothroyd after Doddridge, Campbell, &c. " to take anxious thought," Newcome, and the " Holy Bible" of 1841. In v. 27 we have " by taking careful thought" in Cran. Gen. Bish. In vv. 25, 28, 34 we find " care not" in Tynd. Cov. Cran. Gen. Bish. In v. 31 all Eng. render " take thought," which is the uniform translation of Auth. in all the passages. Cheke, however, has " be not thoughtful," which is somewhat less objectionable. Most English critics have lamented the inadvertence of Auth. which, in bidding us "take no thought" for the necessaries of life, prescribes to us what is impracticable in itself, and would be a breach of Christian duty, even were it possible. The same remark applies to ch. x, 19; Luke xii, 11; 22; 25; 26; and in some measure to Phil. iv, 6. Syr. renders it by ܨܦ, the Latin versions by " solliciti," except that Vulg. uses " cogitans" in v. 27. In fact, there can be no doubt of the inaccuracy of Auth. in this particular.

(II, a). v. 27. προσθεῖναι ἐπὶ τὴν ἡλικίαν αὐτοῦ πῆχυν ἕνα " add to his life one span"]. So correct Luke xii, 25. Syr. Vulg. Beza, Castalio, Cheke and all Eng. render these words with Auth. " add one cubit unto his stature." While I entertain a strong, and I hope a wholesome distrust of novel modes of interpretation, I cannot withhold my assent from the arguments adduced by Hammond, Wolf, Wetstein, Doddridge and Campbell, in behalf of the change I have suggested. The received sense seems to lie under two insuperable difficulties. Our Lord is here dissuading us from worldliness of mind. He even exhorts us not to be over-anxious to secure a due provision for the pressing wants of the body, such as food and raiment. How can we reconcile it with the dignity of his character, or the universal interest of his subject, that he should abruptly turn aside to reprove the foolish vanity of that very small portion of his hearers, who might wish to add to their stature? Whereas, on the contrary, by referring ἡλικία to the duration of life, we establish an intelligible connection between this verse, and the context in which it stands. In the last clause of v. 25, a comparison is instituted between the respective values of life and meat, of the body and raiment. In vv. 26, 28 the leading idea of the passage is expanded in two beautiful similes, each designed to shew the *futility* of our excessive care for food and clothing, since the meanest portions of the creation are abundantly supplied with them, according to their several needs. How natural is it to interpose, by way of parenthesis, between the two members of this single illustration, a new but most important sentiment, that our very life, for the preservation of which these things are necessary, can be prolonged by no foresight or anxiety on our part! Again, is there not almost a contradiction in terms in the common version of this text? "Which of you by taking thought can add *one cubit* to his stature?" Our Lord can only mean, increase his stature by the smallest appreciable measure; by an inch, by an hair's-breadth. And this notion St. Luke, in the parallel text, expresses by the words "If ye then be not able to do that which is least" (ἐλάχιστον Luke xii, 26). Now a cubit is not less than one foot and a half ("an half yard mete," Cheke; but Suidas tells us ὁ πῆχυς ἔχει πόδας δύο·): with what propriety then can it be called ἐλάχιστον? what rational person ever desired to increase his stature in that proportion? Such are the chief objections to the usual rendering of the passage; and they seem to have escaped even Chrysostom's observation, for he quietly dismisses the sentence by saying ὥσπερ γὰρ τῷ σώματι οὐδὲ μικρὸν προσθεῖναι δυνήσῃ μεριμνῶν, οὕτως ....κ. τ. λ.

But how will ἡλικία and πῆχυς bear the senses I have ventured to assign to them? With the former, I conceive, our course is clear. Ἡλικία is used for "age," or "time of life," in John ix, 21; 23; Hebr. xi, 11. In the Attic writers it constantly occurs, as well for the prime of life, or age of military service; as for any particular period of life, even the more advanced. Thus Demosthenes Olynth. 3. (p. 38 Reiske) includes in the expression ὅ, τι καθ' ἡλικίαν ἕκαστος ἔχοι, every possible service that citizens of whatever age can render the state; and Æschines c. Timarch. (p. 19 Stephan.) speaks of τὴν φρονοῦσαν καὶ πρεσβυτέραν ἡλικίαν. I cannot agree with Rose (Parkhurst's Lexicon, voc. ἡλικία) in adding Ezek. xiii, 18; for the Hebrew word (קוֹמָה) there rendered ἡλικία by the LXX, is the very same that is employed by the translator of the Peshito in the New Testament to signify "stature."

Πῆχυς, however, is attended with greater difficulty. Yet even Schleusner, who abides by the usual interpretation of the passage, admits that it may very well (" commodè ") mean the shortest space of time, and refers us to Psalm xxxix, 5. It is in allusion to that memorable Psalm, that I have suggested " span" as an adequate rendering of πῆχυς, though there can be little objection to a more literal translation. Campbell has " prolong his life one hour;"

a version which entirely conceals the tropical form of the passage. Hammond has illustrated the sense of πῆχυς here contended for, by a happy quotation from a fragment of Mimnermus: τοῖς ἴκελοι πήχυιον ἐπὶ χρόνον ἄνθεσιν ἥβης τερπόμεθα. I am not aware that a second example of this usage can be found. The comparison of life to a race in the course is not unfrequent in Scripture (Acts xiii, 25; xx, 24; 2 Tim. iv, 7); with all the circumstances and technical terms of the Grecian games, even the Jews were by this time familiar: thus there is much probability in Wetstein's conjecture, that if πῆχυς is to be taken strictly as a definite measure of length, our Saviour may have reference to the stadium, or race-course, in which a single cubit would be but a very small part of the space over which the contending candidates had to run. That such an allusion is not foreign to our Saviour's mode of teaching, may perhaps appear from Luke xxii, 25.

v. 34. There is a remarkable diversity between the various translations in rendering the last clause of this chapter, ἀρκετὸν τῇ ἡμέρᾳ ἡ κακία αὐτῆς. Auth. is the best, but Tynd. 1. "each day's trouble is sufficient for the self-same day," is decidedly superior to Tynd. 2. "for the day present hath ever enough of his own trouble." See Introd. p. 83.

CHAPTER VII.

(I). v. 2. Read with Griesbach, Scholz, Lachmann, and all recent editors μετρηθήσεται instead of ἀντιμετρηθήσεται, omitting "again," which is found in all Eng. except Cran. Even Bp. Jebb rejects the received reading (which seems to have arisen from Luke vi, 38), on the ground that all the other verbs in this stanza being uncompounded, the preposition ἀντὶ destroys the balance of the couplet. Μετρηθήσεται is given by nearly all the manuscripts of note, by Syr. (though the evidence of that version is of little influence in a question of this kind), and even in some copies of the Italic and Vulg. Indeed Lachmann's revised Vulgate text has " metietur."

(II, b). v. 4. ἡ δοκὸς " the beam"]. So Bish. but manifestly by accident. The promiscuous manner in which all the English versions use the definite and indefinite articles in vv. 3, 4, affords one instance out of a thousand how utterly regardless they were of this little part of speech. In expressing or neglecting the Greek article, they seem to have been guided by no other principle than the caprice or convenience of the moment. Ἡ δοκὸς stands in the same position as τὸ κάρφος in this very verse. There is not the slightest reason for employing our definite article in the one case, and not in the other. I presume that those who, with Bishop Middleton, deny the demonstrative character of the Greek article, would explain its use in vv. 3, 4 by a reference to its *anticipative* property. (Doctrine of the Article, p. 23, 3rd edit.)

Some of my readers will remember that Campbell, in this place, renders τὴν δοκὸν " a thorn ;" a signification which he does not pretend to defend by the authority of any Greek writer whatsoever. The sole reason which he assigns for his bold interpretation is the following. Σκόλοψ, in classical authors, means " a stake." In the LXX, however (Numbers xxxiii, 55), it answers to the Hebrew שֵׂךְ, " a thorn:" it is found in this sense in 2 Cor. xii, 7, and (he might have added) in profane authors also. (See Wetstein *ad loc*). In like manner βολὶς properly is "a dart" or "javelin;" but in Numb. xxxiii, 55 ; Josh. xxiii, 13 it corresponds with צְנִינִים "prickles" or "thorns." "Now it is not more remote from our idiom," he observes, " to speak of a *pole*, or a *javelin*, than to speak of a beam, in the eye." I am surprised that so sagacious a critic as Campbell failed to perceive the broad distinction which subsists between the case of δοκός, and of the words which he cites to vindicate his interpretation of it. For the metaphorical sense, both of σκόλοψ and βολὶς, he has produced sufficient justification; that δοκὸς is ever used in a similar manner he has neither shown, nor endeavoured to show. And with respect to his attempted illustration from the English idiom, it is surely enough to reply, that nothing is more fallacious than to determine what is proper in one language, from the phrases or peculiarities of another. In the present instance there can be no question that the primary signification of δοκὸς is that intended to be conveyed. It is translated "beam" by all the versions. Lightfoot speaks of the passage as a familiar proverb among the Jews; and one of his authorities uses the word קוֹרָה, which is found in 2 Kings vi, 2 (δοκὸς LXX); 5; 2 Chron. iii, 7, and is identical with the Syriac ܩܳܪܝܺܬܳܐ employed by the Peshito in these verses.

(II, c). v. 6. καὶ στραφέντες ῥήξωσιν ὑμᾶς " and they turn again and rend you "]. Auth. renders "and turn again and rend you," after Syr. Vulg. Beza, Cheke, Gen. Bish. But Tynd. Cov. Cran. translate " and [the other] turn again," thereby intimating that this last clause refers not to the swine, but to the dogs. To the same effect Castalio, with his wonted freedom, "ne hi eos pedibus conculcent, illi versi lacerent vos;" and is followed by that disgraceful production, the anonymous English version of 1729. I have already (Introd. p. 121) expressed my gratitude to Bp. Jebb for his valuable illustration of this verse (Sacred Liter. pp. 338-40), and of the kind of stanza which it exemplifies. It will scarcely admit of a doubt that his arrangement of the passage is agreeable to the mind of the Divine Speaker. The whole verse is divided into four clauses or parallel lines, whereof the first is closely connected with the fourth, and the second with the third.* By virtue of an artifice which Bp. Jebb terms Epanodos, the different members of the sentence are thus transposed from their natural order, to situations better fitted for producing a powerful effect.

But without disputing the truth of the principle here stated, we may reasonably question the propriety of imitating Tynd. and Castalio in this particular; and I cannot help assenting to the opinion of Dr. Doddridge, that the practice of Auth. and the later versions is far more judicious. "The transposition [or, as Doddridge might have said, the arbitrary supplying] of words, even where there is a trajection in the sense, is so dangerous a thing where the sacred writers are in question, that no small advantage gained in elegance or perspicuity seems sufficient to counterbalance it." I would fain bear in mind this just and pious sentiment throughout every page of the present work; at the same time I have inserted

---

* The *regular* arrangement of the stanza would be as follows:
  Give not that which is holy to the dogs;
  Lest they turn about and rend you:
  Neither cast your pearls before the swine;
  Lest they trample them under their feet.

the pronoun "they" before "turn," although it is not in Auth., in order so far to disjoin καὶ στραφέντες ῥήξωσιν ὑμᾶς from the preceding clause, as to render our translation *compatible* with Bp. Jebb's idea, to the full extent that reverence for the original will permit.

(I). v. 14. τί στενὴ "how strait"]. So the margin of Auth. after Syr. Vulg. The received reading ὅτι στενὴ " for strait," is adopted by Tynd. 1. Cran. "but strait," Tynd. 2. Cov. Matthew's Bible, Castalio. "because strait," Gen. Bish. Auth. after Beza's " quia." The variation τί for ὅτι has caused me more hesitation and perplexity than any which has yet occurred. Differing as they do only by the omission or introduction of a single letter at the beginning of a sentence, either of them might easily have originated from the other. The balance of external evidence is certainly in favour of τί, which is adopted by Griesbach, Vater, Scholz, and Lachmann. No less than fifty of the best manuscripts are cited in its support by Scholz, and it is read in many others not expressly named. It is found in most of Matthæi's manuscripts, so that it cannot be considered exclusively Alexandrine. It is the reading not only of Syr. Vulg. but of the Æthiopic and several other versions. Although Chrysostom has καὶ in his exposition of the passage ("and the gate is narrow," Cheke), he elsewhere prefers τί. Οὐχ ἁπλῶς εἶπεν, he remarks, ὅτι στενή ἐστιν, ἀλλὰ μετὰ θαυμασμοῦ, τί στενὴ ἡ ὁδός, τούτεστιν σφόδρα στενή (Tom. xi, p. 492): and so say Theophylact and the rest of the Greek commentators. On the other side we have a respectable, but by no means an equal, company of witnesses. They consist of the two uncials B X, of two valuable MSS of about the 12th century, and a crowd of later ones of the Byzantine family. Among the versions ὅτι is supported by the Coptic (*teste Wilkins*), the Armenian, and one or two Italic copies. It is also cited by Origen. In conclusion, then, I am obliged to differ from Bp. Jebb in this matter, though I know not how to refute his arguments, derived from the structure and sense of the passage (Sacr. Liter. pp. 382-4). That ὅτι, *were it the reading of the manuscripts*, ought to be understood in the way pointed out by him, will scarcely be doubted by any one.

(II, b). vv. 24, 25. τὴν πέτραν "the rocky ground."]. See Bp. Middleton. "The article is here used with propriety, because the attention is directed to the *substance*, in respect of its quality, in contradistinction to another (ἐπὶ τὴν ἄμμον, v. 26)." Green, Gram. N.T. Dialect, p. 149. Thus correct Luke vi, 48. It is curious to observe the inconsistency of our old versions (See note on v. 4). They all read "a rock" in v. 24, but in v. 25 Tynd. Cov. Cran. have "the rock." Yet this may possibly be designed to indicate renewed mention. "La roche," Martin, in both verses.

(II, a). v. 25. προσέπεσον "fell upon." v. 27. προσέκοψαν "struck upon"]. These words, which were confounded by Syr. Vulg. Eng. ("beat upon"), as also by Schleusner and most other critics, are accurately distinguished by Castalio ("irruentibus .... impingentibus"), Beza ("inciderunt..impegerunt"), Doddridge and Campbell. I have adopted the version of Bp. Jebb, in whose light we have lately been walking, and whose admirable analysis of the Sermon on the Mount ranks with the most precious treasures of our native theology. "The verb προσπίπτω," observes this great scholar and good man, "is more forcible than προσκόπτω. The rain, the floods, the winds, *fell prone with violence* upon the prudent man's house, and it did not fall; they *struck*, or *impinged* with less of downright impetuosity, on the foolish man's house, and it *did* fall."

(III, c). v. 28. διδαχὴ "teaching"]. So Cheke. "manner of teaching," Campbell. All Eng. have "doctrine," which to a modern ear conveys a different meaning. The verse immediately following renders it clear, that the mode of teaching, and not the doctrine taught, is what is here intended. Διδαχή, ἀντὶ τοῦ διδασκαλία, Suidas. Schleusner approves of my interpretation, but adds that some refer διδαχὴ to the doctrine of a future life and judgment, as taught by our Lord. See ch. xxii, 33.

CHAPTER VIII.

(I). v. 5. Instead of Ἰησοῦ in this verse, Vulg. and all the critical editors read αὐτῷ, except indeed that Lachmann prefers the Alexandrine correction εἰσελθόντος δὲ αὐτοῦ. Ἰησοῦ is found in but one or two good manuscripts, and in Syr., so that its spuriousness is unquestionable. This is another instance of our first translators' disregard of the Vulg., for all Eng. insert "Jesus." The source of such interpolations was explained in my note on ch. iv, 18; and the same remarks will apply to ch. xiv, 22; Mark viii, 1; John i, 29; 44; iii, 2: and perhaps to Mark vi, 34; Luke xxiv, 36.

(III, a). vv. 6, 8. Κύριε "Sir"]. So Tynd. Cov.

Cran. Cheke, Gen. " Domine " of Vulg. was rendered " Lord, " *more suo*, by Wickliffe and the Rhemish translators, but it is to be regretted that Bish. Auth. should have thus altered the earlier versions. Campbell (Prelim. Diss. VII, Pt. 1) has forcibly stated the ingruity of representing our Blessed Lord, " though not acknowledged by the great and learned of the age, and though meanly habited," as addressed by almost every one in the peculiar style by which the Almighty is invoked in prayer. Where an express recognition of his Divine office is intended, it is of course proper to retain the reverential appellation " Lord ;" wherever this is not the case, it both is the safest and most reasonable course to translate Κύριος " Sir, " as is actually done by Auth. in John iv, 11 ; 15 ; 19 ; 49 ; v, 7. In John xx, 15 any other rendering would have been absurd.

(III, c). v. 14. βεβλημένην καὶ πυρέσσουσαν " lying sick of a fever "]. So Tynd. Cov. "lying in bed and sick," Cran. "lying and sick," Gen. Still more harsh is " laid down and sick," Cheke ; and " laid and sick," Bish. Auth. The Syriac ܪܡܝܐ; is constantly used in this sense. The full expression βάλλειν εἰς κλίνην occurs in Mark vii, 30 ; Rev. ii, 22.

(I). v. 15. διηκόνει αὐτῷ " ministered unto him "]. So we ought no doubt to read, instead of αὐτοῖς " to them." Though the latter is contained in Syr. Vulg. the singular is found in Rapheleng's Cologne MS of the Peshito, and in those copies of Vulg. from which the Rhemish divines translated.* All the chief Greek manuscripts *except five* have αὐτῷ, and these (L. 1.

---

* In the Introduction p. 76, I stated that *Wickliffe* also differed from the printed Vulgate in the present passage. But this was an error, for which I entreat the reader's forgiveness.

13. 33. 124) too often conspire in presenting improbable readings, to be regarded, when they stand alone, with much respect. Indeed the Codex L is, next to the Cambridge manuscript, the most suspicious of all the Alexandrine uncial documents. Chrysostom unequivocally favors αὐτῷ, which is cited by Origen and adopted by Scholz and Lachmann. Griesbach's theory here precludes him from admitting the true reading. Considering these five MSS and the Syriac version to represent one of his three families, and the Italic and Vulg. another; he not only rejects the evidence of the Byzantine class, but even that of his special favorites, B, C, and K (Codex Cyprius). A still more unjustifiable application of his principle of recensions occurs in v. 31; where he substitutes ἀπόστειλον ἡμᾶς for ἐπίτρεψον ἡμῖν ἀπελθεῖν, on the poor authority of four manuscripts (certainly B is one of them), and of the Latin and Egyptian versions.* The little influence produced on the sense by such alterations affords us no ground for thinking them slight or frivolous. The uprightness of Griesbach's character places him far above the suspicion of sinister designs; but if his critical canons be once allowed to bias our decisions on matters of minor importance, it will be impossible to offer a consistent or successful resistance to the rashest attempts at innovation, in passages of the highest concern to our Christian faith and practice.

(II, b). v. 16. λόγῳ " with a word"]. So all Eng. except Cheke and Auth., and why should they have changed that rendering into " with his word?" As " his" is not printed in italics in the first edition of

---

* By the term Egyptian I understand the Sahidic, Coptic and Æthiopic versions.

Auth., our common version requires τῷ λόγῳ αὐτοῦ, or τῷ λόγῳ at the least.

(II, b). v. 23. τὸ πλοῖον " the ship"]. So Gen. " a ship," Tynd. Cov. Cran. Bish. Auth. " a boat," Cheke. The vessel in question was that implied in v. 18. See note on ch. iv, 21. In like manner we must correct ch. ix, 1 where Tynd. 1. alone has " the ship." ." la nacelle," Martin, in both places.

(II, b. See Introd. p. 45). v. 24. καλύπτεσθαι " was being covered"]. All Eng. wrongly translate " was covered."

(III, c). v. 26. ἐγένετο " ensued"]. So the Rhemish version. " followed," of Tynd. Cov. Cran. Gen. Bish. is much better than " was" of Cheke, Auth., who seem to agree very often against the rest.

(I)°. v. 28. τῶν Γεργεσηνῶν " of the Gergesenes"]. There are three different readings of this passage. Γεργεσηνῶν, which is given in the textus receptus, and Eng., is retained by Griesbach, though he almost prefers Γερασηνῶν, the word adopted by Vater and Lachmann from the Italic and Vulg. Scholz however edits Γαδαρηνῶν, which is found in Syr. and in the parallel texts Mark v, 1; Luke viii, 26. Γερασηνῶν is contained in no manuscript now extant, although it was a common reading in Origen's age, and besides the testimony of the Latin versions, is supported by Gregory Nyssen and Athanasius, by the Sahidic, and the margin of the Philoxenian Syriac. Still this evidence amounts to so little in itself, and Gerasa was so far distant from the shores of the Lake Tiberias, that we may fairly dismiss Γερασηνῶν from our consideration. The real difficulty consists in choosing between Γεργεσηνῶν and Γαδαρηνῶν. And here again we might readily decide the controversy, if manuscript authority were principally to be regarded.

Γαδαρηνῶν is sanctioned by only eleven MSS (although B C M are among them), and five Evangelisteria, or extracts from the Gospels for ecclesiastical purposes; but into the latter a variation would easily be admitted, which removes the apparent discrepancy between the narrative of St. Matthew, and those of the other Evangelists. Origen says ἐν ὀλίγοις εὕρομεν εἰς τὴν χώραν τῶν Γαδαρηνῶν, and both the Peshito and Philoxenian Syriac, together with the Persic version (see note on ch. vi, 13), and one or two Fathers, favor the same side.

Γεργεσηνῶν, on the contrary, is the reading of the vast majority of manuscripts of both families; of the Coptic, Æthiopic, Armenian and some less important versions, as well as of several ecclesiastical writers of various ages, down to the time of Theophylact. Indeed there would have been little scruple respecting the authenticity of the received text, had it not been imagined by Wetstein, and after him by Michäelis and Scholz (Proleg. N. T. § 15), that Γεργεσηνῶν originated in a gratuitous conjecture of Origen. Now not to insist on the glaring improbability of the supposition, that the unsupported influence of *Origen* was sufficient to procure the insertion of any reading his capricious taste might dictate, into nearly all the manuscripts of Scripture scattered throughout the world; we may reasonably doubt whether, on an attentive examination, his words will bear the construction put upon them by Wetstein. They occur in his commentary on St. John, Tom vi (Opera, Paris. 1759 Delarue, Vol. iv, pp. 140—1). He had taken up a notion (a very idle one perhaps) that the etymology of certain names of places mentioned in the Bible, was prophetically significant of the great events, of which they were hereafter to become the scenes. On this account he prefers the various reading Βηθαβαρᾶ in John, i, 28 to Βηθανία, although the latter was found in *nearly all* his copies. Ἔστι τε ἡ ἑρμήνεια τοῦ ὀνόματος ἀκόλουθος τῷ βαπτίσματι τοῦ ἑτοιμάζοντος Κυρίῳ λαὸν κατεσκευασμένον· μεταλαμβάνεται γὰρ εἰς οἶκον κατασκευῆς· ἡ δὲ Βηθανία, εἰς οἶκον ὑπακοῆς. And he furthermore defends the reading which he approves by the traditional recollections of the inhabitants of the district bordering on the Jordan. We must confess, therefore, that Origen (whether correctly or otherwise is another point) is in *one* passage induced by his fanciful theory to reject the testimony of the majority of his manuscripts; but neither in that place, nor in those which he subsequently cites from the Old Testament (e. g. Gen. xlvi, 11, in p. 141), does he ever hazard a bare conjecture. Why then should we think that he would do so in the case of Matth. viii, 28? He certainly recognises Γερασηνῶν as an established reading (ἀναγέγραπται γεγονέναι ἐν τῇ χώρᾳ τῶν Γερασηνῶν), while he states that Γαδαρηνῶν was found in but a few copies, and is entirely silent respecting the evidence for Γεργεσηνῶν. But can it be thought for a moment, that Origen, a scholar and a man of genius, would have coolly *invented* this word, because forsooth ἑρμηνεύεται ἡ Γέργεσα παροικία ἐκβεβληκότων, ἐπώνυμος οὖσα ΤΑΧΑ προφητικῶς, οὗ περὶ τὸν Σωτῆρα πεποιήκασι, παρακαλέσαντες αὐτὸν μεταθεῖναι ἐκ τῶν ὁρίων αὐτῶν οἱ τῶν χοίρων πολῖται? Moreover, is not his employment of τάχα a sufficient proof that his choice was not determined solely by the etymology of Γέργεσα? It is a certain fact that Γεργεσηνῶν is the reading of the great mass of documents at present. It was appealed to *as such* by several of the antients, who had occasion to notice this passage (see Griesbach). Why then may we not infer that Origen also found it in some of his manuscripts, although through inadvertency he neglected to mention the circumstance?

Thus we are led to conclude, from the pressure of external evidence, that Γεργεσηνῶν is the true reading of St. Matthew. Nor is it hard to reconcile the received text with Γαδαρηνῶν of the other Evangelists. The district wherein Gadara was situated seems to have been called indifferently the country of the Gadarenes, its actual inhabitants, and of the Gergesenes or Girgashites, the Canaanitish nation which had been expelled from those regions by Joshua. Such is Lightfoot's solution of the difficulty, and by its simplicity it proves itself. That Gadara is "the city" alluded to in v. 34, will not be disputed; yet it is not necessary for our purpose to fix its precise locality. A place which was but "sixty stadia" (Joseph. de vitâ suâ, c. 65), or $6\frac{1}{2}$ miles "distant from Tiberias in Galilee;" being itself "above Jordan, opposite Scythopolis and Tiberias, and to the east of them" (Euseb. Onom.); yet "situated on the Hieromax" (Pliny, v, 16) a tributary of the Jordan; *must* have been within three miles of the South-eastern corner of the Lake. Surely a region by the sea-side, so near to Gadara, "the metropolis of Peræa" (Joseph. Bell. Jud. iv, 7), would very naturally be called by its name.

(II, b). v. 32. κατὰ τοῦ κρημνοῦ " down the steep"]. viz. the bank of the Lake Gennesareth. Here is another example of the peculiarity noticed on ch. v, 1, where St. Matthew presupposes in his readers the same intimate acquaintance with Galilee and its vicinity which he himself possessed (Green, Gram. N. T. Dialect, p. 159). This strong though undesigned proof of the writer's good faith, and consequently of the credibility of his history, depends on our accurate observance of the force of the article. " Per præceps," Vulg. whence " headlong," Wickliffe, Tynd. Cov. Cran. Bish. " by an headlong place," Cheke: " from a steep down place," Gen. " down a steep place," Auth.

CHAPTER IX.

(III, a and c). vv. 2, 5. ἀφέωνται " are forgiven"]. So Tynd. 1. and Cov. Cheke in v. 2; Gen. in v. 5. All other Eng. have " be forgiven." Syr. Vulg. render the verb as indicative, and such doubtless was the intention of Auth., though the ambiguity of the expression " be forgiven" is unfortunate in a passage, which so fully demonstrates our Lord's proper divinity (see vv. 3, 6). A similar correction should be applied to Auth. in Mark ii, 5; 9; Luke v, 23. The word is properly translated in Luke v, 20; vii, 47; 48: and the context in every place forbids our taking ἀφέωνται in a mere optative sense. The Doric form ἀφέωνται for ἀφεῖνται is illustrated by Buttmann in his Greek Grammar, Catalogue of Irregular Verbs, pp. 6 and 115, notes, Fishlake's Translation.

(II, a). v. 7. εἰς τὸν οἶκον αὐτοῦ " to his own house"]. So Tynd. 2. Gen. rather more accurately than " to his house," of Tynd. 1. Cran. Cheke, Bish. Auth. The force of αὐτοῦ is not always capable of being preserved in a version, and editions of the Greek Testament perpetually vary between αὐτοῦ and αὑτοῦ. I am ignorant of the grounds of Mr. Field's opinion (Annot. ad Chrysost. in Matth. Hom. II), " pronomen αὑτοῦ reciprocum e Sacro Novi Fœderis codice penitus extirpandum esse."

(III, c). v. 10. ἐν τῇ οἰκίᾳ " in *his* house". viz.

Matthew's: compare Luke v, 29. So Tynd. 1. Cran. Gen. Bish. Scholefield: "in the house," of Tynd. 2. Cov. Cheke, Auth. is indistinct. See note on ch. iv, 21. But this use of the article in the sense of the personal pronoun prevails in every page of Greek. Εἰς τὴν οἰκίαν in v. 28 may be translated in the same manner. It refers, as Rosenmüller has remarked, to our Lord's ordinary residence at Capernaum (see above v. 7, and ch. iv, 13). The transposition of Ἰησοῦ from the last clause to the beginning of v. 10 in Auth. must not be supposed to arise from a various reading of the Greek, as it is done merely for the sake of convenience. Tynd. 1. Cran. Gen. Bish. repeat the word in both places.

(II, b). v. 13. δικαίους "just men"]. So Cheke. All Eng. "*the* righteous." Thus alter Mark ii, 17; Luke v, 32.

(I)°. *ibid.* εἰς μετάνοιαν "to repentance"]. These words are wanting in Syr. Vulg. both here and in Mark ii, 17; so that it might be suspected that they are interpolated from the parallel passage, Luke v, 32. They are rejected both in Matthew and Mark by Griesbach and Lachmann; and in Mark alone by Vater and Scholz. Of the text in St. Mark I will speak hereafter: in the present case I am compelled to consider the evidence for the omission of εἰς μετάνοιαν insufficient. Scholz cites only twelve manuscripts which reject the clause (the great Vatican MS B being one of them), four of which contain it in the margin. They are nearly all of the Alexandrine class, and several of them too closely allied to be regarded with much confidence as separate witnesses (D. 1. 33. 118). The *accordance* of the Peshito with the Vulgate and earlier Latin versions I have before noticed as a little suspicious (see note on ch. vi, 13), and the few other authorities* in favour of expunging the words, are easily counterbalanced by the testimony of the Sahidic version, of Chrysostom, and the vast majority of manuscripts of both families, which favor their authenticity. All Eng. have " to repentance," though Cran.'s attachment to Vulg. led him in v. 15 to render οἱ υἱοὶ τοῦ νυμφῶνος " the bridegroom's children," from " filii sponsi" of Vulg. In v. 25 Cran. alone after " took her by the hand" adds : "and said damsel, arise." I cannot, however, trace *this* interpolation (see Introd. p. 88) to Latin influence.†

(II, a). v. 16. ἀγνάφου " undressed"]. So Campbell: " unfulled," Cheke. This is more literal than " new" of Syr. Eng. and clearer than " rudis" of Vulg. or " raw, unwrought," of the margins of Bish. Auth. Thus correct Mark ii, 21. Doddridge sensibly observes, that cloth which has not passed through the fuller's hands, being less supple than what has been often washed, is likely to tear away the edges to which it is sewed, since it yields less than the old cloth.

(III, a). *ibid.* ἐπὶ " upon"]. So Auth. in Luke v, 36, but " on" in Mark ii, 21, and " unto" here: " in," Cran. Bish. Respecting πλήρωμα in this verse see Störr *de voce* vi. It manifestly denotes " the supplement," " the new part added," that which fills up, or makes perfect, the whole garment. It is called by St. Luke τὸ καινόν, while St. Mark unites

---

* Griesbach cites Clement of Rome as an evidence against the clause. He alludes to a passage in c. 2. of the second or *spurious* Epistle, which is of very little value.

† Mill is mistaken when he says that the words are found in the Vulg. Yet I suppose they may be discovered in some Italic manuscript.

both modes of expression, τὸ πλήρωμα αὐτοῦ τὸ καινόν. It would be well if the signification of the word were equally plain in some other passages of the New Testament (e. g. Rom. xi, 12; Eph. i, 23). The construction of the next clause was entirely mistaken by Tynd. Cov. Cran. (" for then, taketh he away the piece again from the garment") who were probably misled by Vulg. "tollit enim plenitudinem &c." And to the same effect Cheke says " for it taketh away the wholeness of the garment." But Syr. Beza and Castalio rightly make πλήρωμα the nominative to αἴρει. Gen. Bish. are mere translations from Beza (" for then the piece taketh away *something* from the garment," Bish.). Auth. " that which is put in to fill it up taketh from the garment," is as exact and clear as any.

(III, c). v. 17. ἀσκοὺς " leathern bottles"]. So Campbell, Scholefield, but only on the first mention of them; correctly judging " bottles" to be sufficient in all subsequent places : "vessels," Tynd. Cov. Gen. " bottles," Cran. Cheke. Bish. Auth. ; and " utres" of Vulg. is thus rendered by Wickliffe and the Rhemish version. So " His cold thin drink out of his leather bottle." Shakespeare, Henry VI, Pt. iii, Act ii, Scene 5. " Bottle" in this sense is now obsolete.

(III, c). *ibid.* ἀπολοῦνται, " are destroyed"]. So Doddridge, much better than " perish" of Eng. " be marred," Cheke. All the English translations except Cheke and Auth. render the preposition in συντηροῦνται, " preserved together." It is not necessary to the sense, but there can be no good reason for suppressing it. See Introd. p. 35.

(III, c). v. 24. ἀναχωρεῖτε " withdraw"]. So Campbell : " go forth," Cheke : " retire," Doddridge. All are preferable to " get you hence" of Tynd. Cov. Cran. Gen. or " give place" of Bish. Auth. Campbell (Prel. Diss. XI, Pt. 2, 8) complains of the idiomatic phrase " laughed to scorn," by which Eng. render κατεγέλων (" laughed at" simply, Cheke). I do not think that " deride," which he substitutes in its place, so well expresses the intensive κατά.

(III, c). v. 26. ἡ φήμη αὕτη " this report"]. But " this noise," Cran. " the fame of this," Bish. " this fame," margin of Auth. " the fame hereof, " Cheke, Auth. The accordance of Cheke with our common Bible (see note on ch. viii, 26) is very extraordinary. How shall we account for it?

(II, a). v. 30. ἐνεβριμήσατο " enjoined with a threat"]. " charged," Tynd. Cov. Cran. Cheke, Gen. " straitly charged," Bish. Auth. But " comminatus est," Vulg. Castalio; " graviter interminatus est," Beza, whence " défendit avec minaces," Martin; " défendit fortement *d'en parler*," Osterwald. Syr. ݁ܠܐ, which usually implies " to forbid with authority" (κωλύειν, Acts xxvii, 43; 1 Tim. iv, 3). Agreeably to Vulg., Hesychius explains the word by προστάξαι μετ' ἐξουσίας—μετὰ ἀπειλῆς ἐντέλλεσθαι· and Suidas, μετ' ὀργῆς λαλῆσαι—μετ' αὐστηρότητος ἐπιτιμῆσαι. Æschyl. Theb. 443, ἵππους ἐπ' ἀμπυκτῆρσιν ἐμβριμωμένας. Rose compares Psalm cvi, 9; Nahum i, 4. Ἐμβριμώμενος is the rendering of זָעַם " angry" given by one of the Greek translators (Bahrdt thinks by Symmachus) in Ps. vii, 11; where Aquila has ἀπειλούμενος, and the LXX ὀργὴν ἐπάγων. Symmachus also represents גְּעָר " rebuke" by ἐμβριμήσεται in Isai. xvii, 13; where Aquila translates ἐπιτιμήσει, and the LXX ἀποσκορακιεῖ. So correct Mark i, 43.

(III, a). vv. 31, 32. οἱ δὲ ἐξελθόντες ... αὐτῶν δὲ ἐξερχομένων " when they were gone out ... but as they were going out"]. It is easy to perceive the advantage of rendering ἐξέρχεσθαι uniformly in these verses. See Introd. p. 51. All Eng. have " departed" in v. 31, " went out" in v. 32.

(III, c). v. 33. οὐδέποτε ἐφάνη οὕτως ἐν τῷ 'Ισραὴλ " the like was never seen in Israel"]. So Gen. " it never so appeared," Tynd. 1. " it was never so seen," Tynd. 2. Cov. Cran. Bish. Auth.

(II, b). v. 34. τὰ δαιμόνια " the devils"]. So Bish. and even Auth. in the edition of 1611. All other Eng., and the later copies of Auth., wrongly omit "the," which refers us back to τοῦ δαιμονίου, v. 33. Cheke neglects τὰ δαιμόνια altogether.

(I). v. 35. ἐν τῷ λαῷ " among the people," is expunged by Griesbach, Vater, Scholz and Lachmann, and was probably interpolated from the parallel passage, ch. iv, 23. On this ground, more than from the weight of manuscript authority, I am disposed to abandon the clause. It was unknown both to Chrysostom and Theophylact; and is not read either in Syr. Vulg. or in the Italic, Sahidic, Coptic, Æthiopic and several other versions (see p. 132, note). Ἐν τῷ λαῷ is also wanting in about twenty-seven manuscripts (including B C D S. 1. 33. 118. 157); most of them, though not all, being of the Alexandrine recension.

(I). v. 36. ἐσκυλμένοι " (were) harassed "]. This reading is substituted for ἐκλελυμένοι " fainted," by Mill, Wetstein, Griesbach, Vater, Scholz, Lachmann, and most other critics; the common reading being generally regarded as a marginal gloss on ἐσκυλμένοι, which is here employed in a rather unusual sense. A formidable array of the best manuscripts is produced by Scholz to justify the change, while those that favor ἐκλελυμένοι, are either of slight value (such as Codex

L, respecting which see note on ch. viii, 15; and Appendix A), or of recent date. The two words are so nearly synonymous that the testimony of versions should be used with caution: but Syr. ܠܐܝܢ ("lassi," Schaaf) seems best to correspond with ἐκλελυμένοι, while the Italic and Vulg. "vexati" suggest ἐσκυλμένοι, which is also the reading of Chrysostom, and other Fathers; and may fairly be considered as a genuine portion of the sacred text. The renderings of Eng. are various. Thus Tynd. Cov. have "pined away;" Cran. Gen. Bish. "destitute;" Cheke and Auth. "fainted," but in the margin of Auth. "were tired and lay down " (ἐρριμμένοι): "dissipati," Beza. But these are only different modes of translating the same word. See Wolf. Cur. Philog. *ad loc.*

The meaning I have assigned to ἐσκυλμένοι is amply vindicated by the practice of Greek writers. In its strictest sense, as Kypke observes, σκυλμὸς signifies "the plucking of the hair," 3 Macc. iii, 25; iv, 6; vii, 5. Hence it refers to any mode of vexation or annoyance (see Wetstein's note, Æsch. Pers. 583, and Blomfield's Glossary); especially to the weariness felt after a journey: Herodian iv [p. 494, ed. Stephani, 1525], ἵνα δὴ μὴ πάντα τὸν στρατὸν σκύλλῃ. Rosenmüller, after Grotius, understands by ἐσκυλμένοι the effect produced by the harassing and burdensome ceremonies of the Jewish ritual (ch. xxiii, 4); by ἐρριμμένοι the distraction of the people's minds, by reason of the various sects which at that time divided the nation (ch. x, 6). I doubt whether this distinction be not rather far fetched.

CHAPTER X.

(III, a and c). v. 1. ἐξουσίαν πνευμάτων ἀκαθάρτων "power over unclean spirits"]. So Tynd. Cov. and the margin of Auth. "against," Cran. Cheke, Gen. Bish. Auth. after Tyndal's second or quarto edition of 1526. Syr. inserts the preposition ܥܠ. This construction of ἐξουσία with a genitive of the object is not uncommon. See Mark vi, 7; John xvii, 2; Rom. ix, 21, in all which places Auth. has "over." Thus also Raphel cites from Polybius ii, 6, τῶν αὐτῶν ὑπάρχειν καὶ τὰς ὠφελείας ἐκ τῶν ἀπολλυμένων, καὶ τὴν ἐξουσίαν τῶν σωζομένων. In the parallel text Luke ix, 1 we find ἐξουσίαν ἐπὶ πάντα τὰ δαιμόνια.

(II, a). v. 4. Σίμων ὁ Κανανίτης "Simon the Zealot"]. So correct Mark iii, 18. He is the person called Ζηλωτὴς in Luke vi, 15; Acts i, 13; that appellation being in fact nothing more than a Greek translation of the Syriac ܩܢܢܐ or ܩܢܢܝܐ (Κανανίτης), which latter the Peshito employs here and in St. Mark, while it renders Ζηλωτὴς by the kindred term ܛܢܢܐ. Thus Chrysostom: Σίμωνα τὸν ζηλωτήν, ὃν καὶ Κανανίτην καλεῖ. Doddridge objects to this version (which has the sanction of expositors of high reputation; see Poli Synops. *ad loc.*), that the Zealots do not appear to have existed as a sect, till a little before the fall of Jerusalem (Joseph. Bell. Jud. iv, 3, 9). But not to mention that Josephus does not speak of them as a new sect at that period, it is more probable that this cognomen was given to Simon from his *personal* character for zeal for the law of Moses, than on account of his connection with any public sect or order of men. Besides that Doddridge's argument would compel us to expunge Ζηλωτὴς from the text of St. Luke. At any rate, it is clear that "Chananæus" Vulg. (but "Cananæus" in Mark iii, 18), "of Canaan," Cran. "of Canan," Gen. "the Canaanite," Cheke, Bish. Auth. are quite incorrect. The people of the land of Canaan, whom the Jews expelled, are represented both in the New Testament (Matth. xv, 22), and in the Greek versions of the Old (e. g. LXX Deut. i, 7), as Χαναναῖοι, not as Κανανῖται, or Καναναῖοι. A third rendering yet remains, which is that of Tynd. Cov., who translate "of Cana," the town in Galillee where Christ's first miracle was wrought. This interpretation also is open to considerable difficulty. It of course presupposes that the identity in meaning between Κανανίτης and Ζηλωτὴς is purely accidental. Moreover, if the analogy of Classical Greek be observed, from Κανᾶ we should expect Κανίτης, not Κανανίτης: just as we have Ἀβδηρίτης from Ἄβδηρα, &c. The various reading Καναναῖος, which Lachmann adopts after the Coptic and Latin versions, Codices B, C and a few other Alexandrine manuscripts, is liable to a similar exception.

(II, a). v. 5. ἀπέλθητε "go abroad"]. So Cheke. "go off," Bp. Jebb. Sacr. Liter. p. 313. The force of ἀπὸ is lost in Eng.; yet it should be retained in this place, because ἀπέλθητε is pointedly opposed to εἰσέλθητε in the next clause. "Go not away from Palestine, towards other nations."

(II, b). *ibid.* εἰς πόλιν "into a city"]. "civitates," Vulg. whence possibly "the cities," Tynd. Cov. Gen. "any of the Samaritans' cities," Cheke. "*any* city," Auth. "the city," Cran. Bish.; but no particular one is intended.

(I). v. 8. νεκροὺς ἐγείρετε "raise the dead"]. In my

Introduction p. 22, I have been led to condemn Scholz's rash rejection of these words. Griesbach, Lachmann, and Vulg. place them before λεπροὺς καθαρίζετε: Vater, after Syr., agrees with the received text. The clause however is wanting in the editio princeps of the Peshito, in the Sahidic, and in Chrysostom's Commentary. The manuscripts also cited by Scholz in behalf of his decision are numerous and of some consideration, though they are not, perhaps, of the first importance (e. g. E K L M S V X). On the whole there is cause for a *suspicion* that the words were brought into this passage from ch. xi, 5. What I complain of in Scholz is their absolute removal from the text, when so much is still capable of being urged in their defence.

In v. 9, κτήσησθε is well rendered "provide" by Auth., or by its margin "get." In Tynd. Cov. Cran. Cheke, Gen. Bish. we have "possess," an error more than once committed by Auth. e. g. in Luke xviii, 12; xxi, 19.

(I). v. 10. ῥάβδους "staves"]. The received text has ῥάβδον, as also have Syr. Vulg. "a rod," Tynd. 1. Cran. "a staff," Tynd. 2. Cov. Gen. Bish. and the margin of Auth., but only in the later editions.

The present is one of the very few instances in which Auth. departs both from Stephens's third edition and the text of Beza (see Introd. p. 8, and note on ch. ii, 11). Ῥάβδους however is the reading of the Complutensian Polyglott, and of Stephens's first and second editions. It was favored by Beza in the notes to his earlier editions, and is approved by Grotius, Wetstein, Griesbach and Scholz. A great majority of the most excellent manuscripts support this reading, though the singular form is found in B D. 1. 33, and several other Alexandrine documents;

in many later Byzantine copies, as also in Chrysostom, at least in the printed editions. Lachmann and Vater retain ῥάβδον, a form which may possibly have arisen from a misapprehension of the sense of εἰ μὴ ῥάβδον μόνον in Mark vi, 8. Compare Luke ix, 3.

(III, a). v. 11. κώμην "village"] as opposed to πόλιν, uniformly with ch. ix, 35. So Scholefield. All Eng. "town." Cheke omits κώμην altogether. In this verse Cov. alone translates "enquire in it who is meet for you," a transposition of the words which speaks little for his skill and judgment.

(II, b). v. 12. εἰς τὴν οἰκίαν "into *his* house"]. viz. the house of the person who is worthy to receive you. Here all Eng. have "an house," overlooking the article : "any house," Cheke, Martin.

(II, b). v. 16. ὡς οἱ ὄφεις, καὶ ἀκέραιοι ὡς αἱ περιστεραὶ "as the serpents, and harmless as the doves"]. "It is not without reason," Bp. Middleton remarks, "that we have ὡς πρόβατα, but ὡς οἱ ὄφεις [ὡς αἱ περιστεραί]. *All* sheep are not supposed to be in the midst of wolves ; but all serpents are assumed to be prudent, [and all doves harmless]." Bish. alone of Eng. notices this minute distinction. For ἀκέραιοι I prefer "harmless" of Bish. Auth. to "innocent" of Tynd. Cov. Cran. Gen. "plain" of Cheke, or "simple" of the margin of Auth. (which comes from "simplices" of Vulg. Beza, Martin). "Sinceri," Castalio : ܬܡܝܡܐ (perfect) Syr. Chrysostom rightly explains it by εἰς τὸ μὴ ἀμύνεσθαι τοὺς ἀδικοῦντας, μηδὲ τιμωρεῖσθαι τοὺς ἐπιβουλεύοντας. Elsner compares Eurip. Orest. 910 (ed. Matthiæ), ἀκέραιος, ἀνεπίληπτον ἠσκηκὼς βίον (Scholiast ἁπλοῦς). Thus also Plato, Rep. I. (III, 1, 33 ed. Bekker), οὔτε γὰρ πονηρία οὔτε ἁμαρτία οὐδεμία οὐδεμιᾷ τέχνῃ πάρεστιν ... αὐτὴ δὲ ἀβλαβής καὶ ἀκέραιός ἐστιν, ὀρθὴ οὖσα.

(II, a). v. 18. καὶ...δὲ " yea and "]. So Auth. in Acts iii, 24. Both particles are well rendered by Auth. in John viii, 16; xv, 27; Acts v, 32; 1 John i, 3: but one of them is lost in John vi, 51; viii, 17. See Green, Gram. N. T. p. 308.

(II, b). *ibid.* εἰς μαρτύριον αὐτοῖς " for a testimony unto them "]. So Doddridge, Campbell, and all Eng. except Auth. (substituting " witness " for " testimony "). Cheke has " and so shall ye witness me to them :" " en témoignage à eux," Martin : " pour *me rendre* témoignage devant eux," Ostervald. Thus also Vulg. " in testimonium illis," and similarly Castalio and Beza. Syr. ܠܣܗܕܘܬܐ ܕܝܠܗܘܢ (in testimonium ipsorum). Beza however says in his note " ut sint inexcusabiles i. e. adversus eos," whence Auth. has " against them," although it renders the same phrase by " unto " in ch. viii, 4; xxiv, 14; Mark i, 44; Luke v, 14. Thus correct Mark xiii, 9. In Mark vi, 11 (as Campbell has remarked) the context sufficiently vindicates Auth.; accordingly in the parallel text of St. Luke (ix, 5) we read εἰς μαρτύριον ἐπ' αὐτούς: and even on the present passage Theophylact (after Chrysostom) says, τούτεστιν εἰς ἔλεγχον αὐτῶν μὴ πιστευόντων: to the same purport perhaps is the paraphrase of Grotius " hoc facto convincentur auditæ veritatis." Yet it cannot be denied that the construction of the dative which I have adopted is much the more natural of the two; while the sense it affords is perfectly satisfactory: " ut doctrinam salutarem hâc occasione iis et gentibus exteris annuncietis." Rosenmüller.

(I)°. v. 23. Between φεύγετε εἰς τὴν and ἄλλην Griesbach *alone* inserts the clause ἑτέραν, κἂν ἐκ ταύτης διώκωσιν ὑμᾶς, φεύγετε εἰς τὴν ... " flee unto [the next, and if they persecute you from from this, flee unto] another." But not to insist on the offensive tautology thus brought into our Lord's discourse, the additional words are read in but eleven manuscripts of no great value (D and L are the principal), and that too in several different forms: besides which they are contained only in Origen, and in some Italic versions and Latin Fathers. We cannot receive an improbable reading on so little evidence, without overturning every principle of sacred criticism. Even Lachmann dislikes the clause: nor is it in Syr. Vulg.

(II, a and III, c). *ibid.* οὐ μὴ τελέσητε " ye shall in no wise have fully gone through"]. I translate οὐ μὴ like Auth. in v. 42. All Eng. lose its force in this place. Τελέσητε, again, is variously represented by them, though the general sense is the same in all. Tynd. Cov. Gen. and margin of Auth. have "finish" (or "end" Bish. and the margin of Auth): "go through," Cran. "have gone over," Auth. "have done your circuit of," Cheke, very fairly. This use of τελέσητε, as applied to travelling, is perfectly legitimate. Kypke compares Lucian, Toxaris p. 99 [ed. Salmur. 1619, Tom. ii], ἐτέλεσεν ἐκ Μαχλύων ἐς Σκύθας. See also Soph. Elect. 726, τελοῦντες ἕκτον ἕβδομόν τ' ἤδη δρόμον. Xen. Anab. i, 5, 7, ὅποτε ἢ πρὸς ὕδωρ βούλοιτο διατελέσαι, ἢ πρὸς χιλόν· which Xenophon elsewhere (iv, 5, 11) explains by οἱ μὴ δυνάμενοι διατελέσαι ΤΗΝ ὉΔΟΝ. Wetstein illustrates Thucyd. iv, 78, ἐς Φάρσαλον ἐτέλεσε, by ii, 97, ὉΔΩι τελεῖ.

(III, a and c). vv. 24, 25. οὐκ ἔστι μαθητὴς ὑπὲρ τὸν διδάσκαλον " No disciple is above his teacher"]. So Cheke. I have been careful to express the negative exclusive form of this proposition, in compliance with Bp. Middleton's suggestion. Διδάσκαλος is rendered "Master" by Eng. Now not only is the word "master" obsolete in this sense, at least in written language, but our translators found it necessary to change it into "teacher" in several passages (e. g. John iii, 2; Rom. ii, 20; Hebr. v, 12); although they have retained "master" in more than one text, to the great injury of the sense (John i, 38; xx, 16; James iii, 1). A uniform version is far preferable. Thus correct ch. ix, 11; xvii, 24, &c.

(I)°. v. 25. Βεελζεβούλ is the reading of all the Greek manuscripts; "Beelzebub" being found only in Syr. Vulg. and some less important authorities. Yet this latter form is given in the Complutensian Polyglott, and all Eng. (Cheke, however, has "Beelzeboul"). Respecting the marginal rendering of the later editions of Auth. I have spoken in Introd. p. 58, note.

ibid. The words "*shall they call*" (which are not in italics in the first edition of Auth.) are very properly expunged by Gen. So remove "*that*" from all Eng. twice in v. 27. See Introd. p. 63.

In v. 29, there can be little doubt that ἀσσάριον (which is also used in Luke xii, 6) is merely the Greek form for the Latin "as;" which (as is stated by the margin of Auth. in the later editions) was *originally* the tenth part of the Roman denarius. If therefore δηνάριον is to be translated "penny," ἀσσάριον may very well stand for "farthing,"* as it is actually rendered by all Eng. except Gen. which has "half-penny:" "asse," Vulg. Syr. In consequence, however, of the gradual depreciation of the Roman coinage, the denarius came to contain sixteen, or even

---

* But one difficulty still remains. If ἀσσάριον be rendered "farthing," how are we to represent κοδράντης (ch. v, 26; Mark xii, 42) which is probably the fourth part of the ἀσσάριον (Fischer, Prolus. de Vitiis Lex. N. T. xix)? Λεπτὸν (which is half of a κοδράντης) is called "mite" by Auth. in Mark xii, 42; Luke xii, 59; xxi, 2.

twenty asses (Pliny, Nat. Hist. xxxiii, 3); and it has been conjectured, I believe on insufficient grounds, that the *diminutive* ἀσσάριον represents this smaller value, or about one farthing and a half of our money. See note on ch. ii, 8.

(III, c). v. 29. ἓν ἐξ αὐτῶν οὐ πεσεῖται "not one of them shall fall"]. So Tynd. Cov. " none of them doth light," and Cheke " none of them shall fall." But Cran. Bish. have " one of them shall not light," and Gen. Auth. " one of them shall not fall." The precise form of the original is retained by Syr., whose native idiom it perfectly suits : Vulg. Beza less excusably render " unus ex illis (eis, Beza) non cadet." Dr. Symonds ventures to pronounce this clause, as it stands in Auth., unintelligible ; and Macknight (General Preface, sect. ii, note) indulges in some trifling criticism to the same purpose. I certainly do not see why the Hebrew epanorthosis should be retained by our version in this place, since it has been judiciously dropped in several other passages where Vulg. expresses it: e. g. ch. xxiv, 22; Mark xiii, 20; Luke i, 37 ; 1 Cor. i, 29 ; Eph. iv, 29 ; v, 5.

(III, c). *ibid.* ἄνευ τοῦ πατρὸς ὑμῶν " without your Father's will," or " knowledge "]. So Campbell: ἀγνοοῦντος τοῦ Θεοῦ, Chrysostom. All Eng. (even Cheke), after Syr. Vulg. Beza, Castalio, have " without your Father," which is obscure enough. For this sense of ἄνευ compare Homer. Il. E. 185, οὐχ ὅγ᾽ ἄνευθε Θεοῦ τάδε μαίνεται. Thucyd. iv, 78, ἀδικεῖν ἔφασαν ἄνευ τοῦ πάντων κοινοῦ πορευόμενον. Demosth. adv. Lacrit. (p. 935 Reiske), οὐ δανείζειν τούτους ὅτῳ ἂν βούλωνται ἐν τῷ Πόντῳ τὰ ἡμέτερα ἄνευ ἡμῶν : *nobis insciis et invitis.*

(III, b). v. 32. ὁμολογήσω κἀγὼ " I also will confess"]. Dr. Symonds might have added this passage and ch.

xvii, 12; xxiii, 26; xxv, 41 to his examples of the ungrammatical position of " also " enumerated above (note on ch. ii, 8). This error is continuated through all Eng. from Tynd. 2. downwards: yet in the very next verse " also " is used quite correctly.

CHAPTER XI.

(I)°. v. 2. Instead of δύο before τῶν μαθητῶν αὐτοῦ Syr. reads διά, which is found in *all* Lachmann's manuscripts that contain this chapter (B C D P Z), and in one or two of later date. But this reading, although very antient, is too feebly supported to be received with safety, though δύο might possibly have been taken from Luke vii, 19. Vater says "non solet Matthæus ad δύο addere genitivos;" see however ch. xviii, 19.

(II, b). v. 3. ὁ ἐρχόμενος "he who cometh"], he that is expected to come, an ordinary mode of referring to the Messiah (ch. iii, 11; Psalm cxviii, 26). "Qui venturus es," Vulg. which Bois rightly changes into "is qui venit," adding " qui tam certo venturus est, ac si jam adesset;" a use of the present tense which has been noticed in the Introd. p. 46. "Shall come," Tynd. Cov. Cran. " is to come," Cheke, " ought to come," Gen. Martin, " should come," Bish. Auth. So alter Luke vii, 19. Whitby compares Daniel vii, 13; Hab. ii, 3 (LXX, not Hebrew).

(III, a). v. 4. ἀπαγγείλατε "tell"]. So Cheke. Make Auth. here uniform with its rendering in ch. viii, 33; xiv, 12, &c. and thus correct ch. xii, 18: "shew,"Tynd. Gen. " tell again," Cov. " shew again," Cran. Bish. Auth.

o

(II, b). v. 5. Both here and in ch. x, 8; xv, 30; 31; xxi, 14, as Bp. Middleton remarks, the omission of the articles before τυφλοί, χωλοί, &c. intimates that the miracles were performed not on whole classes of men, but only on individuals of each class. It would therefore be strictly correct to omit the English articles: "blind persons," &c. See note on ch. ix, 13.

(III, a). v. 8. οἱ τὰ μαλακὰ φοροῦντες " they that wear soft *raiment*"]. Of course ἱμάτια is understood in μαλακά, indeed the article before that adjective indicates renewed mention. It is strange that Eng. pay so little regard to uniformity as to employ both " raiment" and " clothing " for the same word in the same verse. This error is avoided by Wickliffe and the Rhemish translators.

(I)°. *ibid.* I have already mentioned (Introd. p. 22), that Scholz alone, among all our critical editors, substitutes βασιλείων for βασιλέων in this verse. If he intends βασιλείων to signify " palaces," as in Luke vii, 25; LXX, Esther i, 9; Prov. xviii, 19, no trifling pressure of external proof is requisite to make the expression " houses of palaces " endurable. If he wishes βασιλείων to be rendered " courtiers," he should produce some examples of such a use of the word: βασιλικὸς is employed in this sense in John iv, 46; 49. The Byzantine documents which uphold Scholz's reading are antient and numerous, but it is not countenanced by any authorities of the other family, or indeed by a single version or ecclesiastical writer.

In v. 11, μικρότερος is rendered " less" by Tynd. Cov. Cran. Gen. Bish. " lesser" by Cheke; Cov.'s margin and Auth. alone have " least." The *older* versions are seldom so scrupulous.

(II, b). v. 12. βιασταὶ " violent *ones*"]. I am always

reluctant to differ from Bp. Middleton, but I cannot subscribe to his opinion that by βιασταὶ we are to understand "plunderers" or "extortioners" (" they that thrust men," as the margin of Auth. has it), such as were the soldiers or publicans (Luke iii, 12—14). Not only does this interpretation seem unsuitable to the present context, but it would be hard to reconcile it with πᾶς εἰς αὐτὴν βιάζεται, in the parallel passage Luke xvi, 16. Βιάζεται in this place must necessarily be taken in a moral sense; why should we hesitate to do the same with βιασταί? Πάντες οἱ μετὰ σπουδῆς προσιόντες is Chrysostom's paraphrase : τὸ γὰρ ἀφεῖναι πατέρα, καὶ μητέρα, καὶ τῆς ψυχῆς αὐτῆς καταφρονῆσαι, πόσης βίας ἐστι; says Theophylact. At the same time it is proper to correct Eng., which all translate βιασταὶ by "the violent," or some equivalent expression. Cheke has " is straitly extremely ordered (βιάζεται), and extreme men, they catch it," accurately enough, so far as the article is concerned. But the only discrepancy which thus arises between the Evangelists is, that St. Luke contemplates all who earnestly seek for salvation, St. Matthew only some individuals of that character.*

(II, a). v. 14. αὐτός ἐστιν " he is"] viz. John, who was mentioned in the preceding verse. So Cheke, Kypke, Scholefield. "This is" of Eng. would require οὗτος.

(III, c). v. 17. ἐθρηνήσαμεν ὑμῖν καὶ οὐκ ἐκόψασθε " we have sung dirges unto you, and ye have not smote the breast"]. So Bp. Jebb. Gen. renders ἐθρηνήσαμεν " we have sung mourning songs unto you," and is

---

* This very distinction is largely insisted on by Bp. Middleton in his note on ch. xii, 43. It is therefore the more remarkable that he was misled by the omission of the article in the present case.

followed by the margin of Bish. In a passage whose spirit is nearly unintelligible without some knowledge of Oriental customs, it is desirable that the version should convey as much information as possible, without degenerating into a paraphrase: "we have mourned unto you, and ye have not lamented" of Auth. is very vague.

It is rather surprising that " winebibber" in v. 19 has not come under the lash of Dr. Symonds or some of his compeers. It is used by Cov. Bish. Auth. for " drinker of wine" of Tynd. Cran. Gen. (" wine drinker," Cheke), and correctly : for οἰνοπότης always implies excess, e. g. Prov. xxiii, 20.

(III, c). v. 19. ἀπὸ τῶν τέκνων αὐτῆς " by her children"]. " Of" Eng., which is somewhat too inderminate, in a clause of itself sufficiently obscure. Ἀπὸ is put for ὑπό, as in ch. xvi, 21 (for which we find ὑπὸ in ch. xvii, 12); Mark viii, 31; Luke vii, 35. "Was justified" (ἐδικαιώθη) Bish., with exclusive reference to the rejection first of the Baptist, then of our Lord, by the Jewish rulers; an interpretation which is thus broadly expressed by Cheke, " and wisdom is clean rid from her own children," while in his note he explains δικαιοῦσθαι to mean " clean and utterly rid from a thing, and having no more to do therewith: wisdom was clean separated and taken away from the Jews her children, who was not of them regarded." Such likewise is the view of Castalio, " estque suis aliena sapientia" (not an over-literal translation, surely); and, as it would appear, of Theophylact also, ὑμεῖς ἀπειθήσαντες, δίκαιον ἐμὲ ὡς μηδὲν παραλιπόντα δεικνύετε. If it be thought better to extend τέκνων to believers in general, the aorist-present " is justified" of Auth. and other Eng. may be retained; whether we understand with Bp. Jebb that " *all* true Christians (Luke vii, 35) by the rectitude of their principles, and the purity of their conduct, vindicate the honor of that wisdom from above, which is the parent, the guide, and the instructress of them all" (Sacr. Liter. p. 244): or conceive with Wetstein that the clause rather signifies that " the wisdom of God's dispensations is fully acquiesced in by his children," whatever be the mode of their manifestation to us. "A été justifiée," Martin, Ostervald.*

(III, c). v. 27. βούληται ἀποκαλύψαι " is willing to reveal *him* "]. All Eng. have " will reveal (or, open) *him.*" The ambiguity arising from our two-fold use of "will," both as an auxiliary and an independent verb, sometimes produces great obscurity in Auth. See above v. 14 ; as also ch. xvi, 24 ; xix, 17 ; 21 ; xx, 14 ; 26 ; 27 ; Luke x, 22 ; 2 Tim. iii, 12 ; 2 John v. 12; and particularly 1 Tim. vi, 9. Should any one be disposed to controvert Buttmann's lucid discrimination between θέλειν, " the active wish which looks forward to its own accomplishment," and βούλεσθαι " the bare act of volition, without the means or power of performing it" (Lexilogus, p. 194, English Translation), from the employment of βούληται in this verse, while θέλειν is used in v. 14 ; he must bear in mind Tittmann's remark, that with God to will and to do are the same thing (James i, 18) : and what is here said of the Son, is spoken with relation to his Divine Power and Nature. In all ordinary cases the distinction is carefully maintained. See Demosth. περὶ συντάξ. c. 2. μὴ μόνον ταῦτ' ἀκούειν ἐθέλοντα, ἀλλὰ καὶ πράττειν βουλόμενον.

---

* The exposition in the margin of Gen. is very pithy : " They that are wise in deed, acknowledge the wisdom of God, in him whom the Pharisees contemn."

(III, a). v. 28. οἱ κοπιῶντες " ye that are weary"]. So Gen., uniformly with Auth. in John iv, 6; and more consonantly with the literal meaning of the word. " Labor," Tynd. Cov. Cran. Cheke, Auth. after Vulg. " labor sore," Bish. In v. 29, the article before καρδίᾳ is rendered by Middleton as a personal pronoun, " my heart."

(II, a). v. 30. χρηστὸς " gentle"]. So Syr. (ܚܣܝܐ). Vulg. " suave." But Beza has " facile," Martin and Ostervald " aisé," and all Eng. " easy." Cheke " profitable;" Castalio " commodum," a very convenient subterfuge. Ἀλλ' ὅτι μὲν ἩΔΥΣ καὶ κοῦφος ὁ τῆς ἀρετῆς ζυγός, Chrysostom. In this sense χρηστὸς is a fit epithet for wine, Luke v, 39, and Athenæus xiii, as quoted by Schleusner. See also 1 Macc. vi, 11; Gal. v, 22; Eph. ii, 7; iv, 32; Tit. iii, 4. Wolf too has some remarks which deserve consideration. Cur. Phil. *ad loc.*

CHAPTER XII.

(III, b). v. 2. ὃ οὐκ ἔξεστι "which it is not lawful"]. So correct v. 4. All Eng. (even Cheke) translate " which is not lawful." In v. 11, Auth. falls into the opposite fault; for τίς ἄνθρωπος being nominative to κρατήσει, it is superfluous to insert " he " before " lay hold." This last error is avoided by Tynd. Cov. Cheke.

(I). v. 8. καὶ before τοῦ σαββάτου is rejected by Griesbach, Vater, Scholz and Lachmann, in compliance with the best manuscripts of both families; with Syr. (Bish.) and several other versions; with Origen, Chrysostom, &c. It was doubtless borrowed from

Mark ii, 28; Luke vi, 5, where it should be rendered "even" not "also," as most Eng. translate it in *this* passage. "Even of the sabbath," says Doddridge, "implies that the sabbath was an institution of great and distinguished importance:" yet our Lord's control over it was absolute notwithstanding.

(II, b). v. 14. συμβούλιον ἔλαβον "took counsel"]. So Syr. Tynd. 1. Cheke, Gen. the margin of Auth., Beza and Castalio. But "consilium faciebant," Vulg. whence apparently came "held a council" of Tynd. 2. Cov. Cran. Bish. Auth. which seems a strange version. The phrase is found in four other passages of St. Matthew (ch. xxii, 15; xxvii, 1; 7; xxviii, 12), but no where else in the New Testament. In all these places Auth. has "took counsel," in fact the other rendering would be quite inadmissible (see Grotius). St. Mark's expression is συμβούλιον ποιεῖν ch. iii, 6; xv, 1).

(II, b). v. 15. ὁ δὲ Ἰησοῦς γνοὺς ἀνεχώρησεν "but Jesus knowing *it*, withdrew himself," or "retired"]. So the Rhemish version from Vulg., and Cheke ("Jesus knowing so much went from them"). All Eng. translate "but when Jesus knew *it*, &c." which rendering seems calculated, I am sure through inadvertence on the part of its authors, to exclude the notion of our Lord's *intuitive* perception of the designs of his enemies (compare v. 25). I scarcely need state that in a case of this kind, the context alone can determine whether the action denoted by the participle precedes or coincides with that of the finite verb. For a palpable oversight of Auth. on this point consult Acts v, 30; x, 39; and Scholefield's remarks. See also note on ch. xvi, 8.

(III, b). *ibid.* ἐκεῖθεν "thence"]. So Auth. in v. 9, and all other Eng. here. Yet all Eng. have "from whence" in v. 44, so little was their attention directed to these grammatical niceties. Compare Auth. ch. xv, 21, with v. 29.

(II, a).° v. 20. ἕως ἂν ἐκβάλῃ τὴν κρίσιν εἰς νῖκος "till he send forth judgment unto victory"] i. e. until he make his just ordinance (the Gospel) victorious. So Syr. Vulg. Eng., only that Gen. has "bring forth," and Cheke "until he make right judgment have the victory": "jusqu'à ce qu'il ait rendu la justice victorieuse," Ostervald. It is not easy to elicit any other sense from these words, yet how can they be reconciled with Isai. xlii, 3, from which they are an avowed citation? The prophet there says, לֶאֱמֶת יוֹצִיא מִשְׁפָּט׃ "he shall bring forth judgment unto truth," Auth. "He shall publish judgment, so as to establish it perfectly," Bp. Lowth: εἰς ἀλήθειαν ἐξοίσει κρίσιν, LXX. Now it appears that לָנֶצַח which literally denotes "to victory," is rendered εἰς νῖκος by the LXX in 2 Sam. ii, 26; Job xxxvi, 7; Lament. v, 20; Amos viii, 7, &c. and εἰς νῖκος in Job xxiii, 7; Hab. i, 4: while in every one of these passages it may signify "entirely," "thoroughly," "completely." But this last meaning of εἰς νῖκος approximates nearly to לֶאֱמֶת in Is. xlii, 3, as understood by Lowth, and must therefore be taken to represent that Hebrew word in the text of St. Matthew. I know of no better explanation of the difficulty; but as it does not wholly satisfy me, I propose no alteration in the rendering of Auth. See also 1 Cor. xv, 54.

(III, a). v. 23. μήτι οὗτός ἐστιν ὁ υἱὸς Δαβίδ "is not this the Son of David?"]. So all Eng. (even Cheke) down to Auth. which reads in the original Bible of 1611 "is this the son of David?" Later editors of Auth. have generally (though not universally) inserted the negative, doubtless because they regarded its omission in the early books as a typographical error. It is not, however, perfectly clear that such is the fact, although Auth. uses the negative in John iv, 29, where the form of expression is precisely similar. Both for the sake of uniformity and distinctness Auth. should be altered here. Μή is designed " for throwing out a suggestion of what a person is not disposed to affirm directly, or about which he has still some doubt remaining." Green, p. 129.

(II, a). v. 24. οὗτος " this *man* "]. So Cheke. " He," Tynd. 1. Cov. " this *fellow*," Tynd. 2. Cran. Gen. Bish. Auth. This species of false emphasis, so foreign to the spirit of the sacred writers, is most justly blamed by Campbell (Prel. Diss. III, 23). So alter ch. xxvi, 61 ; 71, where Cov. is correct.

(III, a). v. 28. ἔφθασεν ἐφ' ὑμᾶς " is come upon you"]. So Auth. in the parallel text, Luke xi, 20; and Tynd. Cov. Bish. even here : " to " Cheke, Gen. " unto," Cran. Auth. Schmidt presses the strict and literal force of φθάνω " vestrâ opinione citius pervenit," which interpretation is approved by Fritzche. No trace however of this meaning can be found in Syr. ܐܕܪܟ, Vulg. " pervenit," or Chrysostom (τῆς εὐπραγίας ὑμῶν ἐφέστηκεν ὁ καιρός—ὑμῖν ἥκει τὰ ἀγαθά·); nor can it have any place in Dan. iv, 25 (LXX); Rom. ix, 31 ; Phil. iii, 16. We have προέφθασεν in Schmidt's sense below, ch. xvii, 25.

(II, a). v. 31. ἡ τοῦ Πνεύματος βλασφημία " the blasphemy against the Spirit"]. So Cov. Cran. But Tynd. 1. Gen. Auth. have " against the *Holy Ghost*," as also have Cheke, Bish. " The blasphemy of the Spirit," Tynd. 2. Rhemish version. The adjective " Holy " is totally destitute of authority.

(I).° v. 32. Instead of ἐν τούτῳ τῷ αἰῶνι " in this

world," Scholz reads ἐν τῷ νῦν αἰῶνι "in the present world." About the same number of manuscripts favor both readings, but none of the very highest antiquity agree with Scholz, who consequently stands alone in changing the text. Syr. Vulg. manifestly support τούτῳ, and so also does Chrysostom.

(III, b). v. 33. τὸν καρπὸν αὐτοῦ " its fruit," ter]. " his fruit," all Eng. even Wickliffe, Cheke, and the Rhemish version. See note on ch. v, 13. The general scope of this verse is not perfectly clear. Kypke, who for accurate learning and solid sense has few equals among the Biblical scholars of the last century, thus understands the passage: " if you determine that the tree is good, the fruit will be good also; but if you persist in thinking ME the tree bad, then the fruit, my works of mercy (vv. 13, 22), must needs be bad also;" an inference which his adversaries were not prepared to admit. This is, in substance, Chrysostom's exposition, who adds εἰ γὰρ καὶ τὸ δένδρον τοῦ καρποῦ αἴτιον, ἀλλ' ὁ καρπὸς τοῦ δένδρου γνωριστικός.* For this sense of ποιεῖν (" judicare ") Kypke compares John viii, 53, and Joseph. Antiq. iv, 8, ἐκείνους τοῦ Θεοῦ δυνατωτέρους ποιεῖ. Somewhat similar is 1 John i, 10.

(I)°. v. 35. τῆς καρδίας " of the heart " is removed from the text by Griesbach, Vater, Scholz, Lachmann, and Bp. Jebb, the equilibrium of whose stanza these words disturb. They are wanting in Syr. Vulg. and some other versions; in the best copies of Chrysostom; and in a very large number of Greek manuscripts of every date and class; including codices B C in one family, and all Matthæi's good manuscripts

---

* " Aut agnoscite me bonum esse, et benè agere: aut me malum esse, ac proinde malè agere." Note to Beza's Latin Testament, London, 1592.

in the other. A reading opposed by such authorities can hardly be genuine, and it was probably interpolated from Luke vi, 45; "where τῆς καρδίας is, of necessity, inserted; because that Evangelist, by a transposition with him not unusual, has postponed the clause ἐκ γὰρ τοῦ περισσεύματος τῆς καρδίας, which, in St. Matthew, is preparatory to this couplet" (Jebb, Sacr. Liter. p. 145).

(II, a)°. v. 36. ἀργὸν "idle"]. So Eng. Cheke, Bp. Jebb, after Syr. (ܒܛܝܠ) "otiosum," as it is in Vulg. Beza: "oiseuse," Martin. Castalio, on the contrary, translates "malum," Ostervald "impies," and Campbell "pernicious." Chrysostom wavers between the two interpretations; ἀργὸν δέ, τὸ μὴ κατὰ πράγματος κείμενον, τὸ ψευδές, τὸ συκοφαντίαν ἔχον· τίνες δέ φασιν, ὅτι καὶ τὸ μάταιον· οἷον, τὸ γέλωτα κινοῦν ἄτακτον, ἢ τὸ αἰσχρὸν καὶ ἀναίσχυντον καὶ ἀνελεύθερον. To this latter opinion I confess that I incline. Without wishing to dispute, that by a euphemism common to most languages, ἀργὸς may occasionally be employed as a decorous intimation of something worse; there is every reason for thinking that the primitive signification of the word is that in common use. Even the apophthegm of Pythagoras cited from Stobæus (αἱρετώτερόν σοι ἔστω λίθον εἰκῆ βάλλειν, ἢ λόγον ἀργόν·) may very well be understood literally; and no practice is more fraught with danger than that of assigning to the expressions of Holy Writ the lowest meaning they can possibly bear. "Omne verbum quod non ædificat proximum," says Munster, "indignum est homine Christiano, et conscientia ejus hominem damnabit."

(II, b). v. 41. ἄνδρες Νινευῖται ἀναστήσονται ἐν τῇ κρίσει "men of Nineveh shall stand up in the judgment"]. v. 42. βασίλισσα νότου ἐγερθήσεται "a queen of the

South shall arise"]. All Eng. have "the men of Nineveh," "the Queen of the South." Respecting the omission of the articles see Middleton's notes on this passage, and on Luke xi, 30 (where we find τοῖς Νινευίταις· of so little moment is the variation); also Green's Gram. N. T. p. 183. I have also distinguished between ἀναστήσονται v. 41, and ἐγερθήσεται, v. 42, after Bp. Jebb. They are confounded in Syr. Vulg. Eng. Again Auth. renders "in judgment," v. 41; but "in the judgment," v. 42. On *this* point Cheke and all other Eng. are uniform.

(III, a). v. 43. τὸ ἀκάθαρτον πνεῦμα .. ἀπὸ τοῦ ἀνθρώπου "an unclean spirit .... out of a man"]. So Campbell, who is approved by Bp. Middleton. The article is employed in its inclusive or hypothetic sense in both places; it is therefore very inconsistent that "spirit" in Eng. should have the definite article, and "man" the indefinite (Cov., however, has "out of man"). Ὅταν δὲ should be rendered "but when," as in Syr. Vulg. (δὲ is lost in all Eng.), that the passage may be connected with the preceding verses. Thus also express δὲ at the beginning of v. 46.

(III, c). *ibid.* ἀνύδρων "waterless"], dreary deserts. So Syr. ܐܬܪܐ ܐܝܟܐ ܕܠܐ ܡܝܐ, (in quibus non sunt aquæ). Castalio "siticulosa," Campbell "parched deserts." "Dry" of Eng. and Cheke, at least to a modern ear, conveys this idea very inadequately. It would probably conduce to perspicuity, if the unclean spirit were spoken of in the neuter gender in English, as in the Greek text, throughout vv. 43-45. "It walketh," "it saith," "when it is come," &c.

(II, a). v. 45. γίνεται "becometh"]. So Campbell, after Syr. (ܗܘܐ, the participle of the verb-substantive and not the pronominal copula being used), "fiunt," Vulg. Beza, Castalio. "Is" of Eng. is far from correct. Thus alter Auth. in ch. v, 45; xvii, 2; xxiii, 26, &c.

In my account of the Rhemish translation of the New Testament (Introd. p. 99), I hinted that its diction is occasionally preferable to that of any of the preceding versions. Several proofs of the truth of this remark may be found in the present chapter: e. g. "it was not lawful," v. 4; "withered" for "dried up," v. 10 (adopted by Auth.); v. 15 (see note *ad loc.*); "wicked generation" for "evil nation," v. 45 (also adopted by Auth.). Among these felicitous expressions, however, we cannot class "rifle his vessel," v. 29; "did penance," v. 41, in which last verse even Cov. thus translates from Vulg.

CHAPTER XIII.

(II, b). v. 2. εἰς τὸ πλοῖον "into the ship"]. See notes on ch. iv, 21; viii, 23. Bish. alone is right in this place. All other Eng. Cheke, Martin and Ostervald employ the indefinite article.

In v. 1, ἀπὸ τῆς οἰκίας may be translated with Middleton "out of *his* house," viz. the residence of our Saviour at Capernaum. See ch. ix, 28.

(III, a and c). v. 4. τὰ πετεινὰ "the birds"]. So Wickliffe, Cheke, and even Auth. in v. 32. *Here* all Eng. say "fowls."

(II, a). v. 8. ἐπὶ τὴν γῆν τὴν καλὴν "upon good ground"]. So Cov. and the Rhemish version. "into," Wickliffe, Cran. Bish. Auth. "in," Tynd. Cheke, Gen. Thus change v. 23, and ἐπὶ τὰ πετρώδη in v. 20, for which last even Auth. has "upon stony places" in v. 5.

(III, c). v. 12. περισσευθήσεται "he shall be made to abound "], or "have abundance," as Auth. in ch. xxv, 29, and Tynd. Cov. Cran. Gen. here ("have plenty," Cheke). Symonds censures " *more* abundance" of Bish. Auth.

(I). v. 14. ἀναπληροῦται αὐτοῖς and not ἐπ' αὐτοῖς is sanctioned by all the critics from Mill down to Lachmann. The preposition is omitted in nearly all the older manuscripts of either class, and though Syr. has ⌒ and Vulg. " in," it does not necessarily follow that they read ἐπὶ in their copies. The sense is nearly the same, whichsoever reading we receive. Ἐπ' αὐτοῖς will signify " in them " (as all Eng.) i. e. in their case. Without ἐπὶ the dative may be considered equivalent to ὑπὸ with the genitive, "by them;" as in Homer. Il. E. 465, ἐς τί ἔτι κτείνεσθαι ἐάσετε λαὸν Ἀχαιοῖς; Matthiæ, Gk. Gram. § 392, i. β.

(III, a). vv. 20, 21. εὐθὺς "forthwith"]. As εὐθέως in Auth. v. 5. All Eng. have "anon" in v. 20, and "by and by" in v. 21, except that Cov. reads "immediately" in v. 21, and Cheke "by and by" in both places. From this parable alone it might be shown how seldom the later versions deviated from the language of the earlier, for the sake of obtaining uniformity in the diction.

(III, a and c). v. 21. πρόσκαιρος " endureth but for a time"]. So Auth. in Mark iv, 17; much more perspicuously: "is but a forwhile," Cheke: "il n'est que pour un tems," Ostervald. So Tynd. Gen. have "dureth but a season:" but "dureth for a season," Cov. Cran. Bish. "dureth for a while," Auth. Yet "but" is absolutely needed.

(I). v. 27. The article before ζιζάνια in this verse is rejected by Wetstein, Griesbach, Vater, Scholz and Lachmann. Middleton thinks its spuriousness probable, but Green (Gram. N.T. p. 136) alleges it as a marked example of the demonstrative force of the article.

The present is precisely one of those passages in which we feel our want of a more extensive and accurate collation of the later or cursive manuscripts (see Introd. p. 19). The versions of course lend us no help; but while we find nearly all the few uncial documents in existence conspiring in the omission of τά, and most of Matthæi's good MSS favouring the same reading, we are almost entirely in the dark as to the evidence of the great mass of authorities. We only know that a few of those in cursive characters which have been repeatedly examined (such as the Basle MS Erasmi 1, the Urbino-Vatican 157, and Alter's chief Vienna MS 218) agree with B C D &c. in this place; and we cannot help suspecting that such will be found to be the case with a large proportion of their long-neglected brethren, whenever a systematic collation of them shall be executed. On points connected with the article, more especially, the information afforded by our present critical editions is so little trust-worthy, that we cannot form a positive judgment respecting its authenticity or the contrary in any particular case, from the light which they afford us. (See for instance, Griesbach's or Scholz's notes on vv. 30; 44). In this verse, however, the testimony of Chrysostom, of nine uncial MSS, and the few more recent copies which have been consulted on the occasion, may possibly justify our rejection of the article. If it must be retained, we should translate "the tares," I presume with a reference to vv. 25, 26. Cheke renders "this darnel," as if the article had a demonstrative sense.

(II, b). v. 32. $\mu\epsilon\tilde{\iota}\zeta o\nu$ $\tau\tilde{\omega}\nu$ $\lambda\alpha\chi\acute{a}\nu\omega\nu$ "greater than the herbs"]. So Auth. in Mark iv, 32, Syr. (for Schaaf's version of ܡܢ ܕܢ ܠܗܝ is inaccurate*) Vulg. Campbell, and the "Holy Bible" of 1841. But "the greatest among herbs," Eng. Beza, Castalio, Martin, Ostervald (" plus grand que les *autres* légumes)." Cheke " is one of the biggest herbs." Yet there is not the least reason for thinking that μεῖζον is used for the superlative, and λάχανον is pointedly distinguished from δένδρον.

In v. 33, σάτα is rendered "pecks" by Tynd. Cov. Cran. Gen. Bish. "bushels," Cheke. Since the exact quantity of the meal does not affect the scope of the passage (τρία δὲ σάτα ἐνταῦθα τὰ πολλὰ εἴρηκεν· οἶδε γὰρ τὸν ἀριθμὸν τοῦτον ἐπὶ πλήθους λαμβάνειν· Chrysostom), Auth. judiciously substitutes the more general term "measures" (see Campbell, Prel. Diss. VIII, Pt. I, 6). The Hebrew סְאִים is translated μέτρα by the LXX in Gen. xviii, 6, where Aquila and Symmachus employ σάτα, the word used by St. Matthew (see also Luke xiii, 21). Hesychius and Suidas make the σάτον equivalent to 1½ Italian modii. Now since the modius is one-third of a cubic foot, or somewhat more than our English peck, it appears that the calculation in the margin of the later editions of Auth. " a peck and a half, wanting little more than a pint," is sufficiently accurate.

(II, b). v. 39. οἱ δὲ θερισταὶ ἄγγελοί εἰσιν " and the reapers are angels"]. So Middleton. " the angels," Eng.

(II, a). v. 41. πάντα τὰ σκάνδαλα " all that cause

---

* " Maximum est omnium olerum." He translates the very same words correctly in Mark iv, 32 " fit majus omnibus oleribus." This (as indeed most of his other errors) arises from his treading too closely in the steps of Tremellius.

offence"]. " Scandals," Syr. Vulg. margin of Auth. " all things that do hurt," Tynd. 1. "all things that offend," Tynd. 2. Cov. Cran. Gen. Bish. Auth. " all hindrances," Cheke. The margin of Gen. explains σκάνδαλα to mean " the wicked which hurt others by their evil example;" such as are called τοὺς τὰ σκάνδαλα ποιοῦντας in Rom. xvi, 17. " Seducers," Campbell. " things which have been an offence *to others*," Doddridge.

(II, b). v. 42. τὴν κάμινον " the furnace"]. κατ' ἐξοχήν, as it is rendered by Auth. in v. 50. All Eng. have " a furnace" here, and all except Auth. in v. 50 also. The Rhemish version, Martin and Ostervald very properly translate " the furnace," and Cheke (awkwardly enough) " the chimney," in both places.

(III, c). v. 45. ἀνθρώπῳ ἐμπόρῳ " to a merchant"]. So Tynd. Cov. Gen. " man" is added by Cran. Cheke, Bish. Auth. but without cause. The pleonastic sense of ἄνθρωπος may be regarded as an Hebraism, for it does not very often occur in pure Greek writers (see however Raphel on Luke ii, 15). Thus correct v. 52; ch. xx, 1. This idiom must not be confounded with the common Classical use of ἀνήρ in such expressions as ἄνδρες Νινευῖται (ch. xii, 41), ἄνδρες Ἀθηναῖοι (Acts xvii, 22), ἄνδρες δικασταί, &c.

(I)°. v. 46. Instead of ὃς εὑρὼν " who, when he had found" of the received text, Griesbach inserts εὑρὼν δὲ " but having found," on evidence so extremely weak that nothing but the minuteness of the change could have saved his *amended* reading from general reprobation. Εὑρὼν δὲ is presented by only five of his manuscripts, four of which (DL. 1. 33) lie under the strongest suspicion of Latinising; the

P

fifth being a document of the thirteenth century (Stephens's ιδ', Griesbach's 120 Evan.). It was probably the reading of Syr. and one or two other versions, and *possibly* that of Vulg. also. But it is obvious how little dependence can be placed on versions in a passage like this. On such grounds we are bidden by Griesbach to reject the testimony of all other manuscripts scattered throughout the world.

The management of Scholz in this instance affords us a melancholy specimen of the incorrectness of his great work (See Introd. p. 31). Having almost nothing to add to Griesbach's statement,* he copies his note literatim, but with unpardonable carelessness refers to ὃς εὑρὼν the documents which Griesbach had cited in support of his correction εὑρὼν δέ, while he prints the latter reading as a part of the received text, and pronounces ὃς εὑρὼν a mere Alexandrine variation from it. Lachmann prefers εὑρὼν δέ, in perfect consistency with his peculiar theory: but Buttmann, who compiled the notes for his inner margin, copies Scholz's blundering representation so faithfully, as to make εὑρὼν δέ the reading of the Elzevir text of 1624. And these are the critics in obedience to whose decisions we are called upon to remodel the text of the New Testament!

In the first edition of Auth. we read " who, when he had found . . . , he went." All other Eng. omit " he," which is rejected by the later editions of Auth. itself. See note on ch. xxi, 7.

(III, a). v. 57. ἐσκανδαλίζοντο ἐν αὐτῷ " were of-

---

* Scholz merely adds that the Codex B reads ὃς εὑρών. From whatever quarter he derived this piece of information, it is astonishing that it did not lead him to detect the enormous error into which he had fallen.

fended at him"]. So Auth. in Mark vi, 3; and Cov. Cran. here: " offended with" of Cheke is very good. " Hurt by him," Tynd. 1. " offended by," Tynd. 2. Gen. " offended in," Bish. Auth. which (like many of Bish.'s renderings) is too literal to be perspicuous.

CHAPTER XIV.

(II, a). v. 2. αἱ δυνάμεις ἐνεργοῦσιν " the *spiritual* powers work"]. So Middleton, Green, Vulg. " virtutes operantur." But Syr. Tynd. 2. Cran. Gen. Castalio resemble the margin of Auth. " miracles," or " mighty works are wrought." " His power is so great," Tynd. 1.; so Cov. " This mightiness worketh more in him," Cheke: " mighty (great, Bish.) works do shew forth themselves in him," Bish. Auth. " virtutes agunt in eo," Beza: and, lest his meaning should be doubtful, his editor tells us by " virtutes" to understand " vim illam et facultatem, non autem effecta" (see p. 202, note): thus agreeing nearest with Cheke or Tynd. 1. Ostervald on the contrary entirely coincides with the margin of Auth. &c. " se fait des miracles par lui;" while Martin, as usual, follows Beza more closely, " les vertues montrent leur force en lui;" where " montrent leur force" reminds us of the peculiar turn of the expression in Bish. Auth. On the whole, then, Vulg. of all our versions most favours Middleton's view of the passage. Yet the common interpretation is surrounded with difficulties of no ordinary description. How shall we account for the use of the article before δυνάμεις? Reference seems out of the question, and " if it be the object of the proposition to declare that miracles are wrought by John, it is rather unnatural that their existence should be *assumed*" (Middleton). Besides, in no other place in the New Testament does the active verb ἐνεργεῖν occur in an intransitive sense, such as must be assigned to it here, if by δυνάμεις we are to understand miracles: and so clearly was this perceived by the learned Beza, that he resorted to a forced explanation, in order to avoid the error of Syr. For the Scriptural use of ἐνεργεῖν see 1 Cor. xii, 6; 11; Gal. ii, 8; iii, 5; Eph. i, 11; 20; ii, 2; Phil. ii, 13. Now nothing is more certain than that αἱ δυνάμεις is a term constantly employed by the Greek Fathers to signify the angels and other heavenly powers. Chrysost. Hom. in Matth. i, p. 3, ἄνθρωποι τοῖς ἀγγέλοις ἐκοινώνουν, καὶ ταῖς ἄλλαις ταῖς ἄνω δυνάμεσι. Many examples to the same purpose may be seen in Suicer, *voce* δύναμις (2); indeed it was the common style of ecclesiastical antiquity, and as such is imitated by our Milton, " *Powers* and Dominions, Deities of Heaven," . . . (Par. Lost, ii, 11). Compare 1 Pet. iii, 22; and perhaps Rom. viii, 38; Hebr. vi, 5. If this meaning be given to δυνάμεις, all will become easy. The same Spiritual Influences, which raised John from the dead, are performing in his person the miracles which perplex and alarm Herod. So alter Mark vi, 14.

On the rendering of Auth. " do show forth themselves," Middleton hazards a singular conjecture. He supposes it to be founded on ἐναργοῦσιν, the form exhibited by the Codex Bezæ, which was presented to the University of Cambridge in 1581, and whose peculiar readings might then have been thought of great importance. I fear it is a fatal objection to this ingenious hypothesis, that Auth. merely copied the version of Bish. in this instance: and Bish. was published full ten years before the Codex Bezæ was brought to England.

(III, c). v. 8. ἐπὶ πίνακι "on a dish"]. So correct v. 11. "In a dish," Wickliffe, Cheke, the Rhemish version; "in a charger," Auth. "in a platter," other Eng. In v. 6, the margin of the later editions of Auth. (ἐν τῷ μέσῳ, Gr. "in the midst") is very trifling. In v. 7, ὅθεν Auth. follows the Rhemish N. T. "whereupon." Other Eng. have "wherefore."

In v. 8, προβιβασθεῖσα "enticed," or "induced," is the interpretation of the margin of Bish. and of Cheke ("being set on"). Such is no doubt the ordinary acceptation of the word, according to which the French versions have "étant poussée." Still Vulg. "præmonita," and "before instructed" of Cov. Cran. Gen. Bish. Auth. ("informed before," Tynd.) is probably nearer the truth. See the passages cited by Raphel and Kypke. From Mark vi, 24 it would perhaps appear that the force of πρὸ in composition must not be pressed here. Syr. does not render it, though little stress ought to be laid on that circumstance, inasmuch as the Syriac language can express prepositions compounded with verbs only by means of a periphrasis (e. g. John xx, 4). Compare also the LXX, Exod. xxxv, 34; Deut. vi, 7. In Plato, Protag. (I, 1, 184, ed. Bekker), ἀλλὰ κἂν εἰ ὀλίγον ἔστι τις ὅς τις διαφέρει ἡμῶν προβιβάσαι εἰς ἀρετήν, ἀγαπητόν· Heindorf very properly translates "si quis antecellat in *provehendo* ad virtutem." But this explanation will not suit the passages from the LXX.

(II, a). v. 15. ἡ ὥρα ἤδη παρῆλθεν "the day is now spent"]. "The day is spent," Tynd. "the night falleth on," Cov. "the hour is now (already, Gen.) past," Cran. Gen. Bish. from Vulg. "the time is well gone," Cheke; "the time is now past," Auth. after

Syr. Beza. St. Luke in the parallel place (ch. ix, 12) says ἡ δὲ ἡμέρα ἤρξατο κλίνειν. Ὥρα is thus used by Polybius, as cited by Raphel, ἤδη δὲ τῆς ὥρας συγκλειούσης. Not quite so pertinent is Demosth. c. Midiam (p. 541, Reiske), τῆς ὥρας ἐγίγνετο ὀψέ. Compare also Mark vi, 35.

(I). v. 22. Both ὁ Ἰησοῦς and αὐτοῦ are rejected as spurious by Griesbach, Scholz and Lachmann. Respecting the omission of the name of Jesus at the commencement of a new paragraph, I have already spoken at length (see notes on ch. iv, 18; viii, 5). A few authorities do not read the word in v. 14; but in the present instance there can be little doubt of its spuriousness. It is wanting in Syr. and several other versions, including the Italic; although Vulg. retains it. It is not found in Origen or Chrysostom; nor in five uncial (B C D M P) and about twenty cursive manuscripts. And though these documents are not very numerous, and are chiefly of the Alexandrine family, the internal argument against its genuineness is so strong, that we may confidently (with Vater) remove ὁ Ἰησοῦς from the text.

The evidence against αὐτοῦ is considerably stronger: for most of Matthæi's best Byzantine MSS unite with several Alexandrine, Vulg. Chrysostom, &c. in rejecting it. Griesbach and Scholz quote Syr. as omitting the word. I do not see how any safe conclusions can be drawn from the language of that version as to the pronouns contained in the manuscripts from which it was made: so widely different are the Greek and Syriac idioms in this respect (See Introd. p. 70). No one was better acquainted with this peculiarity of the Aramæan dialect than Scholz (Proleg. N. T. p. cxxii); although he seldom cares to apply his principles to the criticism of the sacred text. But in fact

Syr. here reads ܬܠܡܝܕܘܗܝ "his disciples," though ܗܘ is wanting in the editio princeps, I suppose by an error of the press. To return to αὐτοῦ: it may unquestionably be expunged in this place. The sense is complete without it, and it was probably at first a mere marginal gloss, suggested to the reader by Mark vi, 45.

(II, b). *ibid.* εἰς τὸ πλοῖον "into the ship"]. "a ship," all Eng. See notes on ch. iv, 21; xiii, 2, &c.

(II, b). v. 23. τὸ ὄρος "the mountain-country"]. "a mountain," all Eng. See note on ch. v, 1. So alter ch. xv, 29.

(III, c). v. 24. ὑπὸ τῶν κυμάτων "by the waves"]. "with the waves," Cheke, Bish. "with waves," other Eng.

(I)°. v. 25. Here again ὁ Ἰησοῦς is omitted by nearly the same authorities as in v. 22, with a few of Matthæi's manuscripts in addition to them (V. a., &c.). In this verse it is found in Syr., but not in Vulg. or Chrysostom. Yet though the external evidence is so similar to that in the former case, it is by no means sufficient to *command* our assent: and since the proper name does not here occur at the beginning of a section, it is not equally easy to account for its interpolation. I am therefore disposed to retain it in the present passage; and Vater comes to the same conclusion, it may be on the same grounds. Griesbach, Scholz and Lachmann condemn ὁ Ἰησοῦς as before.

In v. 30, τὸν ἄνεμον ἰσχυρὸν is rendered by Tynd. Cov. Cran. Gen. Bish. "a mighty wind." Auth. has very correctly "the wind boisterous;" Cheke and the margin of Auth. "the wind strong." The same care on the part of Auth. to convey the precise force of the article appears in v. 24, ἦν γὰρ ἐνάντιος ὁ ἄνεμος "for the wind was contrary," where Cheke and all the earlier Eng. except Cov. translate "for it was (they had, Cheke) a contrary wind."

(III, c). v. 35. ἐπιγνόντες "recognised"]. Eng. "had knowledge of," which is very quaint. See also Acts iv, 13. "Knew him," Cheke.

In v. 36, Bish. Auth. rightly express the signification of διά in διεσώθησαν "were made perfectly whole." But "made safe," Tynd. Cran. "made whole," Cov. Cheke, Gen. It is also neglected by Vulg. Beza, Castalio, Martin, Ostervald and Syr., by the last indeed almost of necessity. On this subject I have elsewhere declared my sentiments (Introd. p. 35). Schleusner as usual says "διασώζω i. q. simplex σώζω:" chiefly, it would seem, because St. Mark (ch. vi, 56) contents himself with ἐσώζοντο when narrating the same circumstance. See note on ch. xviii, 31.

CHAPTER XV.

(II, b). v. 1. οἱ ἀπὸ Ἱεροσολύμων γραμματεῖς... "the scribes... from Jerusalem"]. So Cov. Scholefield. But "scribes... from Jerusalem," Tynd. "scribes ... which were come from Jerusalem," Cran. Bish. "certain scribes... of Jerusalem," Gen. "scribes... which were of Jerusalem," Auth. Bp. Middleton is inclined to reject οἱ, which is not expressed by Syr. Vulg. or Origen. Cheke's version would in that case be correct "Then came there from Jerusalem unto Jesus scribes..." Οἱ, however, is found in all Greek manuscripts except B D (Scholz says C, but this is another of his typographical errors) and six cursive; so that in spite of Lachmann's decision, its authenticity is beyond dispute. (Yet compare Mark vii, 1). Οἱ ἀπὸ Ἱεροσολύμων, as Wolf observes, is nearly parallel with οἱ ἀπὸ τῆς Ἰταλίας, Hebr. xiii, 24, and οἱ ἀπὸ τῆς Θεσσαλονίκης Ἰουδαῖοι, Acts xvii, 13. St. Matthew's expression of course implies not that all the scribes and Pharisees of Jerusalem came to Jesus, but that a large number of them came. No difficulty would have been felt in the present passage, but from an indisposition on the part of many good men to concede to the style of Scripture the use of those general and popular forms of speech, which prevail without offence or ambiguity in the most accurate uninspired compositions. Yet (to mention one or two instances out of a thousand), how can such persons defend the strict sense of πᾶς in Matth. iii, 5; iv, 24; Acts ii, 5?

(I). v. 4. Griesbach, Vater, Scholz and Lachmann expunge σου after τὸν πατέρα. It is omitted in so many excellent manuscripts of both families, that it may readily be supposed to be interpolated from Mark vii, 10, where it is repeated after τὴν μητέρα also. Yet we must not allow the Latin versions to have any weight in deciding the point; and since σου is retained in the great majority of the copies of Chrysostom, *he* ought not to have been cited as a witness against the received text. It is chiefly to point out these irregularities of the critical editors that I notice this various reading; for whatever be the fate of σου, the sense is precisely the same. Σοῦ is justly removed by all the critics from the kindred passage ch. xix, 19.

In v. 6, the textus receptus has οὐ μὴ τιμήσῃ "he shall not honor;" where, in compliance with a familiar canon of Greek syntax, we should expect the future indicative. Τιμήσει is actually read by Lachmann, and favorably named by Griesbach: but the manuscript evidence in its behalf is slight, and exclusively Egyptian (B C D. 1. 13. 33. 124. 225. 346, *Scholz*);

so that it bears every mark of being the deliberate correction of some Alexandrian grammarian.* On the licence taken by the writers of the Greek Testament in this matter, consult Green, Gram. pp. 124—127.

(III, c). v. 4. θανάτῳ τελευτάτω "let him surely die"]. So Doddridge. Thus also Auth. renders the same palpable Hebraism (מוֹת תָּמוּת) in Gen. ii, 17; iii, 4; Exod. xxi, 17, &c. "Morte moriatur," Vulg. Beza, and Syr. of course retains the Oriental form. "Meure de mort," Martin; "morte plectatur," Castalio; whence Ostervald "soit puni de mort." Tynd. has simply. "shall suffer death," and Cheke, "let him die." Cov. Cran. Gen. Bish. Auth. exhibit the uncouth phrase, "die the death." So change Mark vii, 10, and perhaps also Matth. xiii, 14.

(II, c. See Introd. p. 46). vv. 5, 6. δῶρον, ὃ ἐὰν ἐξ ἐμοῦ ὠφεληθῇς, καὶ οὐ μὴ τιμήσῃ τὸν πατέρα αὐτοῦ.... "be *that* a gift, by whatsoever thou mightest have been relieved from me, he shall not then honor...."]. I have here united the interpretations of Bp. Jebb and Dr. Boothroyd; and such in substance is the rendering of Whitby, Campbell, Wynne, the translator of the "Holy Bible" of 1841, and the "Layman" of 1840 (Edgar Taylor, Esq. see Introd. pp. 15, 47, notes), who unaccountably praises Wynne's version as "a work of great judgment and ability, which is certainly not known or valued as much as its intrinsic merits justify." Doddridge, with a lack of discretion very unusual in him, adopts Elsner's forced explanation of v. 6, καὶ (λέγετε, ἀπὸ τοῦ κοινοῦ) οὐ μὴ τιμήσῃ, "et ne honoret;" an artifice by the way of which Elsner is

---

* "Grammaticum egit Alexandrinus censor." Griesbach, Proleg. N. T. Sect. III, p. lxxviii.

too fond (see his note on ch. xi, 19). The mode I have suggested makes v. 5 the protasis, and v. 6 the apodosis of a single sentence; καὶ at the commencement of the apodosis being nearly redundant, as δέ often is in a like position in Classical authors. This is the view taken by Grotius and his humble imitator Rosenmüller. Kuinöel also follows on the same side, appealing to Numb. i, 53; 1 Sam. xii, 19, which do not seem altogether apposite. Yet there cannot be a doubt that the Hebrew particle וְ is constantly employed in this manner; and an Hebrew construction is the more natural in the present passage, as our Blessed Lord had just been citing the precise form of a Jewish vow (see Lightfoot, *ad loc.* and Mark vii, 11, 12). Vater quotes Exod. xxx, 33; 38, where וְ is not expressed by the LXX; exactly similar is Gen. iii, 5 (וְנִפְקְחוּ, διανοιχθήσονται LXX): not to insist on countless instances of the pleonastic וְ after וַיְהִי (καὶ ἐγένετο), of which so many traces remain even in the New Testament (Luke ii, 15; v, 1; 12; 17, &c.). For a like use of καί, but not after ἐγένετο, we may refer to Matth. xxviii, 9; Luke ii, 21; 27, 28; vii, 12; xiii, 25; and it is remarkable that nearly all our examples are derived from that Evangelist, who most affects the Oriental idiom. It may tend to prove the commonness of this phrase in the Aramæan dialects, if we observe that the Peshito introduces the same particle (ο) in Luke xiv, 10, where we find τότε ἔσται in the Greek original.

Such, then, are my reasons for resorting to an Hebraism in the present case. My opinion is fortified by Syr., and I may add by those Alexandrine authorities which would remove καί from the text (B C D. 1. 33. 36. 41. 61. Copt. Ital. and Lachmann). It cannot be disputed that this solution is incomparably preferable to the harsh constructions and harsher ellipses of some of our versions. Beza first inserted in the text " *insons erit,*" whence came " *he shall be free*" of Auth. and " *n'est pas coupable*" of Ostervald. Tynd. and Bish. are much nearer the truth. " Whatsoever thing I offer, that same doth profit thee," Tynd. 1. " that which thou desirest of me to help thee with, is given to God," Tynd. 2. " by the gift that [is offered] of me, thou shalt be helped," Bish. but they all add, " and so shall he not honor"... Cov. is very loose, " the thing that I should help thee withal, is given unto God. By this is it come to pass that no man honoreth"... Gen. has "by every gift that *procedeth* from me, thou shalt be holpen. Though he honor not"... Cheke has nearly hit upon the peculiar use of καί, though his translation of the clause before it is bad enough: " Whosoever sayeth . . . whatsoever is given by me, thou shalt take profit by it, he shall not need beside to honor" . . . I can make nothing out of Vulg. " Munus, quodcunque est ex me, tibi proderit; et non honorificabit"... I have chosen to render " *be that* a gift," rather than " *it is* a gift," as in Auth., since the precatory form of the passage seems very evident.

(I)°. v. 8. Griesbach, Vater, and Lachmann remove from the text as spurious the words ἐγγίζει μοι " draweth nigh unto me," and τῷ στόματι αὐτῶν καὶ " with their mouth, and" ... They are wanting in Syr. Vulg. the Italic, Æthiopic and Armenian versions; in Origen, Chrysostom and several other Fathers. This would form a strong reason for questioning their authenticity, were they not found in all existing manuscripts except *five* (B D L. 33. 124), all of which are decidedly Alexandrian. Fully admitting the weight of the versions on a point of this kind, and the *possibility* that the disputed words were inserted from the LXX of Isai. xxix, 13; I still think it unreasonable to reject the reading contained in so immense a majority of the manuscripts of every age, and of both families. Indeed we cannot do so without unsettling the fiist principles of Scriptural criticism.

(III, a). v. 10. προσκαλεσάμενος "called unto *him*"]. Thus all Eng. (even Cheke) except Auth., and even Auth. in v. 32; ch. x, 1; xviii, 2; xx, 25; Mark iii, 13; 23. So alter ch. xviii, 32. " *Him*" only should be printed in italics; and not " unto" (πρός), as is done by Auth. in several places. Turton.

(II, b). v. 12. τὸν λόγον " *thy* saying"]. " This saying," Eng. but the article never bears that meaning.

(III, a). v. 18. τὸν ἄνθρωπον "a man"]. The whole class. So Tynd. 1. Cheke here, and Auth. vv. 11, 20.

(II, b). v. 22. ἀπὸ τῶν ὁρίων ἐκείνων " from those coasts"]. So Cheke, Scholefield. " the same," Eng. a too frequent rendeiing of ἐκεῖνος in these versions. See ch. viii, 13; x, 19; xiii, 1; xviii, 1; 28; xxii, 23; xxvi, 55.

(II, b). v. 26. τοῖς κυναρίοις " to the dogs"] viz. the household dogs. Middleton. So Auth. in Mark vii, 27. "To dogs," Cov. Cran. Auth. " to whelps," Tynd. Gen. (" to the whelps," Cheke), "to little dogs," Bish. Parkhurst, after Bochart, supposes κυνάριον to be a more contemptuous term than κύων: but I must think these distinctions somewhat too finely drawn. See vv. 34, 36; and Introd. p. 33.

(II, a). v. 27. Ναὶ Κύριε καὶ γὰρ τὰ κυνάρια ... " yea Lord; for the dogs"...]. So Bish. Cheke (" yes Lord, for the whelps"..) after Vulg. ("Etiam Domine; nam et catelli"..). But " it is truth Lord, nevertheless"... Tynd. Cov. " truth Lord, yet".. Auth. yet Cran. Gen. more properly "truth Lord, for"... Syr. has اف ܚܒ ܐܠ (" yea Lord, also"..) as if it did not read γάρ. "Ita est Domine, et tamen"... of Castalio is less correct than Beza's "etiam Domine, etenim"... " Il est vrai, Seigneur; cependant les petit chiens".., Ostervald. The fact is that ναί, like the Hebrew נָא (Gen. xix, 7; 8; Numb. xii, 12, *Hebrew*), is a particle of entreaty rather than of assent (Philem. v. 20); yet without absolutely excluding the latter idea (Gen. xvii, 19; Job xix, 4; Rev. xxii, 20). For this last sense see Elsner and Kypke, who produces a passage exactly parallel from Xenophon's Œconom. [p. 488, ed. Stephan. 1581], ἐμὸν δὲ ἔργον ἔφησεν ἡ μήτηρ εἶναι σωφρονεῖν. ναὶ μὰ Δί᾽ ἔφην ἐγώ, ὦ γύναι, καὶ γὰρ ἐμοὶ ὁ πατήρ. In the comic dialogue of Aristophanes ναὶ is *always* used as a particle of affirmation: e. g. Thesmoph. 605, ἔμ᾽, ἥτις, ἤρου;—ναί.—Κλεωνύμου γυνή. Plut. 186-7, ἐγὼ τοσαῦτα δυνατός εἰμ᾽ εἷς ὢν ποεῖν;—καὶ ναὶ μὰ Δία τούτων γε πολλῷ πλείονα. In ναὶ therefore the woman meekly assents to our Lord's statement, while in καὶ γὰρ she urges that very circumstance as an additional reason why her suit should be granted. Chrysostom carefully traces the precise argument which she pleads: ἀπ᾽ αὐτῶν τῶν αὐτοῦ ῥημάτων πλέκει τὴν συνηγορίαν. Εἰ γὰρ κυνάριόν εἰμι, οὐκ εἰμὶ ἀλλοτρία... Ὅτι μὲν γὰρ ἀναγκαία ἡ τροφὴ τοῖς τέκνοις, φησίν, οἶδα κἀγώ· πλὴν οὐδὲ ἐγὼ κεκώλυμαι, κυνάριον οὖσα. Εἰ μὲν γὰρ μὴ θέμις λαβεῖν, οὐδὲ τῶν ψιχίων μετασχεῖν θέμις· εἰ δὲ κἂν ἐκ μικροῦ δεῖ κοινωνεῖν, οὐδὲ ἐγὼ κεκώλυμαι, κἂν κυνάριον ὦ· ἀλλὰ καὶ ταύτῃ μάλιστα μετέχω, εἰ κυνάριόν εἰμι. So alter Mark vii, 28.

(III, c). v. 28. γενηθήτω σοι ὡς θέλεις " be it to thee,

even as thou desirest"]. This is partly taken from Tynd. Cov. Gen. " be it to thee even as thou desirest;" partly from Bish. " be it done unto thee even as thou wilt." Cran. Auth. " be it unto thee even as thou wilt," is a little obscure.

(III, b). v. 31. βλέποντας κωφοὺς λαλοῦντας κ. τ. λ. " when they saw the dumb speak, the maimed whole," &c.]. Bp. Lowth (Eng. Gram. p. 137) points out the impropriety of inserting " to," the sign of the infinitive mood, after a verb of seeing. Tynd. Cov. Cheke, Gen. (and Bish. in part) are accurate in this portion of the verse, but all the versions except Cheke's have " the lame to walk, (" the halt to go," Tynd. Cov. Gen.), and the blind to see." On the omission of the Greek article before κωφούς, κυλλούς, &c. see note on ch. xi, 5. In v. 30, Tynd. Cov. Cheke, Gen. rightly leave out " *those that were*," which words are not in italics in Bish. or the 1st edition of Auth.

(III. a and c). v. 32. ἤδη ἡμέρας τρεῖς προσμένουσί μοι " they have continued with me now three days"]. So Tynd. Cov. Gen. (Gen. " already "). Cheke " they have remained here with me three days now," nearly resembling Auth. in Mark viii, 2; and much more perspicuous than " they continue with me now three days," of Cran. Bish. Auth. All the modern editors read ἡμέραι in both Gospels, and I believe very justly. But this change will not at all affect the sense.

(III, a). v. 37. καὶ ἦραν τὸ περισσεῦον τῶν κλασμάτων " and they took up of the fragments that remained"]. vv. 37, 38 are almost verbally repeated from vv. 20, 21 of the last chapter; and it is fit that this close similarity should not be lost on the mere English reader. Dr. Symonds alleges a further reason for the change of Eng. " they took up of the broken meat that was left." It is disgusting, if we may credit this delicate critic, that the term " meat" should be applied to a meal of bread and fish. Thus alter Mark viii, 8.

In v. 39, for ἐνέβη εἰς τὸ πλοῖον, all Eng. have " took ship," except Cov. " went into a ship" (" a boat," Cheke), which is worse. I would render " went into the ship," mentioned above in ch. xiv, 22, &c.

CHAPTER XVI.

(III, c). v. 1. οἱ Φαρισαῖοι καὶ Σαδδουκαῖοι " the Pharisees and Sadducees"]. So Tynd. 2. Cov. Cheke, Gen. " the Pharisees with the Sadducees," Tynd. 1. Cran. Bish. Auth. it would be hard to tell why. In v. 3, instead of " ye can discern" of Eng. say " ye know how to discern" (γινώσκετε) with Bp. Jebb.

(III, a and c). v. 5. ἄρτους λαβεῖν " to bring bread"]. So correct v. 7, conformably to Auth. in v. 8. Otherwise we must render with all Eng. except Auth. " to take bread (Cheke adds " over") with them ... with us," vv. 5, 7. " To take bread," of Auth. rather implies " to eat." Compare Acts xxvii, 33, 34.

(II, b. See Introd. p. 45). v. 7. διελογίζοντο " began to reason"]. " they thought," Tynd. Cov. Cran. Bish. " they reasoned," Cheke, Gen. Auth. In this verse Tynd. 1. Cov. Cran. do not render ὅτι, but Auth. (" *it is* because"), or Cheke (" saying that it was because"), will suit the passage very well. The ellipsis of ταῦτα λέγει before ὅτι is illustrated by Kypke from Lysias, de cæde Eratosth. (p. 14, Reiske), ἐπειδὴ δὲ ἐγὼ ὠργιζόμην καὶ ἐκέλευον αὐτὴν ἀπιέναι, ἵνα σύ γε, ἔφη, πειρᾷς ἐνταῦθα τὴν παιδίσκην.

(II, b). v. 8. γνοὺς δὲ ὁ Ἰησοῦς εἶπεν "but Jesus perceived *it*, and said"]. So Syr. and Cheke ("Jesus knowing this said"). The renderings of Tynd. Cov. Cran. Gen. Bish. " when Jesus understood (" perceived" Cov.) that, he said," and of Auth. "*which* when Jesus perceived, he said," are equally open to the objection stated in my note on ch. xii, 15. Thus alter Auth. in ch. xxvi, 10, where Gen. and Cheke are quite accurate: " and Jesus knowing that," Gen.

(I). *ibid.* Griesbach, Vater, Scholz and Lachmann omit αὐτοῖς after εἶπεν, with Origen, the Vulg. the Æthiopic, &c. versions, and a respectable number of manuscripts, which however are all Alexandrine (B D K L M, &c.), except a few of the least considerable of Matthæi's, and Birch's Vatican 354 (S). The pronoun has so much the appearance of an addition, that in the present case it is the safest course to acquiesce in their decision.

(1)°. v. 11. Instead of ἄρτου " bread," the reading of all our versions, Scholz and Lachmann edit ἄρτων " loaves," which form Griesbach and Vater judge little, if at all, inferior to the singular. B C K L M S, several of Matthæi's manuscripts, and many others of both families support the plural; and it is possible that ἄρτου was taken from v. 12. But the question is obviously one of slight moment.

(II, c)°. v. 13. τίνα με λέγουσιν οἱ ἄνθρωποι εἶναι, τὸν υἱὸν τοῦ ἀνθρώπου; " who (see the next note) do men say that I the Son of man am?]." This is the construction adopted by Tynd. Cran. Cheke, Bish. Auth. and the margin of Cov. (Introd. p. 86); it is also that of Castalio, and apparently of Syr. also (ܛܒܥܘܢ ܐܢܫܐ ܕܐܝܬܘܗܝ ܐܢܫܐ ܒܪܗ). Vulg. however renders " quem dicunt homines esse Filium hominis?" whence Cov. " whom do men say that the Son of man is," and after him Campbell. I do not conceive that Vulg. and those other versions which pass over με did not find it in their Greek copies (though it is really wanting in Codex B), but that they neglected it in order to relieve a rather embarrassed construction. Gen. translates " whom do men say that I am the Son of man" (sic), which though a literal version of Beza's " quemnam esse me dicunt homines, Filium hominis,* may seem to incline to a mode of interpretation favored by Leclerc and a few other critics; who, by placing a mark of interrogation after εἶναι, and another at the end of the verse, elicit the following sense : " who do men say that I am? the Son of Man ?" i. e. the expected Messiah. The habit of tampering in this manner with the received punctuation I have elsewhere condemned (Introd. p. 47); and it is well urged by Bp. Middleton that so abrupt an interrogation as Leclerc's mode of understanding the passage would render necessary, but little resembles the ordinary ease and perspicuity of the inspired writers. We should naturally expect μὴ or μήτι, or some such word to be prefixed to the second clause of the sentence. Besides, it does not appear that the expression ὁ υἱὸς τοῦ ἀνθρώπου was by any means in common use among the Jews, as an appellation of their future Christ. This name is applied to our Lord in the New Testament by Himself, and only by Himself; for Rev. i, 13 ; xiv, 14, should be otherwise explained. On the whole then we may rest satisfied, that the vulgar construction of these

---

* Beza's French imitators remove the ambiguity by the insertion of one little word : " Qui disent les hommes que je suis, moi le Fils de l' homme ?" Martin, Ostervald.

words, though it may be a little involved, is in all probability the true one.

(III, b). *ibid.* τίνα με λέγουσιν κ. τ. λ. " who do men say" &c.]. So Campbell. " whom," all Eng. even Cheke, and the Rhemish translators, both here, and in v. 15; and all except Cov. in Acts xiii, 25. Bp. Lowth however says " it ought in all these places to be *who;* which is not governed by the verb *say* or *think*, but by the verb *am*, or agrees in case with the pronoun I." Eng. Gram. p. 133.

In v. 14, "*that thou art*" of Eng. is rejected by Cheke without injuring the sense. See Introd. p. 63.

In v. 16, ὁ Χριστὸς is ill rendered " Christ" by all Eng., including Cheke and the first edition of Auth. Most, I believe *all*, the modern impressions of Auth. have " the Christ;" yet the old reading can hardly be considered a mere typographical error. See note on ch. xii, 23.

(I). v. 20. Ἰησοῦς ὁ Χριστὸς " Jesus the Christ," Gen. Auth. " Jesus Christ" is the marvellous version of Tynd. Cov. Cran. Cheke, and even of Bish., after the earlier translators had been set right by Gen. Ἰησοῦς is omitted by Griesbach, Vater, Scholz and Lachmann. Every one must feel that it was needless for our Lord to charge his disciples to tell no man that he was *Jesus*, since by that name he was commonly known while he sojourned on earth. The real point was to desire them to conceal for a time that he was *the Christ;* the great Messiah whom the prophets had foretold. Now Ἰησοῦς is wanting in the Peshito, which was probably translated before the term "Jesus Christ" had become the ordinary appellation of our Blessed Saviour among believers. It is not recognised by Origen, Chrysostom, or Theophylact; and though its constant use in the public prayers of the

Church has procured for it a place in the *printed* editions of the Latin Vulgate, it is not found in most of the Italic manuscripts, nor in the earlier copies of the Vulgate itself; not even in those from which Wickliffe translated his New Testament. At least forty Greek MSS reject Ἰησοῦς, and though only two uncial documents (B L) are among them, yet Scholz's list of authorities contains some of the best of both classes, including twelve of Matthæi's; nor can we doubt that by an accurate survey of all extant cursive manuscripts, many more might be added to the number. Moreover, I fully agree with Mill (Proleg. N. T. p. 64), that the very wording of v. 16, to which v. 20 clearly refers, is fatal to the authenticity of Ἰησοῦς.

(II, a. See Introd. p. 35). v. 22. προσλαβόμενος αὐτὸν " took him aside"]. So all Eng. except Auth., which omits " aside." Yet as Campbell observes, " took him" is quite indefinite. Compare Acts xviii, 26, and so correct Mark viii, 32. Syr. as usual loses the force of πρός. " Assumens," Vulg. " l'ayant pris à part," Martin, Ostervald; " took him by the hand," Doddridge.

The precise sense of ἵλεως is well explained by Wetstein, who compares μηδαμῶς, the Septuagint rendering of חָלִילָה in 1 Sam. xxii, 15, with ἵλεως, that of Symmachus and Theodotion. Auth. " be it far from thee," may stand. " Favor thyself" of Tynd. Cov. Cran. Bish. is very inferior: " look to thyself," Gen. ݣ ܡ Syr. " absit a te," Vulg. " propitius tibi esto," Beza: " parce tibi," Castalio. " Sir, have pity on yourself, Sir" (!), Cheke, which resembles " pity thyself," of the margin of the later editions of Auth. (" a Dieu ne plaise," Ostervald). This use of ἵλεως is purely Hellenistic. Compare the LXX,

2 Sam. xx, 20, with Joseph. Antiq. vii, 2, 8, as cited by Krebs. It is plain that Josephus in the clause ὁ δ' ἵλεω μὲν ηὔχετο τὸν Θεὸν αὐτῷ διαμένειν, had the LXX exclusively in view. See also 1 Macc. ii, 21; 1 Chron. xi, 19, in which last place ὁ Θεὸς is supplied.

(II, a). *ibid.* οὐ μὴ ἔσται "shall in no wise be"]. See note on ch. x, 23. Thus correct Auth. in v. 28; ch. xviii, 3; xxiii, 39; xxiv, 2; 34; 35. Bish. alone of Eng. renders οὐ μὴ fully in v. 28. On the tense of ἔσται see Green, Gram. N. T. p. 126.

In v. 24 (see note on ch. xi, 27) the usual ambiguity occurs with respect to θέλω. In v. 25 there is some difference in sense (not a very wide one certainly) between ὃς ἂν θέλῃ σῶσαι and ὃς ἂν ἀπολέσῃ "whosoever will (is *anxious*, is *resolved* to) save his life shall lose it, and whosoever shall lose."... In the second clause of course no determination, no excessive forwardness to expose our life, is either prescribed or would be lawful (ch. x, 23). This distinction of the Greek is preserved by Tynd. Gen. Bish. "whosoever shall lose;" but disappears in Auth. which employs "will" indifferently in both cases.

(III, a). v. 26. ψυχὴ "life," *bis*] uniformly with Auth. in v. 25. So Doddridge (whose note is worth reading) and Campbell. All Eng. have "soul."

In v. 27, ten or twelve MSS, some copies of Chrysostom, and (if versions can be trusted on such a point) Syr. Vulg. and the Sahidic read τὰ ἔργα for τὴν πρᾶξιν, but this is unquestionably a mere gloss. Yet we must not concede to Schleusner that πρᾶξιν is here put for the plural. It means not a single act, or a multitude of such acts, but the habit, the *practice*, the general character. "Deeds," Tynd. Cov. Cran. Gen. "works," Bish. Auth. "actions," Doddridge, Campbell. Perhaps "conduct" would best express our Lord's exact meaning. In v. 28, ἕως ἂν ἴδωσι "till they shall have seen," Tynd. is better than " till they see" of Cov. Cran. Bish. Auth. or " till they shall see" of Gen.

(I)°. v. 28. Instead of τινες τῶν ὧδε ἑστηκότων ("some of those standing here") Griesbach, Vater and Lachmann prefer τινες τῶν ὧδε ἑστώτων, as they are at perfect liberty to do if they please. Scholz however reads the nominative τινες ὧδε ἑστῶτες ("some standing here," Auth.). The manuscript evidence is pretty evenly balanced, so far at least as such a trifle has been attended to. Vulg. clearly favors the genitive, as also does Chrysostom. Syr. is ambiguous. "Sed τινες in Matthæo sequi solet genitivus," says Vater; whose remark is confirmed by ch. ix, 3; xii, 38; xxvii, 47; xxviii, 11. This may be reason enough on so insignificant a question.

CHAPTER XVII.

(II, a). v. 1. παραλαμβάνει "taketh with *him* "]. The preposition is neglected by all Eng. here and in ch. xx, 17; and by all except Cov. in Luke ix, 28. In Mark ix, 2 it is expressed by Cov. Bish. Auth. In Matth. i, 20; 24, Auth. renders it fully " to take unto."

(I)°. v. 5. In the room of νεφέλη φωτεινὴ " a bright cloud," Griesbach reads νεφέλη φωτὸς "a cloud of light." It might well be called by Mill " lectio singularis," for even now only eight inferior manuscripts, the earliest being of the eleventh century, are known to contain φωτός. Griesbach indeed cites only *six* in favor of his reading; but since they chance to be of different recensions (36. 183. Matthæi's *e*, and perhaps Stephani δ' or 5 of Wetstein being Byzantine; while 13 and 124 are decidedly Egyptian), he alters the common text on that wretched authority; considering no doubt that νεφέλη φωτός, being the harsher and more Hebraic form, is for that reason the more probable. I have already (note on ch. viii, 15) explained my motive for troubling the reader with minutiæ of this kind.

(III, a and c). v. 6. σφόδρα " exceedingly "]. So Auth. in ch. xix, 25. "Sore," all Eng. except Gen., which inadvertently omits σφόδρα altogether. Dr. Symonds would wish us to expunge "sore" entirely from our version, and it may be dispensed with easily enough. See below, v. 15.

(III, c). v. 8. οὐδένα "no one"]. "no body," Rhemish version; "none but Jesus," Campbell; "no man," Eng. Thus correct Mark ix, 8. It is scarcely proper to employ the term " no man " in reference to the glorified apparitions of Moses and Elijah; but when the words are followed by "save Jesus only," they become positively offensive to pious ears. Mr. Walter (2nd letter to Bp. Marsh, p. 48) justly complains of a similar fault in the Authorised rendering of Acts xiii, 38; Hebr. iii, 3; vii, 24; viii, 3; x, 12, in all which texts he proposes to substitute " person " for " man." I need not add that no violence whatever would be done to the original by this alteration of Auth.

In v. 9, the preposition in ἀναστῇ "be risen again" is expressed by all Eng. It may be thought advisable to remove "again" from v. 23; ch. xvi, 21, where we have the verb ἐγείρεσθαι and not ἀναστῆναι.

(I)°. v. 11. Lachmann omits Ἰησοῦς, after B D K (Griesbach says L) Z, about five cursive manuscripts, the Coptic, Vulg. and Italic versions. These are all, or nearly all Alexandrine; yet Griesbach does not agree with Lachmann, although the evidence in favor of a change is considerably stronger than in v. 5: such is the consistency of his judgment. I remember very few passages in the New Testament where ὁ δὲ "and he" occurs *in the singular*, unless it be preceded by ὁ μέν, as in Heb. vii, 23, 24. But it would be rash to speak positively on the point, for in this instance the Concordance affords us no assistance.

(II, a and b). *ibid.* ἔρχεται καὶ ἀποκαταστήσει πάντα " cometh, and shall reform all things "]. " Restituet," says Lightfoot, " non in pristinum statum, sed meliorem." Ἀποκαταστήσει, τουτέστι, διορθώσεται τὴν ἀπιστίαν τῶν Ἰουδαίων τῶν τότε εὑρισκομένων, Chrysostom. " Shall come and restore," Eng. except that Cov. translates " bring all things to right again," and ἔρχεται is rendered by Gen. " must come." " Venturus est, et restituet," Vulg. I prefer taking ἔρχεται strictly as a present, for John had already come, though the ἀποκατάστασις, the fruits of his ministry, had not yet shown themselves. Doddridge, for ἀποκαταστήσει, has " regulate," " reduce to order:" and nearly all the Commentators refer the expression to John's mission of repentance. Beyond a doubt our Lord alludes, as indeed Chrysostom saw long ago, to Malachi iv, 6; where it is said of Elijah ἀποκαταστήσει (Hebr. הֵשִׁיב) καρδίαν πατρὸς πρὸς υἱόν. Campbell lost sight of this prophecy when he rendered the clause " to consummate the whole;" importing that the end of John's coming was to close the old dispensation, and to usher in a new one. This interpretation is certainly countenanced by Syr. (ܢܫܠܡ) and may be made to suit the context in Acts iii, 21; but Campbell produces no examples of the use of ἀποκαθιστάναι in such a sense, whereas it occurs six times in the New Testament in its common and more obvious signification.

(II, a). v. 12. ἐποίησαν ἐν αὐτῷ "they did in his case"]. So Green, Gram. p. 281, comparing 1 Cor. xiv, 11; 2 Cor. iv, 3; Gal. i, 16; 1 John iv, 9. See also Luke xxiii, 31. Thus Eurip. Rhes. 855 (ed. Matthiæ), κοὐδὲν πρὸς αὐτῶν οἶδα πλημμελὲς κλύων· ἐν σοὶ δ' ἂν ἀρχοίμεσθα. So Syr. ܒܗ, Vulg. "in eo." But Beza, Castalio have "ei," and all Eng. "done unto him." This construction of ἐν with persons must not be confounded with its pleonastic use before the dative of the instrument; as in 1 Thess. v, 26; Demosth. adv. Lept. (p. 500, Reiske), λόγους ἐπιταφίους, ἐν οἷς κοσμεῖτε τὰ τῶν ἀγαθῶν ἀνδρῶν ἔργα.

(III, c). ibid. ἠθέλησαν "they pleased"]. So Doddridge, Campbell; "lusted," Tynd. Cran. Gen. Bish. "listed," Auth. "what they would," Cov. It would be more distinct if both here and in v. 22; ch. xx, 22 μέλλει were rendered "is about to," not "shall."

(III, a and c). v. 17. ἀνέξομαι "shall I bear with"]. as in Auth. Acts xviii, 14. All Eng. have "suffer," even Wickliffe and the Rhemish translators. Thus alter Mark ix, 19; Luke ix, 41.

In v. 18, Beza and all Eng. except Cov. transpose τὸ δαιμόνιον and αὐτῷ, translating "and Jesus rebuked the devil, and he departed out of him." Thus also Martin and Ostervald: but Syr. Vulg. and Cov. retain the order of the Greek. Vater thinks that a distinction is here drawn between αὐτῷ, the possessed child, and τὸ δαιμόνιον which possessed him. This however must be fanciful, since both St. Mark (ch. ix, 25) and St. Luke (ch. ix, 42) say plainly ἐπετίμησε τῷ πνεύματι τῷ ἀκαθάρτῳ.

(III, c). v. 24. οἱ λαμβάνοντες "they that were wont to gather"]. So Tynd. Gen. "that use to receive,"

Cran. " that received," Cov. Bish. Auth. probably intending to convey the same meaning.

(II, a). *ibid.* τὰ δίδραχμα " the half-shekels "]. The contribution paid yearly by each adult Israelite, in order to defray the expenses of the Temple-worship: Exod. xxx, 13; xxxviii, 26. No one, I conceive, would gather this circumstance from the indefinite language of Tynd. Gen. " poll money ;" of Cov. " the tribute money ;" and still less from " tribute money " of Cran. Bish. Auth. Vulg. has " didrachma," and Syr. ܠܡܐ ܕܪܫܐ܇ ܐܝܟ ܙܘܙܐ "two drachms of head money." The value of the shekel is accurately stated by Josephus (Antiq. iii, 8, 2), ὁ δὲ σίκλος, νόμισμα Ἑβραίων ὤν, Ἀττικὰς δέχεται δραχμὰς τέσσαρας. In accordance with this interpretation both Aquila and Symmachus translate "shekel" in Exod. xxx, 13 by στατήρ (the Attic stater containing four Attic drachmæ), and Aquila בקע " bekah," or half-shekel, in Exod. xxxviii, 26 by δίδραχμον. On consulting the LXX, however, an unexpected difficulty presents itself: for we there find the shekel called δίδραχμον, and the bekah δραχμή (Exod xxxix, 2, according to the arrangement of the LXX). But this obstacle is soon surmounted. We learn from Varro that the *Alexandrian* drachma, by which the translators of the LXX naturally reckoned, was equal to two Attic drachmæ (see Prideaux's Connections, Preface). It appears therefore that two Attic drachmæ (whose value is pretty accurately given at fifteen pence in the margin of the later editions of Auth.; see note on ch. xviii, 24), were considered equivalent (indeed they were rather more than equivalent) to the Hebrew bekah.

In v. 27, στατῆρα is rendered by Tynd. 1. " a piece of twelve pence;" by Tynd. 2. Cov. Cran. Gen. Bish. " a piece of twenty pence ;" by Auth. with unfortunate vagueness, "a piece of money," which in the margin of the first edition is explained to be "a stater," its value being indicated only in our later Bibles ("it is half an ounce of silver, in value 2s. 6d. after 5s. the ounce"). Since it is necessary to point out the relation subsisting between στατήρ and δίδραχμον (v. 24), we may call the former "shekel," with Pr. Scholefield, though that version is not quite unexceptionable. The half-shekel was in actual use among the Jews, when they presented their legal offering every year. The alleged business of the κολλυβισταί (Matth. xxi, 12; Mark xi, 15), or κερματισταί (John ii, 14), *within the temple* was to supply the worshippers with Hebrew coin, in exchange for the Greek and Roman money then in ordinary circulation. Both on this account, therefore, and from the language of Exod. xxx, 13, there can be no impropriety in speaking of the half-shekel in v. 24. The shekel, on the contrary, seems to have become quite obsolete; and the stater found by Peter was a Greek and not a Jewish piece of money: for few persons, I presume, will believe with Sebastian Schmidt (see Wolf's Curæ Phil. *ad loc.*) that the coin in question was *created* expressly for this purpose; because, forsooth, had it been *lost* in the sea, its former owner would have had good grounds for a law-suit against our Redeemer!

(II, a). v. 27. σκανδαλίσωμεν αὐτοὺς "cause them to offend"]. See note on ch. v, 29. Syr. here, as before, employs the causative conjugation (ܢܟܫܠ): but all Eng. Vulg. &c. have "offend." Piscator renders "offendiculum præbeamus ipsis;" either by inducing them to despise the temple and its services, or to traduce our Lord as an impious subverter of the Mosaic ritual. Thus the general meaning is the same as in

Auth., but our rendering of the verb here is more consistent with its use in other places. See below, note on ch. xviii, 6; 8; 9.

(III, c). *ibid. ἆρον* "take"]. So Tynd. Cov. Cran. Gen. "take up," Bish. Auth. But "up" occurs in the very next line.

CHAPTER XVIII.

(II, a). vv. 6, 8, 9. σκανδαλίσῃ "cause to offend"]. Here vv. 8, 9 are parallel to ch. v, 29, 30; and there is not the least reason for questioning that the verb is used in the full transitive sense. So Syr. and even Tynd. 1. in v. 8 ("give thee an occasion of evil"); Cran. in v. 8, and Cheke in v. 9 ("hinder"); Gen. in vv. 8, 9. All other Eng. have "offend." Auth. is correct in 1 Cor. viii, 13, and its margin in Mark ix, 43; 45; 47 (not in v. 42). "Fait broncher," Martin; "fait tomber," Ostervald in vv. 8, 9, after Beza's "facit ut offendas." It is but candid to admit that Chrysostom (on v. 6) is of a different opinion: οἱ ἀτιμάζοντες,—τοῦτο γάρ ἐστι τὸ σκανδαλίσαι.

The distinction between θάλασσα and πέλαγος in v. 6 is excellently illustrated by Raphel from Arist. Hist. Anim. i, 1, καὶ τῶν θαλασσίων τὰ μὲν πελάγια, τὰ δὲ αἰγιαλώδη.

(I)°. v. 8. Instead of αὐτά "them" Lachmann reads αὐτὸν "it" (i. e. the foot), which is favored by Griesbach and found in the first edition of Erasmus (1516), in Syr. Vulg. Tynd. Cov. Cran. It is supported by only ten manuscripts (B D L inclusive), of which all except two of Matthæi's are Alexandrian. This evidence is far too weak to be considered as authentic, though perhaps αὐτὸν may be thought rather the more probable reading. See note on ch. xxv, 2.

(III, a and c). v. 12. τί ὑμῖν δοκεῖ " what think ye ?"]. So Cheke, and Auth. also in all other places where the phrase occurs (ch. xvii, 25; xxi, 28; xxii, 17; 42; xxvi, 66; John xi, 56). *Here* all Eng. have " how think ye."

(III, b). *ibid.* οὐχὶ ἀφεὶς ... πορευθεὶς ζητεῖ " doth he not leave ... and go ... and seek"]. So Tynd. Gen. and Cheke, *in substance*. But Cov. Cran. Bish. Auth. have " doth he not leave ... and goeth ... and seeketh." This lapse in the grammatical construction is pointed out by Lowth, Eng. Gram. p. 146, and after him by Archbp. Newcome. A similar error occurs Jerem. xxvi, 19. We may here remark that Syr. Vulg. Tynd. Cov. Cran. Cheke, Gen. Castalio, Doddridge and Campbell join ἐπὶ τὰ ὄρη with ἀφείς, " leave the ninety-nine on the mountains," because St. Luke (ch. xv, 4) has ἐν τῇ ἐρήμῳ in the parallel text. Beza, however, the French versions, Bish. Auth. rightly take the words with πορευθείς, " goeth into ('to' would be better) the mountains." I cannot concede to Doddridge that " the original will bear either construction." Ἐπὶ with the *dative* implies rest, with the accusative motion to a place.

(III, c) v. 13. καὶ ἐὰν γένηται " and if it happen that"]. So Tynd. Gen. (omitting " and ") Cov. Cran. It is surprising that Bish. Auth. should have preferred so inelegant a phrase as " if so be that." Again, χαίρει ἐπ' αὐτῷ should be rendered " rejoiceth over it," as in Cov. Other Eng. have " of that *sheep:*" " of that one," Cheke.

(III, c). v. 16. ἐπὶ στόματος " by the mouth "]. So Gen. "By two or three witnesses' report," or "saying," Cheke; " by the testimony," Campbell. " In the mouth" of Vulg. Tynd. Cov. Cran. Bish. Auth. is too obscure. Syr. ܥܠ ܦܘܡ "upon the mouth;" exactly as we have עַל in Deut. xvii, 6; xix, 15. Parkhurst observes "so we say in English, *upon* the word or oath." Thus correct 2 Cor. xiii, 1. Such expressions as ἐπὶ τοσούτων μαρτύρων are very common in Greek, as Wetstein has shown. See 1 Tim. v, 19, and note. In Hebr. x, 28 ἐπὶ is employed with the dative of the person; but this is derived from the LXX, Deut. xvii, 6, which version represents the same Hebrew words by ἐπὶ στόματος in Deut. xix, 15.

(II, a). v. 17. παρακούσῃ "disregard"]. So Doddridge. "Give no ear to," Cheke, "hear not," Syr. Vulg. Tynd. Cov. Cran. Bish. "will not vouchsafe to hear... refuse to hear," Gen. Campbell's "despise" is perhaps too strong, but "neglect to hear" of Auth. is very feeble, for something worse than negligence is intended. Παρακούσῃ is doubtless equivalent to μὴ ἀκούσῃ v. 16, and is used for it in the LXX, Isai. lxv, 12. Καὶ before τῆς ἐκκλησίας should not be lost; "disregard the Church also;" so Syr. Bish. Auth. alone have "Church." See Introd. p. 83, note.

(III, c). *ibid.* ὁ ἐθνικὸς "an heathen"]. So Cov. Cheke. The other Eng. have "an heathen man." See note on ch. xiii, 45.

(I)°. v. 19. Here Griesbach adds ἀμὴν to πάλιν, and Lachmann displaces πάλιν to make room for it. The latter cites Codex B and Cyprian only in behalf of his emendation; a rather poor array of authorities. If Griesbach and Scholz may be trusted, the Codex B adds ἀμὴν to πάλιν, a reading countenanced by the Sahidic and several Italic versions. Ἀμὴν is found also in *seven* other uncial, and in so many of the best cursive manuscripts of both families, that but for the adverse testimony of Syr. Vulg. I should be almost disposed to adopt it. Πάλιν ἀμὴν has so much the air of a pleonasm, that we can readily understand how one of the two words should have been rejected by translators and copyists. It is remarkable that Gen. renders "again verily," and Bish. "again truly." This can scarcely be accidental: but derived (like the variation in ch. ii, 11), from the Complutensian, which reads ἀμήν. In v. 22, Campbell and Vater join οὐ with ἕως ἑπτάκις, not with λέγω σοί, which is thus thrown into a parenthesis; " I say unto thee, not seven times." I see no occasion for the change.

(III, a and c). v. 23. ἠθέλησε συνᾶραι λόγον " wished to reckon"]. So Auth. in v. 24; ch. xxv, 19. Here " would reckon," Wickliffe, Cov. " would come to account," Cheke. " would take account," (or " accounts of,") Tynd. Cran. Gen. Bish. Auth. " settle accounts with," Campbell, Symonds. Syr. Vulg. also are uniform in vv. 23, 24. Συναίρειν λόγον seems to be a Latinism. See Schleusner.

In v. 24, Cov. renders τάλαντον "pound"! Both here and in ch. xxv, 15 the margin of the later editions of Auth. reckons by *Attic* talents, each of which contains 6000 drachmæ. Now assuming that the Attic drachma is equal to the Roman denarius, which the same margin computes at one eighth of an ounce in v. 28; ch. xx, 2; xxii, 19, we shall make the talent weigh " 750 ounces of silver, which after five shillings the ounce, is £187. 10s." Modern authorities, however, have arrived at somewhat different results respecting the relative values of the Attic and Roman money. It appears from actual experiments made on Attic drachmæ of the times posterior to Alexander the Great, which are preserved in the British Museum, that the average weight of *pure* silver in each is 63 grains, whereas our shilling sterling contains 80.7

grains, after deducting the alloy. Hence (80.7 : 63 :: 12 d. : 9.36 d. nearly) the drachma of the later age was equal to about $9\frac{1}{4}d.$ of English money, and the talent ($9\frac{1}{4}d.$ × 6000) to £231. 5s. (Hussey, Antient Weights and Money, pp. 47, 48). And though the Attic drachma became gradually depreciated so as to be considered equivalent to the Roman denarius (Gronov. De Sestertiis, iii, 2), yet at no time were they precisely equal, inasmuch as the denarius itself was undergoing the same process of slow depreciation, until from $\frac{1}{8}$ of an ounce, or 60 grains, it came to weigh under the early Emperors scarcely 51 grains of unalloyed silver, which are convertible into no more than $7\frac{1}{2}d$ of English money (80.7 : 51 :: 12d. : 7.58 nearly. See also Hussey, pp. 141, 142). Some commentators, with little probability, think that the Hebrew talent is here intended. This talent is reduced by Bp. Cumberland to £353. 11s. 10d. English money.

(III, c). v. 26. προσεκύνει αὐτῷ "prostrated himself before him"]. So Doddridge and Campbell nearly. "Bowed himself to him," Cheke. "besought him," Tynd. Cov. Cran. Gen. Bish. and margin of Auth., after "orabat" of Vulg. But there is a broad distinction between the humble entreaty (παρεκάλει) in v. 29, and the formal prostration to a superior in the present case. Syr. has ܣܓܕ "adored." Perhaps "worshipped him" of Auth. expresses this Oriental custom too strongly, and the term is no doubt liable to be misunderstood. The use of προσκυνεῖν in the New Testament is ably examined by Dr. Pye Smith, "Scripture Testimony to the Messiah," vol. ii, p. 270.

(I). v. 28. εἴ τι "what"]. This is the reading of almost all the manuscripts and critics instead of ὅ τι of the received text. Εἴ τι is far more Classical, but still it is frequently found in the N. T.

(I)°. v. 29. Griesbach and Lachmann omit εἰς τοὺς πόδας αὐτοῦ " at his feet." The words are not contained in Vulg. or in any edition of Erasmus, published in his lifetime; nor are they found in Tynd. Cov. Cran. Cheke, among the English versions. See note on ch. xxv, 2. The authority for the rejection of this clause is slight enough: eleven MSS (B C D L. 1. 28. 71. 124, &c.) mostly of the Egyptian class, the Sahidic, Coptic, and Italic versions. There is no ground, therefore, for believing the words spurious.

Before ἀποδώσω Mill and Scholz expunge πάντα, which in the opinion of the former was interpolated from v. 26. The testimony of the manuscripts which favor this omission is so much stronger than that in the case of εἰς τοὺς πόδας αὐτοῦ, that nothing but Griesbach's extravagant partiality for such documents as D L. 1. 124. could have led him to retain πάντα here. It is exhibited however in Vulg. Syr. (Griesbach and Scholz say *not* in the manuscripts of Syr., but I find no various reading in Schaaf), and though it must be confessed that a large number of the earlier Byzantine MSS (including nearly all Matthæi's) neglect it, I am reluctant to dismiss it entirely from the text.

(II, a). v. 31. διεσάφησαν " told plainly "]. So Gen., or perhaps " gave an exact account of," as in Doddridge. " Told," Eng. Vulg. On the force of διά in composition see note on ch. xiv, 36.

(III, a). v. 33. ἐλεῆσαι ... ἠλέησα " had pity," in both cases]. So Cheke: all Eng. " had compassion .... had pity."

(II, a). v. 34. τοῖς βασανισταῖς " to the jailors "]. So Tynd. Cov. Cran. Gen. Campbell, Newcome and

Boothroyd: but "tormentors," Syr. Vulg. Beza, Castalio, Cheke, Bish. Auth. "aux sergens," Martin, Ostervald. Imprisonment, as Grotius observes, was called in the Roman law-books " cruciatus corporis;" and from all we know of the antient jails, very justly too. Nothing further seems intended in the present instance. In v. 35, Cov. Cran. Bish. Auth. render ποιήσει ὑμῖν by "do also unto you." Tynd. Gen. omit "also," which indeed is quite needless.

(I)°. v. 35. Here again Griesbach and Lachmann expunge the clause τὰ παραπτώματα αὐτῶν, on evidence which I cannot help calling weak and inconsiderable. Mill, *more suo*, defends the received text in his note on the passage, but when he came to write his Prolegomena several years later, he had grown bolder, and pronounced the words a marginal gloss, derived either from ch. vi, 15; or from Mark xi, 26. Vater says, "multo facilius addebantur quam delebantur," which I do not think quite true. The words were doubtless removed in order to relieve a somewhat harsh and redundant sentence; for which purpose Syr. and two MSS of Chrysostom read τὰ παραπτώματα αὐτοῦ, a variation, by the way, not noticed by Griesbach or Scholz. The direct authorities for omitting the clause are Griesbach's old favorites B D L. 1. and three other MSS of less note; the Vulg. Italic, Sahidic, Coptic and Æthiopic versions. But a version need be very literal indeed, to be relied on in a case like the present.

CHAPTER XIX.

(II, b and c). v. 4. ὁ ποιήσας, ἀπ' ἀρχῆς ἄρσεν καὶ θῆλυ ἐποίησεν αὐτοὺς " he who made *them*, made them from the beginning a male and a female"]. So Ostervald " qui créa *l'homme*, au commencement *du monde*, fit un homme et une femme." Campbell also renders "a male and a female," and is followed by the " Layman" of 1840 (see note on ch. xv, 5, 6). The course of our Lord's argument requires that it be distinctly stated, that at the creation God made but *one* woman for one man. Such is the view of Chrysostom, οὐ γὰρ εἶπεν ὅτι ἐποίησεν ἕνα ἄνδρα καὶ μίαν γυναῖκα μόνον, ἀλλ' ὅτι καὶ τοῦτο ἐκέλευσεν, ὥστε τὸν ἕνα τῇ μιᾷ συνάπτεσθαι. So too Theophylact, ἐξ ἀρχῆς ἕνα συνέζευξεν ὁ Θεὸς μιᾷ. Thus correct Mark x, 6. All Eng. lose the force of Christ's reasoning in this passage, as if they thought with Grotius and Rosenmüller, that v. 4 is nothing but a general introduction to vv. 5, 6, being prefixed to them merely "ad contexendam orationem." Accordingly in Tynd. Cov. Cran. Cheke, Gen. we find " made them man and woman;" in Bish. Auth. " made them male and female." The Latin versions of course decide nothing where the article is concerned; neither can Syr.; for though both nouns are in the definite state, as it has been called, yet few Orientalists of the present day will lay any stress on that circumstance, or think that the definite or emphatic termination in Syriac had any other end, than that of softening and facilitating the pronunciation of the word to which it is affixed. (See Pfannkuche on the Language of Palestine in the Age of Christ, § 2).

I have also, though not without some hesitation,

adopted the punctuation of Homberg and Macknight (Gen. Pref. to Epistles, sect. iii, note), who join ἀπ' ἀρχῆς with ἐποίησεν, and not with ὁ ποιήσας. Here again the antient versions afford us no light, and all Eng. are against me, except Cheke ("the Maker at the beginning made them" &c). Yet this arrangement appears most suitable to Mark x, 6; it enables us to render ἀπ'ἀρχῆς uniformly here and in v. 8; and it is the construction adopted by Chrysostom, ὁ γὰρ Θεὸς ἐξ ἀρχῆς ἄρσεν καὶ θῆλυ ἐποίησεν αὐτούς. This absolute use of ὁ ποιήσας, for "the Creator," is illustrated by Loesner from Philo, de Opif. mundi, p. 7, ὃ καὶ ἡμέραν ὁ ποιήσας ἐκάλεσε.

(II, b and III, c). v. 5. οἱ δύο "the two"]. "They two," Cov. (but not in v. 6), Cheke, and the Rhemish version. All other Eng. and even Wickliffe have "they twain." Thus correct ch. xxi, 31; xxvii, 21; 51, "twain."

In v. 7 also τί οὖν Μωσῆς . . . Cheke and the Rhemish translators alone say correctly "why then did Moses"... Tynd. omits "then," and the rest misplace it: "why did Moses then," Cov. Cran. Bish. Auth. The rendering of Gen. is even worse; "why did then Moses..."

(II, a). v. 8. πρὸς σκληροκαρδίαν ὑμῶν "against your obstinacy"]. i. e. to meet it, Green, Gram. N. T. p. 303. "Because of the hardness of your hearts," Eng. "for your hearthardness," Cheke. Grotius and Rosenmüller labour to shew that πρὸς is here used like the Hebrew עַל for "propter." Yet is remarkable that Syr. does not render πρὸς by ܠ "on account of," but by ܠܘܩܒܠ "against," which is unquestionably more literal; "ad duritiam cordis vestri," Vulg. With regard to σκληροκαρδία, it is only necessary to refer the reader to Campbell's Prelim. Diss. IV, 22 for a full justification of the change suggested. "Pervicacia," Castalio; μοχθηρία, Theophylact. Syr. agrees with Vulg. and Eng. in rendering " hardness of heart;" but it is only reasonable to expect that this version should retain the Hebrew idiom. Thus correct Mark x, 5.

(III, a). v. 9. λέγω δὲ ὑμῖν " but I say unto you"]. So Cov. Cheke, after Syr. Vulg. Δὲ is omitted by Cran. Bish. In Tynd. Gen. we read " I say therefore," in Auth. " and I say." Yet beyond a doubt the same pointed opposition is intended between the law of Moses and that of Christ, as in ch. v, 32, where Auth. has " but I say."

(III, c). v. 12. ὑπὸ τῶν ἀνθρώπων " by men"]. So the Rhemish version. All Eng. (even Cheke) have " of men," which is equivocal in this place. The Rhemish translators alone have " there are" (εἰσιν) throughout the verse. Wickliffe, Cov. and Cheke render " there be," three times. Tynd. Cran. (Gen.) Bish. Auth. " there are" twice, followed by " there be." So closely in some matters did the later translators copy those that went before them.

(III, a). v. 13. ἐπιθῇ " lay"]. So Cov. Auth. in v. 15, but " put" here. Tynd. Cran. Gen. Bish. have " put," and Cheke " lay," in both places. Παιδία is rendered " young children" by all Eng. except Auth., and by Auth. in Mark x, 13. Yet Gen. translates " little children" in v. 14, as Auth. does here. Cheke does not represent the diminutive here, though he had done so in ch. ii. Bish. alone is consistent in both verses.

(II, b). v. 14. τὰ παιδία " the young children"]. So Bish. a case of renewed mention. All Eng. except Auth. have the article (" these children," Cheke), and even Auth. in Mark x, 14. Thus in v. 17, εἰς τὴν ζωὴν refers us back to ζωὴν in v. 16. Cheke says " y (the?) life," and Campbell " that life ;" but in this case the force of the article can scarcely be preserved in English.

(III, c). *ibid.* τῶν γὰρ τοιούτων ἐστὶν ἡ βασίλεια τῶν οὐρανῶν " for to such belongeth the kingdom of heaven"]. So Tynd. 1. Cov. Bish. Green, Gram. N. T. p. 267. This rendering is much clearer than " of such is," of Tynd. 2. Cran. Gen. Auth. or " such one's is" of Cheke.

(I)°. v. 17. See Introduction, p. 16. Griesbach and Lachmann here admit into the text an important variation, which, both from its extent and obvious bearing, cannot have originated in accidental causes. Instead of τί με λέγεις ἀγαθόν ; οὐδεὶς ἀγαθός, εἰ μὴ εἷς, ὁ Θεός, " why callest thou me good ? *there is* none good but one, *that is* God :" they read, τί με ἐρωτᾷς περὶ τοῦ ἀγαθοῦ ; εἷς ἐστιν ὁ ἀγαθός, " why askest thou me concerning what is good ? He who is good is One." I fear it is but too evident that this text was mangled by some over-zealous scribe, who was displeased with the doctrine of the Son's inferiority which seemed to be implied in it; and who did not perceive that His subordination to the Father in the economy of grace, is perfectly consistent with His equality in respect to the Divine Nature and Essence.* The received text is found in Mark x, 18 ; Luke xviii, 19, with no variety in the manuscripts worthy of notice ; and even in this place Griesbach's reading is contained only in *five* copies (B D L. 1. 22.), and partially in a sixth (Matthæi's x). Now all these documents (except

---

* " Equal to the Father, as touching his Godhead : and inferior to the Father, as touching his Manhood ;" is the accurate and Scriptural statement of the Athanasian Creed.

perhaps one) being Alexandrine, and B alone being of first-rate importance, every rule of sober criticism calls for the rejection of Griesbach's correction, especially since it is clear in what sources of mistaken feeling it took its rise. It is supported, however, by the Italic, Vulg. and the Coptic versions (with the slight addition of *Deus*), and in part by the Sahidic, Æthiopic, and one or two of less weight. Syr. agrees with the textus receptus, but the language of Origen (Tom. iii, p. 664) may shew at how early a period Griesbach's variation had become current: ὁ μὲν οὖν Ματθαῖος ὡς περὶ ἀγαθοῦ ἔργου ἐρωτηθέντος τοῦ σωτῆρος ἐν τῷ τί ἀγαθὸν ποιήσω; ὁ δὲ Μάρκος καὶ Λουκᾶς φασὶ τὸν σωτῆρα εἰρηκέναι, τί με λέγεις ἀγαθόν; οὐδεὶς ἀγαθός, εἰ μὴ εἷς, ὁ Θεός. The process whereby Griesbach and Lachmann persuaded themselves of the genuineness of their new text, is visible enough. The Codices B D, the Italic, Origen and the Vulgate, constitute a clear majority of the authorities admitted by the latter. The former, conceiving that the joint evidence of Codices B L. 1. Origen, the Sahidic and Coptic, is decisive of the testimony of his Egyptian family; while the Codex D, the Italic and Vulg. represent that of the Western recension; infers that their joint influence will more than counterbalance Syr. Chrysostom, and the whole mass of corrupt Byzantine documents of every kind: although numerically they exceed, in the proportion of about ninety to one, the vouchers for both his other classes united. Thus it is only by denying the premises assumed by these critics, that we can avoid subscribing to their perilous conclusions.

In v. 18, Tynd. 2. places the seventh before the sixth commandment, I suppose through oversight, for I know of no various reading. In the parallel passage, Rom. xiii, 9, Pr. Scholefield, in his notes on

Middleton, proposes to express τὸ γάρ "for the commandment." It does not appear advisable to render τό here.

(III, c). v. 21. τὰ ὑπάρχοντα "*thy* substance"]. So Bish. Syr. "quæ habes," Vulg. "that thou hast," Tyn. Cov. Cheke, Gen. Auth. "(all) that thou hast," Cran. from some Italic manuscript (see Introd. p. 88), for Wickliffe reads "all," as also, according to Scholz, does the Sahidic version. Πτωχοῖς should *strictly* be rendered "to poor persons." All Eng. have "to the poor." Indeed Lachmann, after B D and a few editions, reads τοῖς. See note on ch. ix, 13.

(II, b). v. 22. τὸν λόγον "the saying"]. See note on ch. xv, 12. "That saying," Eng. Syr. Here Lachmann reads τοῦτον on the sole authority of the Codex B: for Syr. he cares nothing (Introd. p. 25).

(III, c). v. 23. δυσκόλως "with difficulty"]. So Tynd. 1. "shall hardly enter," Cheke, Bish. Auth. which is very ambiguous: "it shall be ("it is," Tynd. 2.) hard for a rich man to enter," Tynd. 2. Cov. Cran. Gen.

(I). v. 24. Instead of διελθεῖν "to go through," Wetstein, Griesbach, Vater, and Scholz, adopt εἰσελθεῖν "to enter," which is the more difficult reading, and may have been expunged on account of εἰσελθεῖν immediately following (see note on ch. ii, 11).* Campbell says that the sense suggested by εἰσελθεῖν is "odd," and that "should the external evidence appear balanced on both sides, the common reading is preferable, as yielding a better sense." I believe that Griesbach's canon "durior lectio præferatur ei,

---

* Bp. Jebb, however, says that "to depart from verbal repetition, is not the common error of copyists" (Sacred Liter. p. 311). Not of copyists, perhaps; but of critical correctors, a much more meddling and curious race.

quâ positâ, oratio suaviter leniterque fluat" (Proleg. N. T. p. lxv), is grounded on a juster estimate of contending probabilities. In the present case, however, there can scarcely be said to be an equipoise in the external evidence. Not to insist on Syr. and some other versions (which cannot well be trusted in so minute a question), εἰσελθεῖν is read by Chrysostom, and by so many of the most antient manuscripts of both families (including C E F H K L M Z), that it may rightfully claim a place in the text.

(III, a). v. 26. ἐμβλέψας "looking on them"]. So Cheke, and even Auth. in the parallel place, Mark x, 27 : whether *steadfastly*, as Doddridge thinks, or with gracious consolation, ἡμέρῳ ὄμματι καὶ πρᾴῳ φρίττουσαν αὐτῶν τὴν διάνοιαν παραμυθησάμενος, as Chrysostom beautifully expresses it. Here all Eng. have "beheld." Thus correct Mark x, 21. In Luke xx, 17; xxii, 61, the feeling denoted by ἐμβλέψας is widely different, and more in accordance with the common use of the word in Classical authors : e. g. Plato, Charmides (I, i, 307, ed. Bekker), ἐνέβλεψέ τέ μοι τοῖς ὀφθαλμοῖς ἀμήχανόν τι, so that, in confusion, εἶδόν τε τὰ ἐντὸς τοῦ ἱματίου καὶ ἐφλεγόμην, καὶ οὐκέτ' ἐν ἐμαυτοῦ ἦν.

In this verse all Eng., even Cheke and Auth. in the edition of 1611, have "unpossible." We have noticed similar variations in our modern Bibles from the first edition of Auth. in ch. ix, 34 ; xii, 23 ; xiii, 46 ; xvi, 16. For "more" the Bible of 1611 often has "mo ;" e. g. ch. xxi, 36 ; xxii, 46, &c.

In v. 27, Tynd. 2. Gen. omit ἄρα altogether. Tynd. 1. Cov. Cran. Bish. Auth. say "what shall we have therefore?" Rather render "what then shall we have"? Cheke puts "then" last.

(II, c)°. v. 28. ἐν τῇ παλιγγενεσίᾳ " in the regeneration"]. It has been seriously doubted whether these words should be joined with καθίσεσθε, or with the clause which immediately precedes them: and the early editors of the Greek Testament are pretty equally divided between the two opinions. The determination of this question (I cannot pretend to call it a very difficult one) is dependent on the sense we assign to παλιγγενεσία. If we punctuate and translate thus, "ye which have followed me in the regeneration," the "regeneration" can bear no other meaning than that given to it here by Calvin; the then commencing *reformation* of the world, at Christ's first coming: it is something past or present (ἀκολουθήσαντες), or at all events not entirely future. Now I believe it is impossible to produce a single example of this signification of the word; at least I can mention no Commentator who has succeeded in doing so, notwithstanding all the pains that have been bestowed on the passage. Moreover, regeneration in its *moral* sense is always mentioned in the New Testament in close connection with the out-pouring of the Holy Spirit (see John iii, 5; Tit. iii, 5; 1 Pet. i, 22, 23); but it is far from certain that He was at this period known to the Apostles even by name. Much more probable is the method of Bengel, Wetstein, Kypke, and nearly all the best critics, who unite ἐν τῇ παλιγγενεσίᾳ with καθίσεσθε, and regard ὅταν καθίσῃ .... δόξης αὐτοῦ, as a parenthetic explanation of παλιγγενεσίᾳ. This interpretation is confirmed by Syr. which translates ܒܥܠܡܐ ܚܕܬܐ "in the new age," and by Tynd. 1. which renders "in the second generation." The construction of Vulg. Cheke, and other Eng. depends on the punctuation, which, except perhaps in Tynd. 2. Auth., is adverse to my view (Cov. has "new birth"). Theophylact expounds παλιγγενεσία by ἀνάστασις, and

Theophanes adds ὡς αὖθις ἀναγεννῶσαν ἡμᾶς, καὶ εἰς τὸ ἀρχαῖον μετάγουσαν (see Suicer, Thes. Eccles. Tom. ii, p. 551): and such a use of παλιγγενεσία has been amply vindicated by citations from the Classics. Others, however, refer it not so much to the actual resurrection, as to that state of consummate bliss which shall follow it.* But it is evident that both these interpretations are mere modifications of the same general notion, that by the regeneration we are to understand something distant and heavenly; in fact what St. Mark in the parallel passage (ch. x, 30) expresses by ἐν τῷ αἰῶνι τῷ ἐρχομένῳ: "dans le renouvellement *qui doit arriver*," Ostervald.

(III, a and c). *ibid.* ἐπὶ θρόνου " upon the throne "]. So Auth. in the very next line. All Eng. even Wickliffe, Cheke, and the Rhemish version have " in " here. See note on ch. iv, 6. Of course ἐπὶ with the genitive does not *here* differ in sense from the same preposition with the accusative.

(II, b). v. 30. πολλοὶ δὲ ἔσονται, κ. τ. λ. " but many first shall be last, and last first"]. Πολλοὶ refers to ἔσχατοι as well as to πρῶτοι, otherwise it would be οἱ ἔσχατοι, as in ch. xx, 16. See Middleton *ad loc.* Cheke inserts " many " in both clauses. All Eng. have " the last," though I do not suppose that they read, with the Complutensian, οἱ ἔσχατοι. On the omission of the words in italics, see Introd. p. 63. In the Introd. p. 48 I have spoken of the propriety of joining this verse with ch. xx, 1. Ὁμοία ΓΑΡ... See also ch. xx, 16.

---

* Wetstein tells us that παλιγγενεσία here denotes " *summa felicitas,*" on account of the emphasis in the article τῇ. So little did the first critic of his age know respecting the real nature of the Greek article.

CHAPTER XX.

(III, c). v. 1. ἀνθρώπῳ οἰκοδεσπότῃ " unto an householder"]. So Tynd. Cov. Cheke, Gen. " a man that is an householder," Cran. Bish. Auth. Compare note on ch. xiii, 45. In v. 11; ch. xxiv, 43; Mark xiv, 14; Luke xii, 39, we should reject the inelegant rendering " goodman of the house," which Campbell so properly censures, and make those passages uniform with the present: Cov. does so in v. 11.

In v. 2, the marginal note in the later editions of Auth. has been examined above (on ch. xviii, 24). A denarius was the daily pay of a Roman soldier: "denis in diem assibus animam et corpus æstimari," Tacit. Ann. i, 17. So a drachma is proposed as the wages for a day, Tobit v, 14.

(I)°. v. 6. Griesbach, Vater, and Lachmann omit ἀργοὺς after ἑστῶτας, and Mill thinks it may have crept into the text from v. 3. The grounds for its rejection are but trifling. It is read in all the manuscripts except four (B C D L), Origen, the Italic, Vulg. and Egyptian versions; which might easily have neglected it, as not necessary to the sense. Scholz, of course, retains ἀργοὺς in the text.

(II, a)°. v. 12. ἐποίησαν " have wrought"]. So all Eng. including Cheke, Syr.* Vulg. Beza, Castalio, and the French versions. The interpretation of the margin of Auth. " have continued one hour only,"

---

* Syr. here renders ἐποίησαν by ܥܒܕ: whereas in all the passages where ποιεῖν refers to time (except the doubtful instance of James iv, 13), it uses the substantive verb.

makes ποιεῖν express duration of time, as it undoubtedly does in Acts xv, 33; xviii, 23; xx, 3; 2 Cor. xi, 25; and perhaps also in James iv, 13. But Kypke has assigned solid reasons for retaining the common translation. It is unnatural that ποιεῖν should be used in two senses so widely different, in the same verse: if ἐποίησαν signify "tarried," "continued," we should expect ὧδε to be added (but *this* argument would equally apply to the texts just cited from the Acts): and lastly, it is not the time, but the labor expended on the vineyard which is made by the malcontents the ground of complaint; τοῖς βαστάσασι τὸ βάρος κ. τ. λ. Syr. Eng. Cheke, &c. rightly join τὸν καύσωνα with τῆς ἡμέρας. See James 1, 11; LXX. Gen. xxxi, 40, συγκαιόμενος τῷ καύσωνι, in the Alexandrine text; the Vatican reads τῷ καύματι.

(III, c). v. 14. τὸ σὸν "thine own"]. So Cheke. "that which is thy duty," Tynd. Gen. "that thine is," Cov. Cran. Bish. Auth. very awkwardly. Translate θέλω δὲ "for I will." This meaning of δὲ is recognised by Auth. in Mark xvi, 8; Luke xii, 2; 1 Thess. ii, 16. Though it seems necessary to the connection here, yet all Eng. omit it. For θέλω see note on ch. xi, 27.

(III, a). v. 18. παραδοθήσεται "shall be delivered"]. So Auth. in v. 19, and Cov. Cheke here. All other Eng. have "betrayed." The reader cannot fail to observe that Cov. had so little influence on succeeding translators, that they often neglected to adopt his most evident improvements on Tynd. (See Introd. p. 86). Campbell's just distinction between παραδιδόναι "to deliver up," and προδιδόναι "to betray," (Prelim. Diss. III, 23), cannot at all times be expressed in English; but there is the additional motive of uniformity for not overlooking it in the present case.

(II, a). v. 21. εἰπὲ "command"]. So Cheke, Castalio ("jube"), Martin, Ostervald ("ordonne"), which is approved by Vater and Pr. Scholefield. St. Mark (ch. x, 37) has δός, and Kypke supports this view by several Classical quotations: e. g. Xen. Cyroped. vii [p. 107, ed. Stephan.], καὶ εἶπεν αὐτοῖς ἀπιέναι ἐκ τοῦ στρατεύματος τάχιστα. Cov. translates εἰπὲ by "let," the other Eng. by "grant." Syr. Vulg. Beza ("dic") are quite indeterminate.

(I). *ibid.* To εὐωνύμων Griesbach, Vater, Scholz, and Lachmann, after a great majority of the chief manuscripts of both families, add σου: "thy left," as it is in Tynd. 1. Cov. Gen. "The left," Vulg. Tynd. 2. Cran. Bish. Auth. Syr. reads σου, if that is of any weight. See note on ch. xiv, 22.

(1)°. v. 22. Griesbach and Lachmann remove from the text καὶ τὸ βάπτισμα, ὃ ἐγὼ βαπτίζομαι, βαπτισθῆναι, and the corresponding clause in the next verse. Their meagre array of witnesses is of the usual character: six decidedly Egyptian manuscripts in v. 22 (B D L Z. 1. 22. see note on ch. xix, 17), Origen and Epiphanius among the Greeks; the Sahidic, Coptic, Æthiopic, Italic, and Vulg. with their faithful attendants, the Latin Fathers. But even if we grant that the Latin and other versions are more trustworthy in their omissions than in their additions to the text; or concede to Origen the *possibility* that the disputed words properly belong only to St. Mark (ch. x, 38, 39); still it is extravagant to claim for translations so high authority, that they should be held competent to overthrow the positive testimony of manuscripts of the original. The various sources of error to which the versions are *peculiarly* exposed, are admirably summed up by Bp. Horsley, in the Preface to his Translation of Hosea, and ought to be ever present to the mind of the reviser of the textus receptus. How far Bp. Horsley has abided by his own principles in this matter (at least in his posthumous works), I am not prepared to decide. In v. 23, seven other cursive manuscripts, besides those enumerated above, favor the omission of the clause; two of them (Colbert. 33, and Ephes. Lambeth 71) being of some little consequence. But even there the evidence is much too weak to deserve more particular notice. It should be added that for καί, at the beginning of each of the disputed passages, Scholz, on very sufficient authority, reads ἤ.

(II, b). v. 23. οὐκ ἔστιν ἐμὸν δοῦναι, ἀλλ' οἷς ἡτοίμασται ..." is not mine to give, but to those for whom it is prepared"...]. So Tynd. Cov. Bish. merely changing "those," into "them;" "but it shall chance unto them that it is prepared for"... Cran. But Cheke more correctly, "but unto them to whom it is prepared for"... Gen. Auth. translate "but it shall be given to them for whom it is prepared;" the words "*it shall be given to them,*" being printed in italics in the first edition of Auth. though they are not thus distinguished in the parallel text Mark x, 40; so little careful of consistency were our translators in the use of italics (see Introd. p. 62). Modern critics with a rare unanimity, are agreed in thinking that Auth. has wrongly interpolated the clause "it shall be given to them," in this verse. Doddridge, Wynne, Campbell, Macknight, Newcome, Boothroyd, the "Layman" of 1840, and the translator of the "Holy Bible" of 1841, all assent to the rendering I have derived from Tynd. Cov. Cheke, Bish. Dean Turton (Text of English Bible Considered, p. 71, 2nd ed.), Pr. Scholefield, and Mr. Green (Gram. N. T. p. 308) have fully vindicated this interpretation, which had previously been sanctioned by Castalio and Grotius. It goes upon the assumption that ἀλλὰ "but" is here used for εἰ μὴ "except," "unless:" and that these particles were sometimes interchanged is evident. Not only is εἰ μὴ used where we should expect ἀλλὰ in Matth. xii, 4; Luke iv, 26; 27; Rom. xiv, 14; Gal. i, 7; but (what is more to the purpose) the converse takes place in 2 Cor. ii, 5; Mark ix, 8, compared with Matth. xvii, 8; Herod. i, 193 (cited by Raphel), χρέωνται δὲ οὐδὲν ἐλαίῳ, ἀλλ' ἐκ τῶν σησάμων ποιεῦντες. Somewhat similar is the μαρτυρία in Demosth. c. Midiam (p. 554, Reiske), μηδένα ἕτερον εἶναι τὸν Νικοδήμου φονέα, ἀλλ' Ἀρίσταρχον. Other instances may be found in Kypke, of which the most apposite is Joseph. Antiq. xix, 2, 2, τούς τε θεοὺς οὐκ ἄλλοις συμμαχεῖν, ἀλλὰ τοῖς μετὰ ἀρετῆς καὶ τοῦ καλοῦ τοὺς ἀγῶνας ποιουμένοις. If these examples of the employment of ἀλλὰ for εἰ μὴ be deemed sufficient, the passage before us is cleared of all difficulty. There will then be no need of the ellipsis devised by Beza "sed *dabitur* quibus paratum est," which was approved by Bois, and adopted by Gen. Auth. Martin, and Ostervald (*cela* ne *sera donné* qu' *à ceux* à qui mon Père l'a destiné"). Nor will there be any room for the theological objection, that our Lord seems here to disclaim the power of rewarding his people; an objection which drove Augustin and Ambrose to strange modes of evasion (see Poli Synopsis). Yet it is certainly not in favor of the solution I am contending for, that it was not perceived by Chrysostom (οὐκ ἔστιν ἐμόν, ἀλλ' ΕΚΕΙΝΩΝ, οἷς ἡτοίμασται), or Theophylact (τοῦτο εἶπεν ὁ Κύριος πρὸς τὴν ἐκείνων ὑπόνοιαν· οὐκ ἔστιν ἐμὸν δοῦναι ΚΑΤΑ ΧΑΡΙΝ τὸν στέφανον, ἀλλ' ᾧ ἡτοίμασται, τουτέστι τῷ δραμόντι καὶ νικήσαντι ... ἄλλων γὰρ τῶν κοπιασάντων ἐστι, καὶ ἐκείνοις ἡτοίμασται).

This much, however, we may safely say, that it is the least of the two difficulties between which we have to choose. Syr. Vulg. ("sed quibus paratum est,") contain no ellipsis, but are too literal to determine any thing else. In Mark x, 40 Bish. changes sides, in order to copy Beza and Gen. In ch. xix, 11, too, ἀλλά is used in its ordinary signification.

(II, a). v. 24. περὶ "with respect to"]. So Syr. (ܢܠ),* Vulg. "de;" "(were grieved) with," Cheke, "(disdained) at," Eng. "against," Auth. Although Schleusner assigns *adversus, contra*, as the first meaning of περὶ with a genitive, none of the examples he alleges (ch. xv, 7; John vi, 41; Acts xxv, 16, &c.) bear him out in this forced interpretation. In Mark x, 41 Auth. has "with."

(II, a). v. 25. οἱ μέγαλοι κατεξουσιάζουσιν αὐτῶν "the great ones exercise harsh authority over them"]. So Bp. Jebb (Sacr. Liter. p. 223), who has illustrated the whole of this address of our Lord (vv. 25—28) in his happiest manner. Κατακυριεύουσιν he had just before rendered "lord it over." The intensive force of κατά in composition is too familiar to require much defence. For κατακυριεύειν see 1 Pet. v, 3; Psalm x, 10, ἐν τῷ αὐτὸν κατακυριεῦσαι τῶν πενήτων (LXX, *not* Hebrew). Schleusner's adverse instances merely shew, that in translating from a language which admits not of such refinements, the LXX sometimes employed κατακυριεύειν where the simple verb would have sufficed. Cheke has " overmaster them . . . over-rule them." Syr. Vulg. and all Eng.† are nearly

---

* Schaaf renders this word by " contra:" but why should we not prefer " de," " propter ?"

† The margin of Cov. says, " some read, the greatest deal with violence."

as Auth. "exercise dominion . . . exercise authority." See Mark x, 42.

(I). v. 26. Δέ "but," is cancelled after οὕτως by all the modern editors, on the authority of a vast number of good manuscripts; and of the Sahidic, Italic, Vulg. (but not, as Griesbach and Scholz state, of the Syr.) versions. "The insertion of δέ," Bp. Jebb observes, "would serve but to forestall and weaken the succeeding adversative particle ἀλλά." Of Eng. δέ is expressed by Auth. alone. Though the particle is omitted in several of the early editions of the Greek Testament, I conceive that it was merely casually overlooked by the first English translators; *not* that they did not find it in their printed copies. We must not comply with Bp. Jebb in substituting ἔσται for ἔστω here, and in v. 27. The antient versions in such a case prove next to nothing.

(III, c). *ibid.* γενέσθαι "become"]. All Eng. "be." See note on ch. xii, 45. "Εἶναι," Bp. Jebb ingeniously refines, "is an advance upon γενέσθαι: those of a more limited ambition, wish to *become* great; thereby admitting that they *are* and *have been* little: those, on the contrary, whose ambition is unbounded, wish *to be* first, or chief; not making any admission whatever of previous mediocrity." (Sacr. Liter. p. 311; see above p. 152 note.)

On better grounds this eminent prelate adopts Campbell's version of διάκονος "servant" ("waiter on," Cheke, "minister," Eng.), and in v. 27 of δοῦλος "slave" ("servant," Eng. Cheke), that an orderly progression may be visible in every term of each parallel couplet: μέγας γενέσθαι—εἶναι πρῶτος: ἔστω διάκονος —ἔστω δοῦλος. Refer also to ch. xxii, 13, where for διακόνοις Tynd. Cran. Gen. Bish. have "ministers," and Cheke "waiters," not "servants," as in Cov. Auth.

to distinguish them from δοῦλοι in vv. 3, 4, &c. I should state, however, that Dr. Symonds objects to the employment of the word "minister," under any circumstances, lest it should be supposed that a person in Holy Orders is meant! Is not this the very dotage of criticism?

(III, a and b). v. 31. ἐπετίμησεν αὐτοῖς ἵνα... "charged them that"...]. So Auth. in Mark x, 48. In this place Cov. Cheke have "rebuked them that," but all other Eng. "rebuked them because." This obsolete use of "because," for "that," did not escape the keen observation of Bp. Lowth (Eng. Gram. p. 117). Auth. translates ἐπιτιμᾶν "charged," also in ch. xii, 16; Mark viii, 30; "straitly charged," in Mark iii, 12; Luke ix, 21. In the parallel text Luke xviii, 39, Auth. stands as Cov. here.

(II, a). v. 32. ποιήσω "that I should do"] subjunctive aorist. So Tynd. 2. Cheke, Gen. "Shall do," other Eng.

In v. 34, all Eng. render ἀνέβλεψαν "received sight," as in ch. xi, 5. So Syr. Vulg. Castalio, Ostervald. But Beza (who is followed by Martin) has "receperunt," which is approved by Parkhurst and Schleusner. I really do not see why the force of ἀνά should be dropped in this passage and others, because it happens to be inadmissible in the solitary instance of John ix.

CHAPTER XXI.

(II, a)°. v. 1. πρὸς τὸ ὄρος "unto the mount"]. So all Eng. here except Cheke ("beside"). But in the parallel texts Mark xi, 1; Luke xix, 29, all Eng. have "besides," or "at," except Cov. which, after Vulg. "ad," correctly renders "unto" in both places. Syr. translates ܠܘܬ ("ad latus") in Matthew and Luke, but ܠܘܬ ("apud") in Mark. Campbell also ("near"), and Doddridge ("at") fall into the same error. It appears, therefore, that Vulg. Cov. alone saw the distinction between the sense of πρὸς with a dative "at," and with an accusative "unto."

(III, c). v. 3. ὁ Κύριος "the Master"]. So Campbell; "your master," Tynd. 1. "the Lord," other Eng. See note on ch. viii, 6. I think that this is one of the cases, where the appellation "Lord" is clearly improper.

(I). *ibid.* The future ἀποστελεῖ of the received text is mainly supported by B D, Origen, and the Latin versions. A much greater number of valuable manuscripts have the present ἀποστέλλει, a reading received as genuine by Mill, Griesbach, Vater, and Scholz. It is far more easy to acount for the future being substituted for the present in this passage, than for the opposite change. Chrysostom and Theophylact favor the present, and so perhaps does Syr. (ܡܫܕܪ), though Scholz thinks otherwise.* The same altera-

---

* The rendering of Syr. is the same in both texts, Matth. xxi, 3, and Mark xi, 3. In the former instance Scholz cites its evidence in favor of the future, in the latter of the present! But I am

tion is called for, on even higher authority (including both Codices A and B), in Mark xi, 3; where Lachmann also assents to it. The rendering of Auth. "will send" may very well remain. See Introd. p. 45.

(II, a). v. 4. τοῦτο δὲ ὅλον γέγονεν "now all this was done"]. So δέ is rendered by Auth. in ch. i, 18: "but all this was done," Cov. here, and Auth. in ch. xxvi, 56. All other Eng. (like Auth.) in this place neglect the useful particle δέ. In v. 5, the earlier versions translate ὑποζυγίου "an ass used to the yoke" ("subjugalis," Vulg. "an yoked ass," Cheke). But Syr. Auth. rightly say "an ass," simply. Respecting this habit of straining the etymology of words, see Introd. p. 33.

(I). v. 7. We have now come to the first of those texts enumerated in Introd. p. 7, in which Auth. adopts the reading of Beza, in preference to that of Stephens's third edition. Instead of ἐπεκάθισαν "they set him," which we find in Vulg. Beza, Castalio, Tynd. Cov. Cran. Cheke, Gen. Auth., we ought to receive from the Complutensian, one of the editions of Erasmus, and Stephens ἐπεκάθισεν "he sat," the reading of Syr. and Bish., and approved by Bengel, Wetstein, Griesbach, Scholz and Lachmann. I cannot think with Mill and Vater that the external evidence is at all evenly balanced. In favor of the singular form we can produce five of the oldest uncial manuscripts, not only Alexandrine (B C), but Byzantine (Birch's Vat. 354, or S; and Matthæi's H and V, a fine Moscow copy of the eighth century); besides a very great number of the best cursive documents, together with

---

almost tired of exposing this editor's slovenly inaccuracies. In v. 7, Scholz asserts that the Codex Z reads ἐπεκάθισεν. Buttmann informs us that nothing remains of that word in Codex Z, but the first two letters.

Origen, both Syriac, the Sahidic, Æthiopic, and some Italic versions. The Codex D has ἐκάθητο. The Codex Cyprius of the ninth century (K), Marini's venerable Vatican fragment (Γ), and many cursive manuscripts, have ἐκάθισεν, and so far strengthen Stephens's reading. The plural ἐπεκάθισαν rests chiefly on Vulg. and a flood of late copies of so little note, that the authenticity of its rival is placed almost beyond dispute. Ἐπικαθίζειν occurs no where else in the New Testament. It is used by the LXX, not only in the transitive sense here assigned to it by Auth. e. g. 1 Kings i, 44 (ἐπεκάθισαν וַיַּרְכִּבוּ), but also intransitively, as in 2 Sam. xiii, 29. From the parallel passages of the Gospels, nothing certain can be concluded. Mark xi, 7; John xii, 14 have ἐκάθισεν: Luke xix, 35 ἐπεβίβασαν. Where the internal marks are so equivocal, external testimonies alone must decide.

(III, c). *ibid.* ἐπάνω αὐτῶν "upon them"]. "Thereon," Eng. Οὐ τῶν δύο ὑποζυγίων, ἀλλὰ τῶν ἱματίων, says Theophylact, reasonably enough, for ἱμάτια is the nearest antecedent. Thus Beza and Castalio understand the passage (see however Krebs *ad loc.*). Vulg. ("desuper") is doubtful, and Syr. reads αὐτοῦ. Cheke renders "set him on her," αὐτῆς, a reading supported only by one Italic manuscript, and the first edition of Erasmus (1516). It follows therefore that Cheke used *this* edition of the Greek Testament for the purposes of his translation.

In like manner in v. 43, it would be clearer to translate αὐτῆς "of it," viz. the kingdom of God, with Tynd. Cov. Gen. in preference to "thereof," of Cran. Cheke, Bish. Auth.

Dr. Symonds remarks that the nominative "they" before "set" in Auth. v. 7 is quite superfluous.

Auth. seems to have derived it from Bish. "he sat," for no other Eng. have it. But to the sense of Bish. it was absolutely necessary. He also notices the pleonastic " *them* " after " persecute " in ch. xxiii, 34. In this last place Auth. resembles Cov. Cran. Cheke, Bish., for Wickliffe, Tynd. Gen. and the Rhemish version correctly omit the pronoun. Had Dr. Symonds limited himself to the same kind of useful criticism in other cases, I should not have had to speak of him so often in terms of disapprobation. It is never agreeable to be compelled to comment unfavorably on men who have gone before us in the same field of labor, and whose pains and difficulties we can so well estimate, by those which beset ourselves. "To seek rather what to commend than what to censure, a pleasing duty in all instances, becomes in scholarship almost a sacred one. For what is the most successful scholarship? It is little more than to climb on a predecessor's shoulders, and thereby gain a little wider scope of vision: too happy if we can become a temporary step for a successor of still wider eye." These are noble sentiments, Mr. Mitchell: but which of us is so fortunate as at all times to realise them?

(III, c). v. 9. ἐν τοῖς ὑψίστοις "in the highest *heavens*"]. So Gen. and the French versions ("dans les *lieux* très-hauts"), after Beza ("in *cœlis* altissimis"), as also Campbell. "In the height," Cov. "in the highest," Tynd. Cran. Cheke, Bish. Auth. which is too indefinite. Thus change Mark xi, 10; Luke ii, 14; xix, 38. "In altissimis" Vulg. Syr. has ܒܡܪܘܡܐ, which is identical with the Hebrew בַּמְרוֹמִים, translated by the LXX ἐν ὑψίστοις in Job xvi, 20; Psalm cxlviii, 1 (οὐρανοῖς answers to it in the preceding line of the couplet). Mr. Grinfield compares Sirac. xliii, 9. See note on Ephes. i, 3.

(II, b). v. 12. τὰς περιστερὰς "the doves"] used in the temple-worship. Middleton. Thus correct Mark xi, 15. Mr. Green (Gram. N. T. p. 154) remarks that St. John, writing long after the fall of Jerusalem, did not presume upon that familiarity with the Mosaic ritual on the part of his readers, which the article implies. The truth is, that the article could scarcely have been used in John ii, 14, without completely changing the form of the sentence.

·(II, a). v. 16. κατηρτίσω "thou hast ordained"]. So Tynd. Cov. Cran. Bish. "establishest," Cheke, and similarly Syr. (ܐܬܩܢܬ), "condis," Castalio. I prefer this rendering to "perfecisti" of Vulg. Beza, "made perfect" of Gen. and "perfected" of Auth., both because it is more suitable to the context, and as it is actually the rendering given by Auth. to יִסַּדְתָּ in Psalm viii, 2, whence our Lord cites these words. Compare Rom. ix, 22; Hebr. x, 5.

To the end of v. 17 Wickliffe adds "and taught them of the kingdom of God." This spurious gloss is derived from some manuscript of the Vulg. (see Introd. p. 76), or very possibly from the Anglo-Saxon version, to which I have cause for suspecting his obligations. See note on ch. xvi, 20.

In v. 19, the marginal note of the later editions of Auth. συκῆν μίαν "one fig tree," is taken from the scrupulously literal Bish. See Introd. p. 95.

(III, a). vv. 19, 20. παραχρῆμα "immediately"]. So Cov. in v. 19: "anon," Tynd. Cran. Bish. Gen. "by and by," Cheke, "presently," Auth. which is a little ambiguous, and a uniform rendering is desirable in v. 20, where all Eng. have "soon."

(III, a). v. 24. λόγον "question"]. So Auth. in Mark xi, 29; and Tynd. Gen. Bish. here. "Word," Cov. "thing," Cran. Cheke, Auth., the margin of

Auth. in Mark xi, 29, and the text in Luke xx, 3. It is needless to give an unusual or Hellenistic sense to λόγος in the present instance.

Εἴπητε is translated "assoil" by Tynd. Gen. This looks like one of Wickliffe's words, but *he* has "tell," like Auth. and all the rest. "Assoil" in Chaucer signifies "to answer". Thus "Assoileth me this question, I pray," Canterbury Tales, l. 9528 (Merchant's Tale).

(II, b). v. 27. ἔφη αὐτοῖς καὶ αὐτὸς "he likewise said unto them"]. So Tynd. 1. Vulg. "and he likewise" ... Tynd. 2. "then said he" ... Cov. "and he said" ... Cran. Gen. Bish. Auth., which would require καὶ at the beginning of the clause. "Nor I, saith he unto them," ... Cheke, as usual.

(I). v. 30. Instead of δευτέρῳ "second," ἑτέρῳ "other" is read by Mill, Griesbach, Vater, and Scholz. Mill regards δευτέρῳ as a marginal gloss suggested by πρώτῳ in v. 28. The change is sanctioned by five uncial (D E F H K) and very many cursive manuscripts of both families, by Syr. Vulg. the Italic, Æthiopic, and other versions, and (I must add) by considerations of internal probability. The authorities against it, however, are pretty numerous, and include the great Alexandrine documents B Z, and Chrysostom. Yet B (as we saw in v. 3) is rather prone to fall in with plausible grammatical corrections. See note on ch. xv, 6.

In v. 33, all the modern editors reject τις "a certain" after ἄνθρωπος, which *may* be interpolated from Luke xx, 9. It is found, however, in Syr. Chrysostom, and nearly all the manuscripts of the Byzantine family except S V, and six lesser ones of Matthæi. Of the other class it is *omitted* in B C D K L, about twenty cursive manuscripts, Vulg., the Coptic and some Italic versions. But I do not deem this evidence sufficient to prove its spuriousness.

(II, a). v. 33. ἀπεδήμησεν "went abroad"]. So Campbell: "journeyed forth," Cheke. All Eng. render "went into a strange country," except Auth. which has "a far country." In ch. xxv, 15, Auth. has "took his journey." But ἀποδημεῖν does not in itself convey any notion of distance. Demosth. adv. Nausimach. (p. 988, Reiske), οὐδ' ὅλως ἐξέπλευσεν ἐκεῖνος, οὐδ' ἀπεδήμησεν ἐκεῖσε, viz. from Athens to the Bosphorus. Ælian, Var. Hist. xiii, 14, τὸ δὲ ἀγώγιμον τοῦτο ἐξ Ἰωνίας, ἡνίκα ἀπεδήμησεν, ἤγαγεν, referring to the travels of Lycurgus, which, to one living in Ælian's age, would not be thought very extensive. Besides, the whole scope of the parable seems to imply, that the owner of the vineyard was not far distant. Syr. ܐܙܠ simply, as Vulg. Beza, Castalio, "peregre profectus est." Thus alter ch. xxv, 14 (v. 15 is correct); Mark xii, 1; xiii, 34; Luke xx, 9. When remote distance is intended St. Luke (ch. xv, 13) adds εἰς χώραν μακράν. "S'en alla faire un voyage," Ostervald.

(II, a). v. 37. τὸν υἱὸν αὑτοῦ "his own son"]. So all Eng. except Cheke and Auth. which merely have "his son." Vulg. "suum." See note on ch. ix, 7. If αὑτοῦ is ever to be fully rendered, it should be so here.

All Eng. render ὕστερον as if it were ὕστατον πάντων, (see ch. xxii, 27; xxvi, 60) "last of all." Cov. "at the last." Vulg. "novissime." But Cheke has "afterwards," as it is in Auth. ch. xxv, 11.

Ἐντραπήσονται is well translated by Cov. Cran. Bish. "stand in awe of:" "be in some awe of," Cheke. "Verebuntur," Vulg. "fear," Tynd. Gen. "reverence," Auth. are perhaps inferior to Cov.

(III, a). v. 39. λαβόντες " took"]. So Auth. in v. 35. Bish. Auth. alone are wrong, for the rest have "caught" in both places. In v. 40, none but Gen. give οὖν its proper place. Tynd. Cheke pass it over altogether. Cov. has " now when the lord"... and Cran. Bish. Auth. " when the lord therefore of the vineyard"... which certainly sounds ill enough.

At the end of v. 42 Cran. alone has " your eyes," after Codex D, *its Latin translation*, and a few manuscripts of very trifling account. See Introd. p. 88. Wickliffe does *not* agree with Cran. here.

(II, a). v. 44. συνθλασθήσεται " shall be bruised"]. So Cheke, Campbell. " Sorely bruised," Bp. Jebb, Sacr. Liter. p. 127. " Broken," Tynd. 2. Gen. Auth. " alto broken," Tynd. 1. " broken in pieces," Cov. Cran. Bish. "confringetur," Vulg. so Syr. (ܢܫܚܩܝܘܗܝ). In the parallel text, Luke xx, 18, Tynd. 1. has " bruised," the rest " broken " (" in sunder," Cov.). The culprit, at a Jewish execution, was first thrown from a raised platform, and thus *bruised;* he was then stoned to death (λικμήσει).

I would not altogether vouch for Chrysostom's allegorical interpretation: Δύο φησὶν ἀπωλείας ἐνταῦθα· μίαν μέν, τὴν ἀπὸ τοῦ προσκόψαι καὶ σκανδαλισθῆναι· τοῦτο γάρ ἐστιν, ὁ πίπτων ἐπὶ τὸν λίθον τοῦτον· ἑτέραν δέ, τὴν ἀπὸ τῆς ἁλώσεως αὐτῶν, καὶ τῆς συμφορᾶς καὶ πανωλεθρίας, ἣν καὶ σαφῶς προεδήλωσεν εἰπών, λικμήσει αὐτόν.

Tynd. 1. Cran. annex the first verse of ch. xxii to ch. xxi; I know not for what reason.

CHAPTER XXII.

(III, c). v. 2. ἐποίησε γάμους " made a marriage feast"]. Here again Cheke agrees with the best modern interpreters (Doddridge, Campbell, &c.) in presenting to us the correct rendering. Whatever may be thought of the style and general character of his Translation (see Introd. p. 89), in these minor matters he is very accurate. Thus alter vv. 4, 9; ch. xxv, 10. " Married his son," Tynd. Cov. Gen., and "made a marriage for his son," Cran. Bish. Auth., if not positively wrong, would not suggest the notion of a feast to the English reader. After this explanation, "wedding" in vv. 3, 8, 10 may stand. It is evident from these verses that the singular γάμος, as well as the plural, is used in this sense. So in the LXX, Gen. xxix, 22; Tobit viii, 19.

(III, c). v. 6. ὕβρισαν " insulted"]. So Doddridge: " abused, " Campbell: " treated contemptuously, " Symonds: " intreated ungodly," Tynd. " shamefully, " Cov. Cran. " sharply, " Gen. " spitefully, " Bish. Auth. " did them despite," Cheke.

(I)°. v. 7. In the beginning of this verse Griesbach reads ἀκούσας δὲ ὁ βασιλεὺς ἐκεῖνος " that king;" which, after omitting ἐκεῖνος, is the reading of the common text. Scholz adopts καὶ ἀκούσας ὁ βασιλεὺς ἐκεῖνος: Griesbach almost prefers ὁ δὲ βασιλεὺς ἐκεῖνος, without ἀκούσας. Lachmann prints ὁ δὲ βασιλεὺς ἀκούσας, without ἐκεῖνος: while Vater, with some hesitation, retains the received reading. Of all these variations we are concerned only with that which expunges ἀκούσας, and with the authorities which add ἐκεῖνος. The rejection of ἀκούσας is sanctioned only by the Coptic version, and by six thoroughly Alexandrine manuscripts (B L. 1. 22. 118. 209) ; so that it may be at once dismissed from our consideration. The addition of ἐκεῖνος is much better supported : for though it is omitted by Syr. Vulg. and Chrysostom, it is found in most Italic copies, in Theophylact, in ten uncial manuscripts of different families (C D E F K M S, and Matthæi's B H V), and in a respectable number of cursive documents, though not perhaps of the first order. I accede to Vater's decision, "pæne recipiendum, nisi facilius additum quam omissum fuerit." Mill also does not admit ἐκεῖνος.

(II, a). v. 9. ἐπὶ τὰς διεξόδους τῶν ὁδῶν "to the public roads"]. So Campbell: "into the crossings of high ways," Cheke. Whatever we determine respecting αἱ διεξόδοι τῶν ὁδῶν, it is obvious that this expression should not be confounded with the simple ὁδοὶ of v. 10. Yet all Eng. translate them both by "highways," except Tynd. 1. which has "ways" in v. 10. Syr. Vulg. render "exitus viarum" in v. 9, which Beza explains by "compita viarum," Martin and Ostervald by "les carrefours des chemins," and Castalio by "trivia." I conceive that there cannot be much doubt of the fact, that διέξοδοι here means "the crossways, where several roads meet;" not, however, as Kypke gratuitously supposes, *within* the city: at least not so if this be the same parable with that given by St. Luke, ch. xiv; for there, after returning from the streets and lanes of the city (v. 21), the servants are again despatched εἰς τὰς ὁδοὺς καὶ φραγμοὺς of the country (v. 23). Chrysostom paraphrases the word by τριόδους, and an antient gloss has "compita." The ordinary signification of διέξοδος, "a passage" or "outlet," can have no place here.

(II, a). v. 16. τοὺς μαθητὰς αὐτῶν "their own disciples"]. All Eng. have "their disciples." See note on ch. xxi, 37.

In this verse 'Ηρωδιανῶν is rendered "Herod's servants" by Tynd. Cran. Cheke, Gen. "Herod's officers," by Cov. Syr. has ܒܝܬ ܗܪܘܕܣ "Herod's household." "The Herodians," Vulg. Bish. Auth. Chrysostom describes them as τοὺς 'Ηρώδου στρατιώτας. Whether we are to understand a sect or political party of that name, or (as seems more probable) the courtiers and dependants of the Herod family, the version of Auth. may continue. Schleusner observes that Luther translates "Herodis diener," whence Tynd. may possibly have derived its interpretation. Bp. Marsh would have been glad of this example of resemblance between the English and the German versions (see Introd. p. 78); yet to what rational view of the independent origin of Tyndal's New Testament is it adverse?

(II, a). v. 20. ἐπιγραφὴ "inscription"]. So the margin of Auth. and most, if not all, the modern versions. But all Eng. after Vulg. have "superscription," both here and in Mark xii, 16; Luke xx, 24. Vulg. uses "inscriptio" in Mark and Luke. "On writing," Cheke: see Introd. p. 91.

In vv. 7, 22, 33, the ellipsis after ἀκοῦσαι is supplied in three different ways by Cran. Bish. Auth. ("heard *thereof*, heard *these words*, heard *this*). But Tynd. Cov. Gen. render uniformly "heard that," and Cheke "heard this." These are trifles in themselves, but should not be overlooked in judging of the care and skill with which the several versions are executed.

(II, b). v. 23. Σαδδουκαῖοι " Sadducees"]. All Eng. have "the Sadducees," which is not at all called for.

In v. 24, the margin of Gen., over-against τέκνα "children," has "or, sons." Vulg. "filium:" "filios," Beza, Syr. but these languages could scarcely retain the ambiguity of gender, which is found in the Greek original and Eng. It is unquestionably *possible* that בֵּן in Deut. xxv, 5, like the corresponding Syriac form, includes female children; yet the reason assigned by Moses for the institution of the *jus leviratûs* "to raise up unto his brother a name in Israel," would seem to imply that the law contemplated a lack of male children only on the part of the deceased. On the other hand it is difficult to understand how a person who has daughters can be called ἄτεκνος, as in Luke xx, 29; or μὴ ἔχων σπέρμα, as here. On the whole, therefore, the rendering of Auth. is safer, and probably more true, than that in the margin of Gen.

(III, a). v. 25. σπέρμα "seed"]. All Eng. except Cov. translate σπέρμα "seed" in v. 24, and "issue" in v. 25. Cov. very properly has "seed," and Cheke "children" in both places. The marginal note on v. 26, in the recent editions of Auth. ("Gr. *seven*") is extremely weak. Even Bish. does not retain the Hebraism in this instance. See note on ch. xxi, 19.

(II, a)°. v. 35. νομικὸς "a lawyer]. While I entirely assent to Campbell's judgment that the terms νομικὸς and γραμματεὺς are not of necessity identical, merely because an individual who is called in this verse νομικός, is spoken of by St. Mark (ch. xii, 28) as εἷς τῶν γραμματέων, it is proper to state that no stress must be laid on the circumstance that "they are differently rendered in the Syriac version" (Prel. Diss. XII, Pt. v, 12). It is true they are so in the two parallel texts just named; but in Luke xi, 44, 45, which passage is so appositely cited by Campbell to prove that the terms cannot well be entirely coincident, Syr. unaccountably confounds them, rendering them both by ܢܡܘܣܐ. *Here* Tynd. Cran. have for νομικὸς " doctor of law ;" Gen. " expounder of the law ;" Cov. " scribe ;" Cheke, Bish. Auth. Campbell " lawyer." Vulg. translates " legis doctor " here ; " scriba" in St. Mark ; " legis peritus " in Luke xi, 45 (Vulg. does not read γραμματεῖς in the preceding verse).

In vv. 36, 38, μεγάλη is " chief" in Tynd. 2. Gen. " great" in Tynd. 1. Cran. Cheke, Bish. Auth. Cov. reads " chiefest " in v. 36, " greatest " in v. 38. There is some little difference in the order, perhaps in the reading, of Vulg. in v. 38, but it has " magnum " in v. 36. The Hebraism of positive for superlative may be retained without offence in English. Syr., like the Hebrew, has no choice.

CHAPTER XXIII.

In v. 2, all Eng. except Cov. Bish. translate ἐκάθισαν " sit," and very rightly. Cov. has " are set down ;" Cheke " did sit " (Vulg. " sederunt "). Bish. renders it by " sat," with its usual over-scrupulousness, noting however in the margin that " Beza readeth, sit " (" sedent ").

(III, c). v. 6. τὴν πρωτοκλισίαν " the first places "]. So the Rhemish version : " the first sitting places," Wickliffe, Scholefield nearly ; " the highest places," Cheke ; " to sit uppermost," Tynd. Cov. " the uppermost seats," Cran. Bish. " the worthiest place," Gen. Thus it is remarkable enough that Auth. alone, in this passage, employs the obsolete and ambiguous expression "the uppermost rooms." Thus alter Mark xii, 39; Luke xiv, 7; 8; xx, 46; in which texts however all Eng. except Cov. have " rooms," as well as Auth.; and even Cov. in Luke xiv, 8.

(I)°. At the end of v. 7, Syr. Vulg. the editions of Complutum and Erasmus, and (as a necessary consequence) Tynd. Cov. Cran. Cheke read ῥαββὶ but once (see note on ch. xxv, 2). This variation is supported by only eleven manuscripts, nearly all of them Alexandrine, by Chrysostom, the Sahidic, Coptic, Italic, and some lesser versions. The received text, therefore, is undoubtedly genuine, although Lachmann has decided to the contrary.

(I)°. v. 8. Here again two changes have been proposed by the critics, both on insufficient authority. Syr. Vulg. reject ὁ Χριστός, which is rendered in all Eng., and the omission has been approved by Griesbach and Lachmann. It may not be very unlikely that ὁ Χριστός was brought into this place from v. 10; but such a conclusion is by no means a necessary one: since the disputed words are contained in all the manuscripts but about fourteen (B D L. 1. 22. 71. 118. 124, &c.); while the Sahidic, Coptic, Æthiopic, and Italic versions, Chrysostom and Theophylact, are the only other authorities adverse to their genuineness.

The other alteration is more feebly supported. Beza, Grotius, and Lachmann would fain substitute διδάσκαλος for καθηγητής, although it is pretty clear, as Loesner observes, that the former is but a gloss, intended to explain the latter, which is met with but seldom. Διδάσκαλος, however, is read in many manuscripts, including eight of Matthæi's (but only in B among the uncials), and in Chrysostom. Syr. and several other versions are also alleged in its behalf, but on very precarious grounds. In Syr. καθηγητὴς in v. 10 is rendered by a different word from that employed in v. 8, though it is derived from the same root. Such a circumstance can prove but little on either side of the question.

(III, a). v. 12. ταπεινωθήσεται "shall be humbled"]. No Eng. renders ταπεινοῦν uniformly in this verse, although the antithetic form of the sentence so plainly requires it. Cheke has "abase" in both places.

(I. See Introd. p. 7). vv. 13, 14. All Eng. and Vulg. read these verses in the same order as Beza and the received text. But they are transposed in Syr. the Complutensian, and Stephens's third edition; and this latter arrangement has been approved by Wetstein, Griesbach, Scholz and Vater. Lachmann cancels the verse ὅτι κατεσθίετε τὰς οἰκίας κ.τ.λ. altogether: and Mill (Proleg. N. T. p. 42), after Grotius, thinks that it is borrowed from Mark xii, 40; or Luke xx, 47. The authorities for Lachmann's reading are far from strong. They are ten decidedly Alexandrine manuscripts (B D L Z. 1. 33. 118. 208. 209. 346; for which last see Appendix I); a few copies of the Italic and Vulg., and probably Origen* and Eusebius. If we lay this reading out of the question, we can have little hesitation in placing ver. 14 of Auth. before v. 13, as it is in both Syriac, the Sahidic, Coptic and Æthiopic versions, in Chrysostom and Theo-

---

* Origen's words are (Tom. iv, p. 352) ἐν τῷ κατὰ Ματθαῖον ὁ πρὸς τοὺς Γραμματεῖς καὶ Φαρισαίους ΔΕΥΤΕΡΟΣ ταλανισμὸς οὕτως ἔχει .... (quoting v. 15). But δεύτερος was very possibly an oversight.

phylact: as well as in almost all the manuscripts which do not favor Lachmann's view. Scholz, with his usual inaccuracy, cites the Codex Z both for the omission of v. 14, and for placing it before v. 13. Of course the variation in this place must be attributed to the circumstance, that the commencing clauses of vv. 13, 14, 15 are the same.

(II, b). v. 14. καὶ προφάσει μακρὰ προσευχόμενοι ,"and that, making long prayers for a pretence"]. Thus correct Mark xii, 40; Luke xx, 47 (where Auth. has "shew," which perhaps is better than "pretence"). The rendering of Auth., besides that it loses much of the force of the passage, would require προσεύχεσθε instead of the participle. All other Eng. are preferable: "and that under a color of praying long prayers," Tynd. Cov. Gen. (Gen. omits "praying"); "and that under a pretence of long prayer," Cran. Bish. so Syr. Καὶ ταῦτα, διὰ προσχήματος τοῦ μακρὰ προσεύχεσθαι, Theophylact: "nay, and use long prayers for a disguise," Campbell. For this intensive force of καὶ Raphel compares Polybius, μόνοι τῶν κατὰ Συρίαν ὑπέστησαν, καὶ πάσας ἐξελέγξαντες ἐλπίδας. In v. 15, Cov. has "a child of hell." This is better than "the child" of other Eng.

(III, a). vv. 16, 18. ὀφείλει "is bound"]. Thus the margin of Auth. in v. 18, though Auth., most strangely, has "he is a debtor" in v. 16, and "he is guilty" in v. 18; the latter rendering approximating to nonsense. All other Eng. are uniform in both places. Tynd. 1. Bish. "is (a) debtor" (a very fair version); "offendeth," Tynd. 2. Gen. "is guilty," Cov. Cran. "debet," Vulg. Syr. "is bound to perform it, vel, he fauteth," Cheke. I suppose "is guilty" of Cov. Cran. Auth. originated in "reus est" of Erasmus, retained by Beza. But this, I need not say, is a pure Latinism: *voti reus.*

In v. 23, Tynd. Gen. render ἀφιέναι uniformly throughout the verse, "leave undone." But perhaps this is unnecessary. Cheke has "dill" for ἄνηθον, like the margin of Auth. in the later editions.

(II, a and b). v. 24. οἱ διυλίζοντες τὸν κώνωπα . . . τὴν κάμηλον " who strain out the gnat . . . the camel"]. Bp. Middleton remarks that the article here intimates, that our Lord is alluding to a familiar proverb. See Suicer, Tom. ii, p. 29. Cheke also has " strain away the gnat . . . the camel." Since all Eng. except Auth. read " strain out," it has been reasonably conjectured that " at," in the first edition of Auth. is but a typographical error for " out." At all events it must be corrected, for as Bishop Lowth remarks, " the impropriety of the preposition has wholly destroyed the meaning of the phrase."

(I). v. 25. There are at least three readings of the last word of this verse: ἀκρασίας " excess," of the received text, Lachmann and Eng.; ἀκαθαρσίας, favored by Vulg. and noticed by Cov. in his margin ("some read, uncleaness"); and ἀδικίας " injustice," which is adopted by Griesbach, Vater, and Scholz. Syr. has ܡܶܐ, which, though it stands for ἀνομία in v. 28; ch. vii, 23; xiii, 41; xxiv, 12, represents the cognate term ἀδικία in Luke xvi, 8; 9; 11, &c. Besides two or three versions, ἀκαθαρσίας is found in only two manuscripts of inferior value, and may therefore be rejected at once. The received reading is contained in some copies of the Italic, and in about ten manuscripts, all Alexandrine (B D L. 1. 13. 33. 69. 106. 124), except perhaps one of Matthæi's (e). Since I am perpetually refusing to receive readings proposed by Griesbach, supported by the same or similar evidence, I cannot dispute the ἀκρασίας is spurious, though the comparative rarity of the word makes somewhat in its favor. In the N. T. it occurs only in 1 Cor. vii, 5. Ἀδικίας is read in Chrysostom and Theophylact, in several versions, and (what is of much greater consequence) in the countless majority of manuscripts of both families ; for some of the best of the Egyptian class (e. g. C K) support it. Scholz cites Codex 33 (Colbert. Reg. 14) both for ἀδικίας and ἀκρασίας.

Since γέμειν is not followed by ἐκ, but by a simple genitive, in all other places where it is found in the N. T., Mr. Green (Gram. p. 280) thinks that the present expression may be translated " are full *of the fruits* of rapine and injustice." I cannot help regarding this construction merely as a vestige of the Aramæan use of a preposition after the verb of fulness. For though I cannot discover that מָלֵא is ever accompanied by מִן in the Hebrew Bible ;* and though Syr. does not render ἐκ even in the present passage; the employment of ܡܢ after ܡܠܐ is both frequent and legitimate. It occurs no less than six times in the Pseudo-Peshito version of the Apocalypse (ch. iv, 6 ; 8 ; v, 8 ; xv, 7 ; xvii, 4 ; xxi, 9 ; but not in ch. xvii, 3), although there is no preposition in the Greek. St. Matthew's style is certainly less tinged with Orientalisms than that of one or two other writers of the N. T.: yet he often uses the preposition after the verb, quite in the Hebrew manner (e. g. ch. v, 34 ; 35 ; 36 ; x, 28 ; 32 ; xxiii, 16). I lay no stress on the

---

* Grotius indeed cites תִּמְלָאֵמוֹ Exod. xv, 9. This must be a mistake ; the termination מוֹ- is nothing more than a poetic form of the pronominal affix ם- or ָם.

hypothesis of the Aramæan origin of this Gospel, because I have never been able to satisfy my mind, as to the validity of the arguments on which it rests.

(II, b). v. 31. μαρτυρεῖτε ἑαυτοῖς " ye testify concerning yourselves"]. So Syr. (ܥܠ), "de vobis," Castalio, "of yourselves," Cheke, "testimonio estis vobismetipsis," Vulg. whence "unto yourselves," Eng. Campbell, Beza, and Rosenmüller say "against," a meaning which Syr. also will bear. Eng. at all events are either very obscure, or the sense produced by them is poor enough. Compare Luke iv, 22; John iii, 26; Col. iv, 13. The construction with περὶ and a genitive, is frequently met with in St. John.

(III, c). v. 33. κρίσεως "judgment," or "condemnation"]. "Punishment," Cheke. All Eng. have "damnation," both here and in v. 14 (except that, in v. 14, Cran. translates "shall be the sorer punished"). For obvious reasons it may be advisable to correct Eng. in both places. In the present instance I see no difference between κρίσις the act of judging, and κρῖμα the resulting sentence.

(II, a). v. 35. τοῦ ναοῦ "the sanctuary"] the holy place, to which the priests alone had access, as distinguished from τὸ ἱερόν (ch. xxi, 12), which included the surrounding courts. Syr. Vulg. Eng. render both indifferently "the temple." In most cases, it is perfectly needless to mark the difference between the two words (e. g. vv. 16, 17, 21, &c.), but here strict accuracy is essential to the sense. The θυσιαστήριον, or altar of burnt offerings, was itself in the ἱερόν, "outer court," or "court of the priests" (see Dr. Lee's Hebr. Lex. Append. A, p. 634), though it was opposite to the entrance of the "Holy Place" (οἶκος or ναὸς), at about ten cubits' distance from its gates.

Within this small space Zacharias was slain. Castalio properly translates ἱερὸν "templum," ναὸν "ædem." So also Campbell. Thus correct ch. xxvii, 51; Mark xv, 38; Luke i, 9; 21; 22; xxiii, 45.*

CHAPTER XXIV.

(II, a). v. 6. πάντα "all things"]. "All these things," Eng. Beza; though Cran. Beza, Bish. Auth. indicate that "these," is not in the Greek. Πάντα ταῦτα is read in four lesser manuscripts, Syr. and one or two other versions. Vulg. and some others have "hæc," but this is rather an explanatory gloss, than a various reading. Eng. merely added the Vulgate rendering to the Greek.

In the next verse Tynd. Cov. Cran. Gen. place "pestilence," before "hunger," like Vulg. Syr. Cheke, Bish. Auth. follow the order of the Greek. Since the Vulgate reading is found in only four manuscripts, *and in no early edition of the N. T.*, I will fairly admit that in this trifling particular Tyndal copied from the Vulgate. But it is the first instance of the kind we have yet seen; for ch. x, 5 must not be insisted on.

(III, a). v. 10. παραδώσουσι "shall deliver up"]. Uniform with v. 9. " Betray," Eng. Cheke. See note on ch. xx, 18.

(II, b). v. 12. τῶν πολλῶν "of the many,—the

---

* In ch. xxvii, 5, Judas cast down the money ἐν τῷ ναῷ. Since we cannot venture with Kypke to translate ἐν "near," we must suppose that the anguish of Judas led him to the very threshold of the Holy Place, within which the Chief Priests were sitting, when he threw down the silver pieces at their feet.

greater number"]. So Campbell. See Matthiæ's Gr. Gram. § 268. Cheke translates "the people's love," very suitably; but he has the same rendering in ch. xx, 28; xxvi, 28, where the article is omitted after the preposition in Greek, and should scarcely be supplied. I know not how to interpret τῶν πολλῶν otherwise than I have here suggested, yet all Eng. have "many." Syr. and the Latin versions cannot readily express the force of the article; but even Chrysostom (whose temper might be supposed to lead him to embrace the more emphatic sense) contents himself with saying, πολλοὶ γὰρ ψευδάδελφοι γεγόνασιν.

(I). v. 17. In the room of τι " any thing," τὰ (ἐκ τῆς οἰκίας αὐτοῦ) " the *things* (out of his house)," is read by Mill, Wetstein, Griesbach, Vater, Scholz, and Lachmann. Bp. Jebb approves of the change, which is confirmed by Syr. Origen, Chrysostom, and so decided a preponderance of manuscript authorities, as to leave no doubt of its propriety. Bp. Middleton prefers τι, as being more exclusive, but he is misinformed when he says that it is the reading of the great Vatican MS. (B).

(II, a). v. 22. καὶ εἰ μὴ ἐκολοβώθησαν . . . οὐκ ἂν ἐσώθη "and except . . . had been shortened . . . would be saved"]. This is the form into which the parallel text Mark xiii, 20, is thrown by Tynd. 1. Cov. Gen. Bish. Auth., only that they have "should," for "would," as usual (see Introd. p. 54). Tynd. 2. Cran., however, in St. Mark, and all Eng. here use "should be shortened . . . should be saved" ("were shortened . . . should be saved," Cheke). Besides the awkwardness of this arrangement, it does not lead us to infer, what is implied in the Greek, that the decree for shortening the days was contemplated by our Lord as past in the Divine

Mind, though with that rapid change of time so common in Prophecy, the future immediately follows.

(II, a)°. v. 24. δώσουσι "shall shew"]. So Cran. Bish. Auth. "give," Tynd. 1. (too literally), "do," Tynd. 2. Cov. Gen. "perform," Campbell, "work," Cheke. This is unquestionably the meaning of the phrase διδόναι σημεῖα in Exod. vii, 9; Deut. vi, 22; and especially in Deut. xiii, 1; where the Jewish people are expressly warned against the false teachers who shall work miracles in attestation of their mission. See also 2 Thess. ii, 9. This last text alone might have removed the scruples of Kypke, as to the *reality* of the wonders to be wrought by the deceivers mentioned by our Saviour: and I cannot think either him or Schleusner (*voce* διδόναι No. 13) at all successful in their attempt to affix to the verb the signification of "to promise, profess." Chrysostom at any rate entertained no doubt that the signs and marvels were actually performed: καὶ γὰρ πολλὴ τότε ἡ ἀπάτη, διὰ τὸ καὶ σημεῖα γίνεσθαι ἀπάτης.

(III, b). v. 24. ὥστε πλανῆσαι, εἰ δυνατὸν "so as to deceive, if possible"...]. The version of Bish. Auth. "insomuch that, if *it were* possible, they shall deceive," is almost self-contradictory. For "shall," Tynd. Cov. Cran. Cheke, Gen. have "should," which is materially better.

(I). v. 27. After οὕτως ἔσται Scholz and Lachmann would omit καί, as if it were interpolated from vv. 37, 39. It is wanting in Syr., in some copies of Chrysostom, in twelve uncial Greek manuscripts of both families (B D F G H K L S U X, and Matthæi's B V), and so very large a number of cursive, as to render it surprising that it should be retained by Griesbach, who often removes words from the text, on a tenth part of the present evidence. But the *printed* Vulg. has "et;" and that, I suppose, biassed him.

(II, b). v. 31. μετὰ σάλπιγγος φωνῆς μεγάλης "with a loud-sounding trumpet"]. So Cheke "loud sounded," Syr. ܒܩܠܐ ܪܒܐ ܕܫܝܦܘܪܐ ("with a loud trumpet"), Castalio "cum vocalissimâ tubâ," and Campbell. Beza, however, and Eng. have "with a great sound ("voice," Tynd. Cov. Cran. Gen.) of a trumpet." But this sense is more clearly expressed in Rev. viii, 13 by τῶν [λοιπῶν] φωνῶν τῆς σάλπιγγος. The Greek language admits of an inversion in the order of two genitives, so that the governing noun may follow the governed, which according to the more natural arrangement it would precede. Thus in Herod. vi, 82 we find within a few lines of each other ἐκ τοῦ ἀγάλματος τῶν στηθέων, and ἐκ τῆς κεφαλῆς τοῦ ἀγάλματος employed quite indifferently. But this trajection, I believe, takes place only *where no ambiguity can possibly arise.* If there be any difficulty in determining which is the governing noun, and which the governed, we may rest assured that they ought to be construed in the order in which they stand. This remark may prove of some importance in enabling us to decide between contending interpretations in Acts vii, 30; 1 Cor. i, 21; Eph. iv, 16. In the present passage I understand the second genitive to be used as an adjective, after the ordinary Hebrew idiom (e. g. ch. xxv, 31; Luke xvi, 8; Eph. i, 18, &c.), and to be equivalent to ἐν σάλπιγγι Θεοῦ, 1 Thess. iv, 16. The margin of Auth. ("with a trumpet and a great voice"), follows Vulg. which inserts "et" between "tuba," and "voce." Codex D, and seven cursive MSS of little consequence, give καί. Chrysostom and a few others have μετὰ σάλπιγγος μεγάλης, as Syr. But this is more an interpretation, than a various reading.

At the end of this verse Cran. translates ἀπ' ἄκρων οὐρανῶν " from the highest parts of heaven," I presume from a misapprehension of Vulg. "a summis cœlo-rum."

(II, a and b). v. 32. ὅταν ἤδη ὁ κλάδος αὐτῆς γένηται ἁπαλός, καὶ τὰ φύλλα ἐκφύῃ " when its branch has now become tender, and the leaves shoot forth"]. Thus correct Mark xiii, 28. I am persuaded that the propriety of a change in the first clause of this passage, will readily be conceded. All Eng. have nearly the same as Auth. " when his branch is yet tender" . . . 'cum jam ramus ejus tener fuerit," Vulg. which is somewhat dubious. Syr. is much more perspicuous " immediately that its branches grow-tender" (ܿܿ); " tener fit," Beza : " tenerescunt," Castalio : " commencent à être tendres," Ostervald. The *first* sign of approaching summer is the softness of the branch. The construction of τὰ φύλλα ἐκφύῃ is more questionable. Yet Syr.* Vulg. Castalio, and all Eng. except Auth. translate " the leaves spring " (" her leaves bud forth," Cheke). This view is confirmed by ὅταν προβάλωσιν ἤδη, Luke xxi, 30. Ἐκφῦναι is perpetually used intransitively ; thus Eurip. Ion. 1533, Ξούθου τέ φησι παῖδά μ' ἐκπεφυκέναι ; and in many other passages of the same tragedian. Beza, however, Martin, Ostervald, and Auth. take the verb transitively, " and putteth forth leaves." Thus it was used by Symmachus in Psalm civ, 14, εἰς τὸ ἐκφῦσαι τροφὴν ἀπὸ γῆς, where the LXX has ἐξαγαγεῖν,

---

* Grotius thinks otherwise, I suppose because Syr. has the noun (τὰ φύλλα) *after* the verb (ἐκφύῃ). Yet though ܿܿ be of the common gender in the plural, it would hardly be joined with two participles ܿܿ and ܿܿ standing together, the former of them being feminine, the latter masculine.

(II, b). v. 33. ἐγγύς ἐστιν "He is near"] viz. the Son of Man, mentioned in v. 30. So Beza, and the margin of Auth. in the later editions. Gen. supplies "the kingdom of God," from Luke xxi, 31. Vulg. Castalio are doubtful. Syr. Eng. have "it is near," viz. the advent of Christ. My correction is sanctioned by Bishop Horsley, in the first of his elaborate Sermons "On the coming of the Son of Man" (that on James v, 8): discourses which may well be admired as models of profound reasoning and ingenious research, though perhaps we may not adopt their author's solution of the difficulties with which he grapples.

In v. 41, "*women,*" is not in italics in the original edition of Auth. Since the gender is distinctly marked by the participle, our modern Bibles are wrong in their change. See Introd. p. 62.

The use of the present for the future in vv. 40, 41, to express the certainty of the event here foretold, is perfectly legitimate. See Introd. p. 46. Παραλαμβάνεται is variously rendered in Eng. "Received," Tynd. Cov. Cran. Gen. Bish. ("taken," Cheke); ἀφίεται being translated "refused," by Tynd. Cov. Cran. Gen. "forsaken," by Cheke, "left alone," by Bish.: all evidently referring the words to election and its contrary, although Bish. tries to soften the expression. This exposition is approved by Vater, who compares παρέλαβον in John i, 11. A more probable opinion is, that παραλαμβάνεται alludes to the being carried away captive out of Judæa by the Romans; and agreeably to this notion Doddridge has "seized ... dismissed," and Campbell, "taken ... escape." In this uncertainty it is surely wiser to say "taken ... left," as it is found in Auth. Syr. Vulg. This interpretation is perfectly literal, and happily retains the ambiguity of the Greek. Beza "accipietur... relinquetur;" "pris ... laissé," Martin, Ostervald.

(I)°. After v. 41, Cov. Cran. insert within brackets "two in a (" the," Cov.) bed, the one shall be received, and the other refused." This sentence is of course derived from Luke xvii, 34, and is contained in Wickliffe, who took it either from the Anglo-Saxon version (see note on ch. xxi, 17; and Introd. p. 88), or from some early MSS of the Italic and Vulg. It was printed in Pope Sixtus' Vulgate Bible, but was expunged from the present Clementine text. Besides the Latin copies, and the Æthiopic version, it is found in but three Greek manuscripts, all notorious for Latinising: viz. the Codex Bezæ (D), the Colbert. Reg. 14. (13), and the Leicester MS, of the 14th century (69).

(III, a and c). v. 43. διορυγῆναι "to be broken through"]. So Auth. in ch. vi, 19; 20; Luke xii, 39. All Eng. have "broken up" here, as also have Tynd. Cov. in ch. vi, 20. In ch. vi, Gen. uses both "dig through," and "pierce through," the former of which terms is perhaps the best rendering of the word. So Aristoph. Plut. 565, πάνυ γοῦν κλέπτειν κόσμιόν ἐστιν, καὶ τοὺς τοίχους διορύττειν (Parkhurst). Demosth. c. Aristog. i (p. 787, Reiske), τὸ δεσμωτήριον διορύξας ἀπέδρα. The ἂν after ἐγρηγόρησεν is translated "utique," by Vulg. "surely," by Tynd. Cov. Cran. Gen.; a rendering in every way worthy of Macknight's approbation (Prelim. Ess. to Epist. iv, 82).

(II, b, and III, c). v. 45. τὴν τροφὴν "*their* food"]. "Meat," Eng. See note on ch. xv, 37, and thus alter ch. xxv, 35; 42. The employment of the article as a personal pronoun is constantly acknowledged by Auth. See v. 49 ("*his* fellow-servants," but there the chief critical editions read αὐτοῦ); ch. xxv, 32, &c. So in v. 32, τὴν παραβολὴν should be rendered "*its* parable," i. e. that which the fig-tree teaches. Scholefield.

On "but and if," in v. 48, see Introd. p. 82, note. The phrase occurs also in Auth. 1 Cor. vii, 11; 28. "What and if," John vi, 62.

(II, a)°. v. 51. διχοτομήσει "shall cut asunder"]. So Auth. Cheke, Doddridge, Castalio: "divide," Tynd. Syr. Vulg. "hew him in pieces," Cov. Cran. Bish. "cut him off," Gen. the margin of Auth. and the "Layman" of 1840. "Separabit," Beza, and his French disciples. The sense of Beza and the margin of Auth., that of excommunication, or separation from spiritual privileges, was the favorite exposition of the Greek Fathers. Τῆς διχοτομίας νοουμένης κατὰ τὴν εἰς τὸ παντελὲς ἀπὸ τοῦ πνεύματος ἀλλοτρίωσιν, says the great Basil: γυμνωθήσεται τοῦ προσιόντος αὐτῷ χαρίσματος, is Theophylact's explanation. I do not see how this view is promoted by the remark of Grotius, that Aquila on Gen. xxxiii, 1, expresses the division of Jacob's children into three or four companies by ἡμίσευσεν (יֶחֱצִ).

But why should not the word be understood literally? Our Lord often accommodated his language and allusions to the customs and ideas of the people He was immediately addressing. If He proposed the unjust steward as an example of prudence and forethought, without condescending to stigmatize his manifest villany; why should He not represent the householder in this parable as cruelly vindictive towards the slave who had abused his trust; the rather as in the very next words He turns aside from his subject to intimate the *bitterness* of the hypocrite's portion in the unseen world? Now it is well ascertained that the punishment here referred to was familiar to the Jews (see 2 Sam. xii, 31; 1 Chron. xx, 3; Amos i, 3; Hist. Susann. 55; 59), in common with other nations of antiquity (Herod. vii, 39; Sueton. Calig. c. 27):—no unfit retribution for the double-hearted dissembler, as Bois quaintly observes. Because in the parallel text Luke xii, 46 διχοτομήσει is found in the same context with δαρήσεται πολλάς (v. 47), some have fancied that nothing more than a severe scourging is here intended. But they fail to produce instances of this signification of ΔIΧΟτομεῖν: for "scindo," "discindo," τέμνω, or even διατέμνω are quite insufficient for their purpose.

CHAPTER XXV.

(I)°. v. 1. To the end of this verse Cran. adds " (and the bride)." These words are found in Syr. Vulg. the Italic, and eight Greek manuscripts, chiefly such as are suspected of Latinising (D. 1. 36. 124. 209). Lest it should be thought that this gloss was brought into Syr. from Vulg. (see note on ch. vi, 13, p. 159), I remark that it is contained in the Philoxenian and Persian versions, although the margin of the Philoxenian states that *all* the Greek manuscripts do not read it.

In v. 2, Griesbach and Scholz have αἱ before the second πέντε, and this is also the reading of Stephens's third edition. External evidence is not very favorable to the insertion of the article, though it is given by many Byzantine manuscripts, by most copies of Chrysostom, and by Theophylact. Bp. Middleton says, "the omission may have arisen from the want of the article before the *former* πέντε: the first five, however, are not definite, whilst the latter are so, being those which remain of the ten." This is just such a nicety of the Greek as would escape the apprehension of the copyists of the Codices B C D L Z &c., whose native language was either Coptic or Latin.

Φρόνιμοι " wise," and μωραὶ " foolish," are transposed in Vulg. Tynd. Cov. Cran. Cheke, Gen., in a few Greek manuscripts (B C D L Z. 1. 33. 102. 157. 209, &c.), and in the Complutensian Polyglott and the editions of Erasmus and Lachmann.

Since this is almost the last instance in St. Matthew's Gospel, with which I am acquainted, wherein Tyndal's version agrees in reading with the Vulgate, against the received Greek text, it may be well to recapitulate those which have already passed under review. In ch. vi, 13, Tyndal's first edition agrees with the Vulgate in omitting the doxology; but the doxology is also omitted in the Complutensian Polyglott. In ch. x, 25, &c. "Beelzebub" is the form employed by all Eng. after the Vulgate; but here again they are countenanced by the Complutensian Testament. In ch. xviii, 8, Tyndal and the Vulgate read αὐτὸν not αὐτά: but this is also the reading of the first edition of Erasmus (1516). In ch. xviii, 29, εἰς τοὺς πόδας αὐτοῦ is not found in Tyndal or the Vulgate; nor is it found in any edition of Erasmus published before 1551. In ch. xxiii, 7, the second ῥαββὶ is rejected by Tyndal and the Vulgate: it is rejected too by the editions both of Complutum and Erasmus. The same may be said respecting the transposition of μωραὶ and φρόνιμοι in the present verse. See also below, on ch. xxviii, 20, note. From these premises the inference is tolerably clear. If Tyndal adopted the readings of the Vulgate in those cases *only*, in which the first editors of the Greek Testament agree with the Vulgate against the textus receptus; he did so in compliance with the authority, *not* of the Vulgate translation, but of the original Greek, as represented by the Complutensian and Erasmian editions (See Introd. p. 108). The single exception to these remarks has been pointed out in my note on ch. xxiv, 7.

(II, b). v. 8. σβέννυνται " are going out "]. So the margin of Auth. and Campbell. See Introd. p. 45, and note on ch. viii, 24. " Go out," Tynd. Gen. " are gone out," Cov. Cran. Bish. Auth. " be out," Cheke, Syr. (ܥܕܟܝܠ). " Extinguuntur," Vulg. It is absolutely necessary to express the full present meaning in this place, since ἐκόσμησαν in v. 7, proves that they were not as yet extinguished.

(II, b). v. 9. μήποτε οὐ μὴ ἀρκέσῃ " *we fear* lest there be not enough "]. So Gen., a softer and less direct denial than " *not so,* lest there be not enough " of Eng. Cheke's " there is not then sufficient " is very bad. Μήποτε, however, in the original is still more courteous than Gen. represents. It rather suggests than states the probability of the contingent event. See note on ch. xii, 23, and Gen. xxiv, 5, LXX.

(I). *ibid.* I have cited the text above as reading μήποτε οὐ μὴ ἀρκέσῃ. A similar use of οὐ μὴ where we should have expected οὐ occurs in ch. xxiv, 21; Mark xiii, 2; Luke xviii, 30. It is also found in the textus receptus of ch. xxiv, 2, where however it must have been interpolated from Mark xiii, 2, since all the critics and nearly all the manuscripts reject μή. In the present verse μὴ has been admitted as genuine by Scholz and Lachmann. It is read in eleven uncial manuscripts (B C D F G H K M S and Matthæi's H V, but not in the venerable Codex Alexandrinus or A, which commences at v. 6 of this chapter), and in so vast a number of cursive documents of both recensions, that we ought not to think of rejecting it; the rather as it is an Hellenistic anomaly, such as no copyist or critic would forge. Μὴ is found in several of Matthæi's copies of Chrysostom, and in all Mr. Field's except one.

(I)°. *ibid.* After πορεύεσθε all the modern editors omit δέ. It is wanting in nine uncial manuscripts of both classes, and in sixteen cursive: we might safely say in many more, for collators have been very careless in noting these minute variations (see note on ch. xiii, 27). It is also deficient in Vulg. and possibly in Syr. I might add that Chrysostom rejects it; but since he rather abridges than quotes the whole paragraph (v. 1—30), he cannot be appealed to with any great confidence. Until more manuscript readings are collected, we cannot decide with certainty for or against δέ. If it is not to be retained (and all Eng. retain it), I must protest against Campbell's arrangement of the verse ("Lest there be not enough for us and you, go rather" . . . .) as violent and improbable.

In v. 21 a similar question arises respecting the omission of δέ after ἔφη. It is not in Syr. Vulg. the Italic, nor in Greek manuscripts at least as numerous as those which reject it in v. 9. The particle is neglected in Tynd. 1. Cran. Bish. Auth., but carefully introduced by Tynd. 2. Cov. Gen.

(I). v. 13. The clause ἐν ᾗ ὁ υἱὸς τοῦ ἀνθρώπου ἔρχεται "wherein the Son of man cometh," is expunged by Griesbach, Vater, Scholz, and Lachmann..

Mill guesses that it was removed to this place from ch. xxiv, 44, by the compilers of the Church Lectionaries, who wished to avoid so abrupt an ending of the Lessons as τὴν ὥραν would be. It is omitted in six uncial MSS (A B C D L X), chiefly Alexandrine; in about twenty good cursive documents, mostly of the same family; and in Chrysostom. The words are wanting also in Syr. Vulg. (yet all Eng. have them), the Italic and Egyptian versions; and versions claim much consideration on a point of this nature. On the other hand they are found in the great mass of Constantinopolitan documents, and (as if to confirm Mill's conjecture) in *all* the Lectionaries. This circumstance, coupled with the testimony of Chrysostom and nearly all the versions, induces me to judge the clause spurious. The manuscript evidence against it, though weighty, is not of itself convincing.

(II, c). v. 14. ὥσπερ γὰρ ἄνθρωπος ἀποδημῶν " For *it is* as when a man " . . .]. So Beza supplies the ellipsis "ita enim *est* ut *quum* " . . as Cheke had done before him " for it is even like as " . . Syr. Vulg. Castalio retain the deficiency of the Greek; for which Vulg. receives the somewhat ambiguous commendation of Bois. Thus also Tynd. Cov. Cran. " likewise as a certain man" . . and Bish. " likewise as *when*" . . . "car *il en est* comme *d*' un homme *qui*" . . . Ostervald. Gen. first tried to render the sentence fully complete: "for certainly the kingdom of heaven is like as when" . . . Auth. renders here " for *the kingdom of heaven is* as a man " . . ., but in the parallel text, Mark xiii, 34, Gen. Auth. both read "*for the Son of man is* as a man" . . . Whether the words I have inserted be sufficient to make the passage perspicuous, the reader must determine. At any rate, we must prefer the rendering of Auth. in St. Mark to that in St. Matthew, since "the kingdom of heaven" and its dispensation cannot so properly be compared with ἄνθρωπος ἀποδημῶν, as "the Son of man" may.

(III, a). v. 15. κατὰ τὴν ἰδίαν δύναμιν "according to his own ability"]. Thus ἴδιος is rendered in v. 14. "After his ability," Eng. but "according to his several ability," Auth. "according to his power," Cheke. "Secundum ipsius facultatem," Beza. "Secundum propriam virtutem," Vulg., and so Syr. (ܐܢܫ ܐܢ ܐܝܟ ܣܘܟܠܗ). Some persons have felt a difficulty in distinguishing between δύναμις, the natural ability of the heart and understanding, and τάλαντα, the acquired gifts of fortune, rank, or learning. Yet that δύναμις will bear the meaning here given to it will scarcely be questioned. Wetstein cites Jambilich. Pythag. 19, πολλὰς ὁδοὺς Πυθαγόρας παιδείας ἀνεῦρε, καὶ κατὰ τὴν οἰκείαν φύσιν ἑκάστου καὶ δύναμιν, παρεδίδου τῆς σοφίας τὴν ἐπιβάλλουσαν μοῖραν. Were we to consider δύναμις as equivalent to τάλαντον, in the sense of *riches, abundance*, the clause κατὰ τὴν ἰδίαν δύναμιν would be almost redundant; a supposition very unworthy of the Divine Speaker, and of the solemnity of the occasion. I do not quite comprehend the drift of Kypke's objection to the more common interpretation, which is found in Auth. &c. "Deus sane dona et naturæ et gratiæ quæcunque hominibus largiens, aut etiam partes diversas in se suscipiendas illis injungens, vires recte istis utendi et in iis versandi non supponit, sed ipse largitur." Undoubtedly this ability to use our talents, no less than the talents themselves, flows entirely from God's free bounty. Yet if the former be a part of our individual character, while the latter may be given or taken away by the thousand Providential changes of life; what is there unreasonable in the supposition, that God's temporary and fortuitous gifts (if such an expression be allowable) are regulated and apportioned to faculties and capacities which were planted in us at our birth; and which, in the natural course of things, can neither be increased nor diminished?

(II, b). v. 17. τὰ δύο "the two"] named in v. 15. So the Rhemish version. All Eng. omit the article here, although in v. 16 they had said "the five talents." Correct in like manner vv. 18, 20, 22, 28. All are right in v. 24; as are Tynd. 2. Cov. in v. 18 "the one," for which Cran. Gen. have "that one."

(III, b). v. 24. ἔγνων σε ὅτι . . . εἶ "I knew that thou art"..]. So Cov. Cheke. "I considered that thou wast," Tynd. Gen. "I knew thee, that thou art".. Cran. Bish. Auth. No advantage can be obtained from preserving the Greek idiom, which sounds very awkwardly in our ears. Thus alter Auth. in Mark i, 24; John ix, 8; Acts iv, 13; xxvi, 5; 1 Cor. xv, 1, 2, &c.

(III, c). v. 25. ἴδε, ἔχεις τὸ σὸν "lo, thou hast thine own"]. So Tynd. Cheke, Gen. "there" is inserted by Cov. "*there* thou hast *that is* thine," or "that thine is," Cran. Bish. Auth. See note on ch. xx, 14.

(III, c). v. 27. τοῖς τραπεζίταις "to the bankers"]. So the Rhemish version, Doddridge and Campbell. "Tablers," Cheke, absurdly enough. Wickliffe and Eng. have "changers," or "exchangers." In their time all exchangers of money may have been bankers. Τράπεζα and its derivatives are perpetually used in this sense by the Attic orators.

(III, c). *ibid.* σὺν τόκῳ "with interest"]. So Doddridge, Campbell. "Gain," Cheke: "vantage," Eng. except Auth. which after Wickliffe and the Rhemish version, has "usury," a word at present always used in a bad sense.

In v. 28, Tynd. 2. alone reads " five" for " ten" talents, I suppose by a typographical error. Codex D indeed has πέντε, yet it is most unlikely that Tyndal ever saw that suspicious document.

(II, b). v. 30. τὸ σκότος τὸ ἐξώτερον "the outer darkness"]. Thus correct ch. viii, 12; xxii, 13. See Bp. Middleton's valuable note. All Eng. render " outer" or " utter darkness," except that Tynd. 1. has the article in ch. viii, 12; Cov. in ch. xxii, 13; and Cheke in ch. xxii, 13, and here ("the uttermost").

(I)°. v. 31. Ἅγιοι " holy" is here expunged by Mill, Griesbach, and Lachmann. This epithet is applied to angels in three other passages of the New Testament: Mark viii, 38; Acts x, 22; Rev. xiv, 10; in the two former of which texts no doubt rests on its authenticity, and very little in the third. Its opponents in the present verse are pretty exclusively Alexandrine: our old acquaintance B D L of the uncial MSS (A reads ἅγιοι), and about fourteen of later date, including 1. 33. 61, or the too-famous Codex Montfort of Dublin, the voucher for the authenticity of the Three Heavenly Witnesses in 1 John v, 7. Of the other leading authorities Syr. reads ἅγιοι, as does Chrysostom; but the Italic, Vulg. Coptic, and some lesser versions agree with Origen in omitting the word. Unless the critical principles I have adopted be fundamentally wrong, ἅγιοι is indisputably genuine.

I do not know whether it is quite just to revive every crude opinion that Mill may have pronounced with regard to the goodness of each reading which he incidentally mentions in his Prolegomena. His judgment was usually decided by the occasion of the moment; and in truth any enlarged view of the whole mass of evidence on both sides of a question could hardly have been taken in his age. The same remark applies to Bengel, and (though not in its full extent) to Wetstein; a scholar both in vigour of mind and extent of learning greatly superior to his predecessors. It therefore seems desirable, for the future, not to allege the decisions of these earlier critics respecting particular readings, unless when they have communicated to us the precise grounds on which their judgment was formed.

(III, c). vv. 35, 37, 42, 44. ἐπείνασα "I was hungry"]. So Cov. Cheke: " an hungred" of Eng. is obsolete. Thus alter ch. iv, 2, &c.

(II, b). v. 41. τὸ πῦρ τὸ αἰώνιον " the everlasting fire"]. Cov. Bish. alone of Eng. have the article.

In vv. 40, 45, ἐφ' ὅσον is translated " quamdiu" in Vulg. Yet all Eng. are correct " inasmuch as;" except Cov. " look, what ye have done," and Cheke in v. 40 " whatsoever you have done " ...

(I). v. 44. After ἀποκριθήσονται the pronoun αὐτῷ is cancelled by Griesbach, Vater, Scholz and Lachmann. It is not found in twelve uncial manuscripts (A B D E F G K L S and Matthæi's B H V), in a multitude of cursive documents, in Syr., in the Egyptian versions, and in some copies of the Italic and Vulg. There can be little doubt of the spuriousness of αὐτῷ: and St. Matthew frequently suppresses the pronoun after ἀποκριθείς. See ch. xv, 13; 24; 26.

(III, a). v. 46. αἰώνιον " everlasting"]. Follow Cov. and Cheke in rendering this much-controverted word uniformly in the same verse. Other Eng. vary between " everlasting" and " eternal," for no possible reason. I so often appeal to Cov. in favour of slight verbal alterations, which I conceive to be improvements on Auth., that the reader may possibly think I have spoken too slightingly of his merits in my Introduction, p. 85. The fact is, that in more importrant matters Cov. generally fails us: though doubtless such minutiæ are not without their importance.

CHAPTER XXVI.

(II, a). v. 2. τὸ πάσχα γίνεται "the passover cometh"]. "Shall be Easter," Tynd. Cov. Cran. Cheke: "is Easter," Gen. a rendering of πάσχα still retained by Auth. in Acts xii, 4: "is the feast of the passover," Bish. Auth. But neither here, nor in v. 17 (where Gen. alone resembles Auth.) should "the feast" be expressed.

(II, a). v. 3. εἰς τὴν αὐλὴν "into the court"]. So Cheke. This *must* be the meaning of αὐλή in vv. 58, 69; Mark xiv, 54; 66; Luke xxii, 55; John xviii, 15, as will be clear on comparing the several accounts given by the four Evangelists. In Rev. xi, 2, it is thus rendered by Auth. Hence it is desirable to give the same interpretation to it in Mark xv, 16; Luke xi, 21, where it may possibly be used with a rather wider signification. The αὐλή of an Oriental house, I need scarcely observe, was the enclosed area or court-yard, surrounded by buildings, and open above, to which there was access from the street through the porch πυλών v. 71, or προαύλιον Mark xiv, 68. In this chapter Cheke uniformly translates αὐλή "court," but all Eng. "palace" (except Gen. "hall" in vv. 3, 69), to the serious injury of the sense. Campbell has "palace" here, and "court" in vv. 58,

69 : to which, excepting on the score of consistency, there can be no objection. Syr. ܠܨܝܢ, and Vulg. "atrium," in every place. Doddridge has "hall" only in v. 69.

(II, a). v. 5. ἐν τῇ ἑορτῇ " during the feast"], the whole Paschal festival, for no particular day is meant. Hence " the holy day" of Tynd. Cov. Cran. Cheke, and " the feast day" of Gen. Bish. Auth. are improper. Γένηται is translated " arise" in Tynd. Gen. This is much better than "be" of the other Eng.

Again in v. 7, ἀνακειμένου is better rendered by Tynd. Cran. Gen. Bish. " sat at the board," or " at the table" by Cov., than by Cheke and Auth. " sat at meat." In v. 20 Auth. has " sat down," which is far preferable.

(III, c). v. 8. ἠγανάκτησαν "were indignant"]. "Had indignation," Eng. "disdained," Cov. the rendering of all but Auth. in ch. xx, 24; xxi, 15: " were discontented," Cheke.

(I)°. v. 9. τὸ μύρον " ointment" is expunged by Griesbach, Scholz, and Lachmann. Granting that it has some appearance of being a marginal gloss, we must not reject the noun of the sentence, on the slender evidence hitherto produced against it. It is not found indeed in Syr. Vulg. the Italic, and Egyptian versions; but I hesitate to confide in translations, in the case of an omission so comparatively trifling. The direct testimony against τὸ μύρον is slight enough: namely A B D L of the uncial, and eleven cursive manuscripts. But all these are very decidedly Egyptian, excepting Codex A, which is mixed, and Matthæi's e. This last, however, is frequently found in very suspicious company; see note on ch. xxiii, 25.

At the end of the verse, Chrysostom countenances all the modern editors in reading τοῖς before πτωχοῖς.

It is so well supported by manuscripts, that we may justly assume its genuineness; the rather as πτωχοῖς is anarthrous in ch. xix, 21. All Eng. have " the poor;" but no one will imagine that *they* read τοῖς. See note on ch. ix, 13.

(II, a). v. 12. πρὸς τὸ ἐνταφιάσαι με " for my embalment," or "to embalm me"]. " Bury," Eng. Syr. Vulg. But since ἐνταφιάζειν necessarily means " to embalm" in John xix, 40, it is advisable with the great Casaubon, Campbell, Newcome, and Boothroyd, so to render the verb here, and ἐνταφιασμὸς in Mark xiv, 8 ; John xii, 7. The LXX employ this word for חנט in Gen. l, 2, where the ἐνταφιασταὶ must be illustrated from the minute description given by Herodotus, ii, 86.

(III, b). v. 13. καὶ ὃ ... " this also which"]. So Cov. Other Eng. wrongly place " also" before " this." See notes on ch. ii, 8 ; x, 32. Thus correct v. 71, by putting " also" before " was." Auth. is accurate in vv. 69, 73.

(II, a). v. 15. ἔστησαν αὐτῷ " weighed him"]. So Beza, Campbell, Newcome, and Scholefield. "Offered him," Cov. " appointed unto him," Tynd. Cran. Cheke, Gen. Bish. Boothroyd: " covenanted with him," Auth. " constituerunt ei," Vulg. and thus Syr. (ܐܘܦܝܘ); " pacti sunt," Castalio. To the same effect Theophylact paraphrases ἔστησαν by συνεφώνησαν, ἀφώρισαν δοῦναι, and Ostervald has " ils convinrent," though Martin abides by Beza's judgment " ils lui comptèrent." The truth is that St. Mark (ch. xiv, 11), and St. Luke (ch. xxii, 5) merely state that the Jewish Rulers " promised" or " covenanted" to give Judas money: whereas in the present text St. Matthew pointedly alludes to that great prophecy of Zachariah (ch. xi, 12), which he expressly cites in

v. 9 of the next chapter, where וַיִּשְׁקְלוּ "and they weighed," is represented by καὶ ἔστησαν in the LXX. The same Greek answers to the same Hebrew word in Ezra viii, 25; Jerem. xxxii (LXX, xxxix), 9. Mr. Grinfield compares likewise 1 Esdr. viii, 55. See also Herod, ii, 65, ἱστᾶσι σταθμῷ πρὸς ἀργύριον τὰς τρίχας· τὸ δ᾽ ἂν ἑλκύσῃ ... Demosth. adv. Timoth. (p. 1200, Reiske), οὐ γὰρ δήπου ἄνευ γε σταθμοῦ ἔμελλεν οὐθ᾽ ὁ ὑποτιθέμενος παραλήψεσθαι, οὐθ᾽ ὁ ὑποτιθεὶς τὸν χαλκὸν παραδώσειν, οὐδ᾽ αὖ ὁ πατὴρ ἔμελλεν αὐτὸς οὔτε οἴσειν τὸν χαλκόν, οὔτε στήσεσθαι.

At the beginning of this verse " unto them" is not in Tynd. Cov. Cheke, Gen. It is wrongly added by Cran. Bish. Auth. from Vulg. It is also found in Syr. and some other versions, and in *one* Greek manuscript, the notorious Codex D. Thus we see how even Cov. follows Tynd. in preference to Vulg.

Ἀργύρια is rendered by Cov. " silver pence," both here and in ch. xxvii, 3; 5: " silverlings," by Cheke; by Eng. " silver pieces" or "pieces of silver" here, but in ch. xxvii, 3 " plates of silver," by Tynd. Cran. " argenteos," Vulg. and Syr. By "silver pence," Cov. of course means denarii, or Attic drachmæ, which is probably the true sense in Acts xix, 19. But it is generally supposed that by ἀργύρια in this place we are to understand *staters* (see note on ch. xvii, 24); in fact Codex D and one or two other Greek and Italic MSS have στατῆρας as a various reading. The strangers' burial-ground would certainly be more likely to cost thirty staters than thirty drachmæ (ch. xxvii, 7); and thirty silver shekels is the sum fixed in Exod. xxi, 32 for the compensation of a master, whose man or maid-servant should be slain by accident. But this latter argument I must confess to be rather precarious. See also Campbell, Prelim. Diss. VIII, Pt. I, 4, 5, 10.

In v. 17, τῶν ἀζύμων is called " of unleavened bread" by Tynd. 1. " of the unleavened," by Cheke: " of sweet bread," by Tynd. 2. Cov. Cran. Bish. " of the feast of unleavened bread," by Gen. Auth. (see note on v. 2); " of the Azymes" (!) by the Rhemish version. Tynd. 1. is obviously the best of them all.

(III, c). v. 18. πρὸς τὸν δεῖνα " to a certain man"]. So Gen. " To such a man," Eng. The word δεῖνα occurs no where else in the New Testament, nor is it ever used by the LXX, but by Aquila and Theodotion in 1 Sam. xxi, 2.

Bish. renders ποιῶ " I make :" other Eng. " I will keep." The use of ποιεῖν in this sense is familiar to all Greek writers. Wetstein cites Hebr. xi, 28; a far more certain example is Acts xviii, 21.

(III, c). v. 24. ὑπάγει "departeth"]. So Campbell. Thus alter Mark xiv, 21. "Goeth his way," Cheke. "Goeth," of Eng. is ambiguous, and "goeth forth," of Cov. positively wrong. Syr. Vulg. have " vadit" merely; Beza, Castalio " abit." There is little doubt that ὑπάγειν is here intended, by a euphemism common to all languages, to denote departure from life. Thus the Greeks use ἀπέρχεσθαι, διοίχεσθαι, and the Hebrews הָלַךְ (Psalm xxxix, 13).

(II, b). v. 26. τὸν ἄρτον "the loaf"]. "The bread," Cov. Bish. "bread," Tynd. Cran. Cheke, Gen. Auth. There was little reason for Middleton's following Chrysostom, and a few Alexandrine authorities (BCDLZ.1.33,&c.) in removing τὸν before ἄρτον. It is certainly not found in the parallel texts Mark xiv, 22; Luke xxii, 19, which circumstance, together with ignorance of Oriental customs on the part of the Alexandrine correctors, was the probable cause of its being cancelled here. Ὁ ἄρτος, as Mr. Green remarks (Gram. N. T. p. 219), is nothing more than the *single* loaf ordinarily placed on the table at meals (Luke xxiv, 30, where Auth. needs correction), and has no peculiar reference to the Paschal supper.

(I). *ibid.* Instead of εὐλογήσας " blessed," the margin of Auth. informs us that " many Greek copies have *gave thanks*," εὐχαριστήσας (See Introd. p. 58). The latter reading is approved by Scholz, and almost adopted by Griesbach. It is found in ten uncial documents (A E F H K M S, and all Matthæi's Byzantine B H V), and in a large majority of the cursive MSS of every kind hitherto collated. Chrysostom supports it, and there seems little doubt of its authenticity. Εὐλογήσας (which may have been derived from Mark xiv, 22) is in the received text, and is read by Griesbach, Vater, and Lachmann. Its advocates are four uncial MSS (B D L Z), strongly Alexandrine, and about six cursive copies of various descriptions. The versions are worth but little in such a case, but Syr. Vulg. have the same rendering in both Gospels, and so far countenance the common text. Matth. xiv, 19; Mark vi, 41 favor εὐλογήσας, and Mark viii, 6; Luke xxii, 19 εὐχαριστήσας.

(II, a). v. 28. διαθήκης " covenant "]. So Castalio, Beza, Doddridge, Campbell, Ostervald (" de la nouvelle alliance "), Scholefield, and nearly all our modern translators. Vulg. Eng. have " testament ; " Syr. writes the Greek word in Syriac characters. Chrysostom seems to agree with Vulg. κἀντεῦθεν δείκνυσιν, ὅτι καὶ μέλλει τελευτᾷν· διὸ καὶ διαθήκης μέμνηται· a visible allusion to Hebrew ix, 15-17, in the note on which passage the whole question may be more conveniently discussed. Here, at all events, the course seems plain. Our Lord's Διαθήκη can be called " New " only in allusion to the Old one, that of Moses. · But the Law was consecrated not by the death of Moses the legislator, but by the blood of calves and goats. Since "Testament," therefore, would be quite impertinent when applied to the dispensation of Moses; it can hardly be appropriate *in this place*, as a designation of the religion of Christ.

It has been proposed to give to διδόμενον in Luke xxii, 19, to ἐκχυνόμενον here, and to κλώμενον in 1 Cor. xi, 24 the full present sense, "being given," "being shed," "being broken." Undoubtedly this is quite allowable; but then we must conceive the present to be used in a popular manner, where the future would be more strictly accurate; as we have ποιῶ in v. 18; γεννᾶται in ch. ii, 4; ἐγείρομαι in ch. xxvii, 63 (Introd. p. 46). I do not recommend a change in the rendering of Auth.; the rather since it has been suggested with oblique reference to a doctrine unwarranted by Scripture, and which the formularies of our Church emphatically condemn.

In v. 29, Bish. translates οὐ μὴ " in no wise ;" in v. 35 " by no manner of means." Other Eng. neglect it in both places.

(II, a). v. 30. ὑμνήσαντες " when they had sung the hymn "] viz. the great Hallel, or hymn of praise, with which the Jews concluded the Paschal supper. This Hymn was Psalms cxv-cxviii; for Psalms cxiii, cxiv had been sung at an earlier stage of the feast (see Lightfoot *ad loc.*). Dr. Doddridge seems miserably afraid of binding our Lord to the ritual observances of the Jews, and deems it " uncertain whether (as Grotius and some others think) it might not be some other hymn more closely adapted to the celebration of the Eucharist." More closely adapted, be it observed, than the cxvi[th] or cxviii[th] Psalm! Tynd. Cov.

Cran. have " said grace :" " sung a song of thanksgiving," Gen. " praised [God]," Bish. so Cheke. " Sung an hymn," Auth. " the hymn," Campbell: " psalm," margin of Auth : but it was rather a collection of psalms, than any one in particular. "Hymno dicto," Vulg. ܫܒܚܘ ("they praised") Syr. " le cantique," Martin, Ostervald.

(I). v. 33. After εἰ all the modern editors omit καί, and Griesbach inserts δὲ after ἐγώ, where all Eng. (by accident, no doubt;—see v. 35) have " yet." These minute variations are not noted by critics with sufficient care, to enable us to determine to which side the balance of manuscript testimony inclines: but if we confine our attention to the uncial, and the more remarkable cursive documents, we shall perhaps conclude, that the former of these changes is necessary, but the other not. Syr. Vulg. favor the received text in both instances. The same observations apply to the insertion of δὲ after ὁμοίως in v. 35, which is sanctioned by Griesbach and Scholz, on the authority of Syr. Chrysostom, nine uncial, and numerous later MSS.

(II, b). v. 34. ἀλέκτορα " a cock"]. So Wakefield, Middleton, and Boothroyd : "the cock," all Eng. even Wickliffe, and the Rhemish version. There is nothing in the Greek to answer to the English article; nor were cocks in Judæa the domestic birds they are with us, or which the article implies. It appears from the Rabbinical writers (see Lightfoot *ad loc.*) that they were accounted unclean, and forbidden to be kept by the priests, or by any person within the precincts of the Holy City. Hence the cock mentioned in v. 74, must have been without the walls, nor was his crowing 'a familiar sound in Jerusalem. Thus alter vv. 74; 75; Mark xiv, 30; 68; 72; Luke xxii, 34; 60 (see note *ad loc.*); 61; John xiii, 38; xviii, 27.

In v. 31, ἐν ἐμοί is rightly rendered "because of me," by Tynd. 1. Auth.; Tynd. 2. changes it into "by me." See Introd. p. 83.

In v. 36, χωρίον is translated "field," by Cov. "farm-place," by Cran. Vulg. has "villam." Syr. Tynd. Cheke, Gen. Bish. Auth. "place." The common rendering is amply sufficient, though that of Cov. is justified by the practice of Greek writers. See in particular, Philo de Agric. in Loesner.

(II, a). v. 37. ἀδημονεῖν "to be overwhelmed with anguish"]. Doddridge complains, and not altogether without cause, that "the words which our translators use here, are very flat, and fall vastly short of the emphasis of those terms, in which the Evangelists describe this awful scene." No single Greek word, indeed, can be more expressive of deep dejection than ἀδημονεῖν, to which I hope my rendering will be found adequate. Eurip. Frag. lxxxi, 3, ἀδημονοῦντα συμφοραῖς. Plato, Phædr. (I, i, 50, Bekker), ἀδημονεῖ τε τῇ ἀτοπίᾳ τοῦ πάθους, καὶ ἀποροῦσα λυττᾷ, καὶ ἐμμανὴς οὖσα ... Vulg. is very weak "mœstus esse;" "heavy," Cran. Bish. "very heavy," Auth. "full of pain," Cheke; "in an agony," Tynd. Cov. (fairly enough), "grievously troubled," Gen. "gravissimè angi," Beza, whence Martin has "fort angoissé," which Ostervald dilutes into "dans une amère douleur." Castalio merely "angi." Syr. ܡܬܬܥܝܩ "coarctari," a very forcible word.

(I)°. v. 38. After λέγει αὐτοῖς the nominative ὁ Ἰησοῦς is added by Griesbach and Scholz. It is not in Chrysostom, Syr. Vulg. or the Sahidic; but it is supported by nearly all Matthæi's manuscripts, and six or seven uncial besides, together with many cursive documents, mostly though not exclusively Byzantine. I suppose that Griesbach (who has little partiality for this class of authorities) admits it into his text, chiefly on account of its inherent improbability; for it is not at all wanted, and is so much like a marginal note taken from the Evangelistaria, that I cannot receive it with implicit confidence.

ibid. "Unto the death," Tynd. Cov. Cran. Gen. Bish. after Wickliffe. Auth. follows the Rhemish version in leaving out the article here, but retains it in ch. xv, 4; Acts xxii, 4, &c. "I am even like to die for sorrow"(!), Cheke.

(I)°. v. 39. In the room of προελθών "went farther," of the received text, Syr. Vulg. &c., Scholz reads προσελθών "having approached," or "come to." The manuscripts of Chrysostom fluctuate, but no less than twelve uncial documents of both recensions (A C D E F G H L S, and all Matthæi's), together with full eighty cursive documents, chiefly Byzantine, favor προσελθών. The received reading is supported by the Codices B K, and a crowd of others, of little influence perhaps considered individually, but possibly forming a majority of the whole; since they are loosely cited by Scholz as "permulti alii." But if ever there be a case in which common sense should prevail over authority it is the present. What rational meaning can we attach to προσελθών? whereas the textus receptus is perfectly intelligible. The critical canon "quo difficilior lectio, eo verior," must have some limit, or it would compel us to adopt the grossest blunders of the copyists. The difference between ΠΡΟΕΛ... and ΠΡΟΣΕΛ... is far from considerable; and the former had not hitherto occurred in the New Testament, whereas the latter had been used ten times already. But the variation must have arisen very early, for in Mark xiv, 35 even Syr. falls into it.

(II, a). v. 45. τὸ λοιπὸν "henceforth"]. So Tynd. Gen. Bish. Syr. Beza, Castalio, Martin ("dorésnavant"). But Ostervald "encore;" "jam," Vulg. "now," Cov. Cran. Cheke, Auth. It would not be easy to defend by examples this last interpretation, which makes τὸ λοιπὸν equivalent to ἤδη or νῦν, yet such seems the view of Chrysostom, καὶ μὴν TOTE γρηγορῆσαι ἔδει, ἀλλὰ δεικνὺς κ. τ. λ. I have chosen to make τὸ λοιπὸν in this place uniform in rendering with Auth. in 2 Tim. iv, 8; Hebr. x, 13: the same version would very well suit Acts xxvii, 20. "Henceforth," is most agreeable both to the primary signification of the word, and to its actual use in Greek authors. See Æschin. c. Ctesiph. (p. 86, ed. Stephani), οὔ τὴν γλῶτταν, ὥσπερ τῶν αὐλῶν, ἐάν τις ἀφέλῃ, τὸ λοιπὸν οὐδέν ἐστιν. Referring τὸ λοιπὸν then not to present but to future time, I see nothing unbecoming our Lord's character, or the awfulness of the occasion, if we understand the words to be spoken in a tone of expostulation and of gentle irony,* and thus reconcile them with ἐγείρεσθε in v. 46. Something in the same manner, though more stern in spirit, may be observed in ch. xxiii, 32. So Fritzche explains the present passage. See also Green, Gram. N. T. p. 321. Thus alter Mark xiv, 41.

(II, a). v. 47. ξύλων "clubs"]. "Fustibus," Vulg. here, and in v. 55; Luke xxii, 52. But "lignis," in Mark xiv, 43; 48. Campbell draws a very fair distinction between ξύλα "clubs" in these parallel texts,

---

* Much to the same purpose is Bp. Hall's explanation in his "Hard Texts." "Since my so serious admonition could not keep open your eyes, go to, now sleep on, take your rest *if you can;* behold ye are now entering into a busy and perilous time, for now is the hour of my suffering at hand."

and ῥάβδους "staves" in ch. x, 10; Mark vi, 8; Luke ix, 3, in which last places Vulg. has "virgam." Syr. also seems to recognise the same difference, calling ξύλα ܟܺܐܦ̈ܐ, and ῥάβδους ܚܘܛܪܐ. Auth. renders both words "staves" alike. Cheke has "staves" here, and "walking staves" in ch. x, 10. Other Eng. vary between "rods" and "staves," but with no fixed purpose.

(II, b). v. 48. ἔδωκεν "had given"]. So Tynd. 2. Cov. Gen. Syr. "avait donné," Martin, Ostervald: "gave," Vulg. Tynd. 1. Cran. Cheke, Bish. Auth. See note on ch. xxviii, 17. For χαῖρε " hail," of Eng. in v. 49, Gen. has "God save thee," and its margin "or, rest thee merry!"

(II, b and III, a). v. 51. τὸν δοῦλον " the servant"] viz. Malchus (John xviii, 10), a well-known person. So Cheke, and even Auth. in Luke xxii, 50: "a servant," Eng. here. Thus correct Mark xiv, 47.

(I)°. v. 53. After παραστήσει Cran. adds (" even now"). Ἄρτι is placed in this position by Syr. Vulg. and a few manuscripts and versions, but Cran. has it after δύναμαι also. Bish. translates παραστήσει " cause to stand by," very literally, as is its wont; but in the present instance more clearly than "give," of Tynd. Cran. Gen. Auth. " send," of Cov. or " aid with," of Cheke. Syr. resembles Bish. (ܢܩܝܡ), Vulg. "exhibebit."

(II, b). v. 54. πληρωθῶσιν αἱ γραφαί " can the Scriptures be fulfilled?"]. "Should," Tynd. 2. Cov. Cheke, Gen. " shall," Tynd. 1. Cran. Bish. Auth. On the deliberative sense of the subjunctive, see Green, Gram. N. T. p. 41.

(II, a). v. 55. λῃστήν " a robber"]. So Doddridge, Campbell, Syr. (ܓܰܝܳܣܳܐ not ܓܰܢܳܒܳܐ), Vulg. (" latro," not " fur"), " murderer," Cov. Other Eng.

have " thief," thus confounding λῃστής with κλέπτης, although they are expressly distinguished in John x, 1; 8: and all these precautions would be futile against a petty thief, though very proper against a bandit, such as Barabbas for example. Compare Luke xxiii, 19 with John xviii, 40 (where Auth. has " robber"). Thus alter ch. xxi, 13; xxvii, 38; 44.

(I)°. v. 60. Καὶ before πολλῶν, and οὐχ εὗρον after προσελθόντων are expunged by Griesbach; the καὶ only by Lachmann: ten unimportant manuscripts also omit the intermediate words, πολλῶν ψευδομαρτύρων προσελθόντων. The appearance of tautology presented by the whole clause, has given rise to several other varieties of reading, especially among the Italic versions. Vulg. supports Griesbach throughout, and Syr. rejects the second οὐχ εὗρον. All the Greek manuscripts, however, retain the disputed words, except the ten above mentioned, three Alexandrine uncials (B C L), and seven cursive, five of which are decidedly of the same family (1. 102. 118. 124. 209), and another of them (51) so much addicted to Latinising, that Mill (whether rightly or not is another point) was inclined to think it the identical Vatican copy, which formed the basis of the Complutensian text (Mill, Proleg. N. T. p. 156-7). It is not on such evidence, seconded only by Vulg. the Coptic, and some inferior versions, that we ought to disturb a reading sanctioned by the great mass of the manuscript authorities.

(III, a). v. 61. διὰ τριῶν ἡμερῶν " within three days"]. So Cheke, and Auth. in Mark xiv, 58, though it has " in" here. I propose this petty correction chiefly that I may notice Pr. Scholefield's version " after three days." That διὰ is frequently used with the genitive in this sense, can need little proof. See

Mark ii, 1; Acts xxiv, 17; Gal. ii, 1, in all which places it is so rendered by Auth. Herod. iv, 1, τοὺς δὲ Σκύθας ἀποδημήσαντας ὀκτὼ καὶ εἴκοσι ἔτεα, καὶ διὰ χρόνου τοσούτου κατιόντας ἐς τὴν σφετέρην ... Compare Matthiæ, Greek Gram. § 580. d. Vulg. has "post," Syr. ܒ, which *perhaps* may have this meaning, since it is employed in Mark ii, 1; Acts xxiv, 17. But Beza and Castalio have "triduo," the French versions and Eng. "in three days;" a rendering which I prefer to that of Vater and Pr. Scholefield for one reason only; namely, that the first two Evangelists, in quoting the taunt addressed to our Saviour on the cross, both say ἐν τρισὶν ἡμέραις (ch. xxvii, 40; Mark xv, 29); which is also the interpretation given by Chrysostom to the present passage, for his ἐν τρισὶν ἡμέραις ἐγερῶ αὐτὸν is not a various reading.

In v. 64, for δυνάμεως the *printed* copies of Vulg. (but not Lachmann's Latin text) read "virtutis Dei." Hence Cov. Bish. translate "of the power (of God)," Gen. "of the mighty *God;*" but Tynd. Cran. Cheke, Auth. reject "Dei."

(III, c). v. 66. ἔνοχος θανάτου ἐστὶ "he is deserving of death"]. "Worthy to die," Tynd. Cran. Cheke, Gen. Bish. I cannot guess why Auth. should have borrowed the uncouth phrase "guilty of death," from Wickliffe, Cov. and the Rhemish version. Thus correct Mark xiv, 64; 1 Cor. xi, 27, where "guilty" is used in the same obsolete sense. So in v. 67, Cheke has "spit" (Cov. "spitted"), instead of the less antiquated "spat" of Tynd. Gen. Thus alter Auth. in ch. xxvii, 30.

(II, a)°. v. 67. ἐρράπισαν "smote *him* with the palms of their hands"]. So Auth. preceded by Tynd. Cran. Bish. Vulg. who all add "on the face." Cov. Cheke simply say "smote upon the face," and Syr. "smote" only. Castalio "alapis ferire." The margin of Auth. ("or, rods") follows Gen. and Beza (so "*le* frappaient de leurs verges," Martin, "avec leurs bâtons," Ostervald), who after Hesychius and his tribe derive ῥαπίζω from ῥάβδος, whence the epic χρυσόρραπις, and appeal to such instances as Herod. vii, 35 (Schleusner should not have added viii, 59), where the verb is used generally for any kind of beating. But whatever we may think of the derivation (that most uncertain of all guides to the interpretation), both authority and the *usus loquendi* are adverse to Beza. See Matth. v, 39 and Kypke's note; Mark xiv, 65; John xviii, 22 (where Auth. has the same marginal note as here); xix, 3. Moreover, this verse manifestly contains a fulfilment of Isaiah's prophecy (ch. l, 6) " (I gave) my cheeks לְמֹרְטִים to the pluckers of hair:" τὰς σιαγόνας μου εἰς ῥαπίσματα, LXX. Compare the same version in Hosea xi, 4 with Symmachus and the Hebrew. Suidas too explains ῥαπίσαι by πατάξαι τὴν γνάθον ἁπλῇ τῇ χειρί, and so the Etym. Magnum. That ῥαπίζειν cannot well mean " to beat with rods" may also appear from Demosth. c. Aristog. i (p. 787, Reiske), τὸ μὲν πρῶτον ῥαπίσας [τὴν ἄνθρωπον] καὶ ΑΠΕΙΛΗΣΑΣ, ἀπέπεμψεν ἀπὸ τῆς οἰκίας.

(I). v. 70. Between ἔμπροσθεν and πάντων Griesbach and Scholz place αὐτῶν. " Them" is found in all Eng. (but not in Vulg. or Cheke), in Chrysostom and Syr., though I lay no stress on this last fact. It is read by all authorities of note except BDL. 13. 33. 69., the Sahidic and Latin versions. These purely Alexandrine witnesses are not sufficient to counterbalance the testimony of those opposed to them; although αὐτῶν looks very much like an addition of some scribe.

In v. 75, εἰρηκότος is rendered " quod dixerat," by

Vulg. Syr. " which he said," by Tynd. 1. Cheke: " which said," by other Eng. This would require τοῦ εἰρηκότος. Without τοῦ it should *strictly* be " when he said."

CHAPTER XXVII.

(II, a). v. 2. τῷ ἡγέμονι " the Procurator"]. So Campbell, and this no doubt was Pilate's correct official title; yet it seems scarcely worth while to alter Auth., unless perhaps here, where he is named for the first time. Syr. retains the Greek word untranslated. Vulg. Beza, Cheke, " præsidi," but this appellation belonged to Pilate's immediate superior, the President of Syria (Luke ii, 2). Castalio " prætori," which I presume he intends to use in the wider acceptation of *early* Roman history. " Deputy," Tynd. Cov. Cran. Gen. Bish., but this word is reserved by Auth. to designate a Proconsul (ἀνθύπατος) in Acts xiii, 7; 8; 12; xviii, 12; xix, 38. "Governor," Auth. here.

(III, c). v. 4. αἷμα ἀθῶον " innocent blood"]. So Cov. Other Eng. unmeaningly prefix " the." See note on ch. xxvi, 38.

It is worth while to notice in this place a curious example of the operation of Griesbach's critical theory. Instead of ἀθῶον he places δίκαιον in his inner margin, with a mark denoting that it is " equal or perhaps preferable to the received reading" (Proleg. N. T. Sect. vi, p. xc). What then is the authority for a variation thus highly eulogised by Griesbach? *One* Greek manuscript (L), a marginal note in a second (B), Origen in four places (though in a fifth he has ἀθῶον), Syr. Vulg. the Italic, Sahidic, and Armenian versions, together with three or four Latin Fathers, who naturally followed their own Bibles. Now this eminent critic must have arrived at his strange conclusion by some such process as I shall describe. B L and Origen represent the judgment of the whole Alexandrine family; the versions and Latin Fathers that of the Occidental. These being united would overpower not only the recusants of their respective classes (a tolerably numerous body), but the whole heap of documents of every kind which comprise the Byzantine recension. The internal evidence certainly does not favor δίκαιον, which looks very much like an explanation of the rarer word ἀθῶον. And it is self-evident how very precarious the testimony of versions must be in such a case. With respect to Syr. both Griesbach and Scholz are utterly mistaken. It renders ἀθῶος by ܕܟܐ "clean," but δίκαιος in vv. 19, 24 of this chapter, and in other places without number by ܙܕܝܩ "just." Respecting the Sahidic and Armenian I can say nothing: but possibly they stand on the same footing as Vulg. which uses " justus" for ἀθῶος here, and for δίκαιος in vv. 19, 24 ; while it renders ἀθῶος by " innocens" in v. 24. Far be it from me to detract from Griesbach's hard-earned reputation; but what would be the fate of the editor of a classical author, who should venture to reason and to decide, as he has done in the present instance, and in several others noticed in the preceding pages?

(II, b). v. 8. ἐκλήθη " is called"]. So Tynd. Cov. Cran. Cheke, Gen. and even Wickliffe. "Was called," Vulg. Bish. Rhemish version, Auth. Compare ch. xxviii, 15, Auth. Cran. after Vulg. and some Italic versions, interpolates ("Haceldema, that is") before "the field," from Acts i, 19.

In v. 9, Ζαχαρίου is found in but *one* manuscript of inferior rank, written in the eleventh century (22), so that however Ἰερεμίου may perplex us, it is unquestionably the true reading. No solution seems so easy as Lightfoot's, who supposes that the book of Jeremiah, being actually arranged by the Jews as the first of all the prophets (Bava Bathra), gave its name to the whole body of their writings; an opinion which is somewhat countenanced by ch. xvi, 14.

ibid. The marginal note of Auth. "whom they bought of the children of Israel" is the rendering of all Eng. before Auth. It is perhaps derived from an over-literal interpretation of Vulg., "quem appretiaverunt a filiis Israel." But without stopping to enquire whether τιμᾷν can properly be used in the two different senses of "value" and "buy" in the same verse, or whether that verb ever signifies "to buy," any farther than such a notion is included in the act of valuing; it is a fatal objection to this mode of rendering, that it is neither suitable to the sense of the passage, nor to the language of Zechariah (ch. xi, 13). Christ cannot well be said to have been bought of (i.e. from, ἀπό) the children of Israel, though their elders and chief magistrates bargained for him at a certain sum: and the whole clause τὴν τιμὴν ... Ἰσραηλ is but an expansion of the prophet's words אֶדֶר הַיְקָר אֲשֶׁר יָקַרְתִּי מֵעֲלֵיהֶם "a magnificent price at which I was prized by them." I acquiesce then in the version of Auth. "whom they of the children of Israel did value:" the only difficulty of which arises not from ἐτιμήσαντο, but from the construction of ἀπό υἱῶν Ἰσραηλ as a species of nominative before it; for which compare ch. xxiii, 34 ἐξ αὐτῶν ἀποκτενεῖτε. Syr. resembles Auth. (ܘܢܩܛܠܘܢ ܡܢܗܘܢ), but translates τοῦ τετιμημένου in the preceding clause by ܐܝܩܪܐ, with a view to the Hebrew text of Zech. xi, 13. For ܝܩܪ see ch. xx, 2. Beza also has "pretium æstimati, qui æstimatus fuit a filiis Israel."

(III, c). v. 10. συνέταξέ μοι " appointed to me "]. "Commanded me," Cov. "Appointed me" of Eng. is susceptible of another meaning. Thus correct ch. xxviii, 16, and perhaps ch. xxvi, 19, where Gen. has " given them charge."

(III, a). v. 11. σὺ λέγεις " thou sayest right," or " truly "]. So Campbell. " Thou sayest it, " Cov. " thou sayest so, " Cheke, Gen. " thou sayest " of Tynd. Cran. Bish. Auth. is very obscure. In ch. xxvi, 64, Cov. Gen. add "it," but not in v. 25; where Cheke has " so thou sayest," but in v. 64 " thou hast said so."

In v. 14, for πρὸς οὐδὲ ἓν ῥῆμα (" to never a word," Eng.), Cov. neatly renders "not one word."

(II, b). v. 15. κατὰ ἑορτὴν " at the feast "]. The great feast, the Passover. Middleton. "That feast," Eng.

(III, c). v. 16. ἐπίσημον " famous "]. So Wickliffe, Campbell, or "notorious," Rhemish version, Symonds. "Notable" of Eng. is now always employed in a good sense, unless the tone be ironical. For this use of ἐπίσημος with a bad meaning see Schleusner, and Joseph. Antiq. v, 7, 1, οἱ διὰ πλῆθος ἀδικημάτων ἐπίσημοι. Eurip. Orest. 239, ἐπίσημον ἔτεκε Τυνδάρεως ἐς τὸν ψόγον γένος θυγατέρων, δυσκλεές τ.'

(II. b). v. 20. αἰτήσωνται τὸν Βαραββᾶν " ask for Barabbas"]. "Ask Barabbas." Eng. and even Wickliffe, Cheke and the Rhemish version. But this is either ungrammatical or obsolete. In v. 18, Symonds proposes to render παρέδωκαν by "delivered up," instead of "delivered," as in Eng. It is actually so translated by Auth. (though not by the rest), in Acts iii, 13. " Brought him in," Cheke.

(III, c). v. 27. ὅλην τὴν σπεῖραν "the whole band"]. So Cheke. Auth. adds "*of soldiers*," but this surely is an idle repetition. See Introd. p. 63. "All the company," Tynd. Cran. "the whole multitude," Cov. (very badly); "all the band *of their company*," Gen. "all the band *of soldiers*," Bish. Scholefield suggests "*their* whole company." "Universam cohortem," Vulg. By σπεῖρα we must of course understand the whole cohort then on duty at the Palace: "toute la bande," Martin.

ibid. Πραιτώριον is termed "common hall," by Eng. "the governor's house," in the margin of Auth. Since in the parallel text Mark xv, 16, it is spoken of as an αὐλή or "open court" (see note on ch. xxvi, 3), it seems as well not to disturb the Authorised rendering. In John xviii, 28; 33; xix, 9, however, πραιτώριον can only signify "Pilate's house" *within* the αὐλή: for the Jews would not venture into it, for fear of pollution; although that they did go into the judgment-hall or αὐλή is plain from the mention of βῆμα in v. 19, compared with John xix, 13. In Acts xxiii, 35; Phil. i, 13 it is used for the residence of the chief magistrate.

(III, a). v. 33. κρανίου τόπος "the place of a skull"]. So Auth. in Mark xv, 22; John xix, 17. Here Bish. Auth. have "a place of a skull;" through a morbid anxiety to be very literal, and from ignorance of the licence of the article after verbs nuncupative. See Middleton's Treatise, Part I, Chap. iii, Sect. iii, § 2

p. 43. "A place of dead men's skulls," Tynd. Cov. Cran. "the place...," Gen. correctly. "The skull-place" (!), Cheke.

(I)°. v. 34. In the place of ὄξος "vinegar," Lachmann reads οἶνον "wine," as in Mark xv, 23. He is supported by four uncial (B D K L), and ten cursive manuscripts, all, or nearly all, Alexandrine, and by the Egyptian, Italic and Vulgate versions. Even Griesbach thinks this evidence insufficient to vindicate οἶνον from the suspicion of wilful alteration. Yet while we retain the received rendering, it were unreasonable to doubt that ὄξος μετὰ χολῆς μεμιγμένον here, is the same draught as the οἶνον ἐσμυρνισμένον of St. Mark. Χολή, therefore, is nothing more than a bitter mixture, whether of myrrh, or (as Campbell thinks) of wormwood, intended to flavor the wine.

(I). v. 35. It ought not to be questioned that the words ἵνα πληρωθῇ κ.τ.λ. and the accompanying citation from Psalm xxii, 18, were interpolated by the copyists from John xix, 24. All the critics, from Mill and Wetstein down to Lachmann, reject them. They are omitted in a considerable majority of the manuscripts; and though they are found in not a few cursive documents (Scholz, however, enumerates but nine), yet these should weigh but little when we regard the vast preponderance on the other side: nor are some of them of very high intrinsic value (e. g. 1. 17. 61). The whole clause is wanting in the Egyptian and most Italic versions; and although it is printed in Schaaf's edition of Syr. and the Clementine Vulg., it is omitted in many manuscripts and the Sixtine edition of the latter; while, for any thing that appears, it is contained in no Syriac MS whatever, being absent from the editio princeps, and the Antwerp, Paris, and London Polyglotts. Tremellius was the first editor who placed it in the margin. It is little creditable to Schaaf's sagacity, that both here and in Acts viii, 37 ; 1 John v, 7 he should have followed Gutbirius (Hamburg, 1664) in corrupting the Syriac text: but since he has explained the true state of the case in his "various readings," it is neither candid nor just to accuse him (as by some he has been accused) of ill-faith or a deliberate intention to mislead.

(III, c). v. 39. κινοῦντες " shaking "]. So Cheke. " Wagging," of Eng. and the Rhemish version has now become almost ludicrous.

In v. 37, instead of " accusation " of Bish. Auth. αἰτία is rendered " cause of death " by other Eng. Syr. and Campbell (" causam ipsius," Vulg. " his cause," Cheke). I see no need of a change in Auth.

(III, c). v. 44. ὠνείδιζον " were upbraiding "]. So Cheke, Doddridge, Campbell, nearly: "reproached," Rhemish version. I suppose no reader of Scripture would wish " cast the same in his teeth, " of Eng. to be retained.

In v. 45, ἐπὶ πᾶσαν τὴν γῆν is translated by Cov. Cheke " over the whole earth," mistaking (as do Wickliffe and the Rhemish version) "super universam terram " of Vulg. " Over all the land," other Eng. correctly. Syr. is ambiguous like the Greek. " Super universam regionem, " Beza ; whence " sur tout le pays," Martin, Ostervald.

(III, a). v. 46. ἀνεβόησεν " cried out "]. So Auth. in Luke ix, 38, " cried aloud," in Mark xv, 8. Here all Eng. neglect ἀνά. See Introd. p. 35. Perhaps instead of " will come," in v. 49, ἔρχεται should be translated " is coming." See note on ch. xvii, 11. Grotius and Rosenmüller think that ἄφες does not mean " let be," " forbear," as in Eng. Cheke ("soft"), Syr. Vulg. Beza, Castalio, &c., but that it is used pleonastically, as in such expressions as ἄφες κολαζώμεθα, &c. Compare ch. vii, 4. Theophylact's exposition differs a little from the common mode of understanding the passage, yet it lends no countenance to the opinion of Grotius : μὴ ποιήσῃς αὐτὸν ἀποθανεῖν, ὡς ἂν γνῶμεν εἰ βοηθήσει αὐτῷ Ἠλίας.

(II, b). v. 50. τὸ πνεῦμα " *his* spirit "]. So Campbell, Middleton, &c. the article being employed in its ordinary sense as a possessive pronoun. " The ghost," Eng. Wickliffe, and the Rhemish version, here and in John xix, 30.

In v. 51, " the rocks were rent," of the Rhemish N. T. is noted by Symonds as more grammatical than "rent" of Cov. Cran. Bish. Auth., or "did rent," of Tynd. Gen. " were torn asunder," Cheke.

(II, a). v. 55. ἠκολούθησαν "had followed"]. So Cov. Cheke, Vulg. Syr. " followed," Eng. Thus Auth. renders the aorist, v. 60.

(III, a). v. 60. μνημείῳ .. μνημείου "sepulchre," uniformly]. Since the latter word is used with a direct reference to the former (as indeed the article intimates), μνημεῖον should not be rendered, as it is by Auth., both " tomb " and " sepulchre " in the same verse : though it would be vexatious to object to " grave " in vv. 52, 53. Cov. Cheke alone are uniform here ; other Eng. vary like Auth.

(III, a). v. 62. τὴν παρασκευὴν " the preparation "]. So Auth. in Mark xv, 42 ; John xix, 14 ; 31. In John xix, 42 " *day* " is put in italics in the modern editions ; but it can be dispensed with altogether. In Luke xxiii, 54 ἡμέρα is expressed. Here παρασκευὴ is called by Tynd. Cheke " Good Friday," a rendering not more unreasonable than " Easter" for τὸ πάσχα (see note on ch. xxvi, 2). " The day of preparing," Cov. Cran. Bish. " the day of the preparation," Auth.

to which Gen. adds "*of the Sabbath*," from St. Mark's explanation ὅ ἐστι προσάββατον.

(I). v. 64. Νυκτός is cancelled by all the critics, and certainly may have come from ch. xxviii, 13 : Syr. and Codex S are the chief witnesses in its favor, but it is not in Chrysostom, nor in the Coptic, Italic or Vulg. versions. Ten uncial MSS (A B C D E H K L, and Matthæi's H V) reject it, as do many cursive copies of both recensions, so that its authenticity should not be insisted on. In v. 65, δὲ after ἔφη is not rendered by Syr. Vulg. Eng., by the last probably through accident. All the editors expunge it, and it is omitted in very many manuscripts.

(II, a). v. 65. ὡς οἴδατε " as ye know how "]. So Syr. Vulg. Beza. "Ye know how well enough," Cheke, "vestro modo," Castalio: "as ye know," Bish., literally, as usual: "as ye can," other Eng., but οἴδατε is not quite equivalent to δύνασθε. "Ut fieri oporteat, pro *sollertiâ* vestrâ indicabitis," Rosenmüller.

(II, a or b). v. 66. μετὰ τῆς κουστωδίας " together with the watch "], the watch aiding them in securing the sepulchre, and setting the stone. Such is Wetstein's explanation, and it completely removes all the difficulties which have been raised, respecting both the construction and punctuation of the verse. Chrysostom asserts that Pilate, suspecting now more than ever the real character of the Person he had murdered, οὐκ ἀφίησι τοὺς στρατιώτας ΜΟΝΟΥΣ σφραγίσαι, lest the Jews should hereafter pretend that the Roman soldiers were suborned by Christ's disciples: but compelled the chief priests themselves to take their share in sealing the tomb, that every doubt or subterfuge might be cut off. He then adds respecting the Jewish rulers, εἶδες πῶς σπουδάζουσιν ὑπὲρ τῆς ἀληθείας ἄκοντες; καὶ γὰρ αὐτοὶ προσῆλθον, αὐτοὶ ᾔτησαν, αὐτοὶ ἐσφράγισαν ΜΕΤΑ

ΤΗΣ ΚΟΥΣΤΩΔΙΑΣ, ὥστε ἀλλήλων εἶναι κατήγοροι καὶ ἔλεγχοι. This would appear to be the sense of Syr. Vulg. " cum (ܥܡ) custodibus"; and such a use of μετὰ with the genitive, denoting the union of several agents in a single act, is almost too common to need illustration. See ch. viii, 11; ix, 11; xii, 41; 42, &c. Tertullian says " sepulcro conditum magnâ militari manu custodiæ diligentiâ circumsederunt," thus joining μετὰ τῆς κουστωδίας with ἠσφαλίσαντο, and giving to μετὰ the meaning of διά (compare Acts xv, 4 with v. 12). This inversion (which I must be allowed to think rather violent) is sanctioned by Beza and several of the earlier editors of the Greek Testament (so far as the punctuation expresses their views), as well as by Tynd. Cov. Cran. " made the sepulchre sure with watchmen;" " sure with a watch," Gen.; " sure with the watch," Bish.; "kept the grave safely with watchmen," Cheke. The interpretation of Auth. " and setting a watch," and of Ostervald " *en y mettant* des gardes," most resembles that of Castalio, "et lapidem, præter adhibitam custodiam, sigillârunt." But how can such a rendering be extracted from the words of the original ?

CHAPTER XXVIII.

(III, c)°. v. 1. Ὀψὲ δὲ σαββάτων " Now at the end of the Sabbath"]. So Auth. nearly, omitting " now." St. Matthew means early in the morning after the Sabbath ; a period sometime before day-break on the first day of the week : for Bois is right in stating that τῇ ἐπιφωσκούσῃ εἰς μίαν σαββάτων, is a mere explanation of ὀψὲ σαββάτων. The Syriac idiom whereby in

Luke xxiii, 54 ἐπέφωσκε denotes the approach of evening, has no place here. The sense of ὀψὲ σαββάτων, as Theophylact remarks, is exactly ascertained by comparing it with διαγενομένου τοῦ σαββάτου, Mark xvi, 1; ὄρθρου βαθέος, Luke xxiv, 1; and πρωί, σκοτίας ἔτι οὔσης, John xx, 1. Both our French versions ("après le Sabbat," "après que le Sabbat fut passé"), and Campbell agree with Auth., and Campbell observes that " ὀψὲ before a genitive *often* means ' after.' " I wish he had furnished us with a few examples, for while I agree with Krebs and Loesner that such *must* be its meaning here, the only satisfactory instances I have yet seen alleged, were cited long ago by H. Stephens (Thesaurus) from Plutarch. Num. ὀψὲ τῶν βασιλέως χρόνων, and by Bos from Philostrat. Vit. Apoll. iv, 18, ὀψὲ μυστηρίων,* " when the mysteries were over." Syr. has " on the evening (ܒܪܡܫܐ) on the sabbath," perhaps retaining the Oriental phrase above alluded to. Yet Vulg. says " vespere sabbati ;" Tynd. " the sabbath day at even;" Cov. " upon the evening of the sabbath holy-day ;" Cran. " upon an evening of the sabbothes" (!); Cheke, " on the sabbath day, at night ;" Gen. Bish. " about (" in " Bish) the latter end of the sabbath day," after Beza's " extremo sabbato." All these interpretations are in substance the same, and though perfectly unobjectionable so far as ὀψὲ is concerned, cannot easily be reconciled with the accounts given by the other Evangelists.

(II, b). v. 2. ἐγένετο " had been"] " ante adventum mulierum," Rosenmüller. So the margin of Auth.,

---

* Ælian, Var. Hist. II, 23, Νικόδωρος ὁ πύκτης ... ὀψὲ τῆς ἡλικίας καὶ μετὰ τὴν ἄθλησιν, καὶ νομοθέτης .. ἐγένετο, might look like a case in point But ἡλικία seems here to be used in that wider signification which I spoke of in the note on ch. vi, 27.

Campbell, Vater. " Was," Eng. " was made," Cov. Vulg. Syr. See note on ch. xxvii, 55. " The angel," Eng., see note on ch. i, 20.

In v. 4, for "did shake" (ἐσείσθησαν) of Cheke, Bish Auth., we find " were troubled, " in Cov. " were astonied, " in Tynd. Cran. Gen. Was Cheke's MS used by Parker for Bish., or by our own translators at a later period? These repeated coincidences can scarcely be fortuitous. See Introd. p. 88, and notes on ch. viii, 26; ix, 26.

(III, a). vv. 8, 9, 10, 11. ἀπαγγεῖλαι " to tell," or " inform"]. Without the least desire to enforce a rigorous uniformity in rendering the same Greek word (see Introd. p. 51), I do not think it right that ἀπαγγεῖλαι should be translated, as it is by all Eng., in three different ways within the space of four verses: " to bring word," in v. 8; "tell," in vv. 9, 10; "shew," in v. 11, in which last however Cov. has " tell." In vv. 8, 9, Cheke has " shew," but his manuscript breaks off at " go" (ὑπάγετε) in v. 10. In v. 10 all Eng. *except Cov.* run into the opposite fault of rendering both ὑπάγετε and ἀπέλθωσιν by " go." Thus also in v. 8, Cov. has " ran" for " did run," of other Eng., and in v. 9 " were going" (ἐπορεύοντο), instead of " went" of Eng. See note on ch. xxv, 46.

(I)°. v. 9. The first clause of this verse ὡς δὲ ἐπορεύοντο ἀπαγγεῖλαι τοῖς μαθηταῖς αὐτοῦ, is wanting in Syr. Vulg., B D., and some twenty other manuscripts, chiefly Alexandrine (e. g. 33. 69): nor is it found in Origen or Chrysostom, in the Coptic or Italic versions. Nevertheless the preponderance of evidence is so clearly in its favor, that Lachmann alone dares to expunge it; although Vater urges some trifling objections against the diction, of which the construction of καὶ ἰδοὺ after ὡς ἐπορεύοντο is the principal (see note on ch. xv, 5, 6). Bowyer, in his Conjectures, sagaciously suggests the rejection of these words, inasmuch as by so doing we should facilitate the harmonising of the different narratives of our Lord's appearances after his resurrection, which are recorded in the Gospels. More patient and cautious critics than Bowyer would trace in that very circumstance, the origin of the omission of this clause in so many manuscripts and other authorities.

(III, c). v. 12. ἀργύρια ἱκανὰ " much money"]. So Wickliffe. " Money enough," Cov. " large money," other Eng. In v. 13, "*away*," is not in italics in the first edition of Auth. Our modern Bibles, by printing "away" in italics here, but not in ch. xxvii, 64, have introduced another inconsistency into the English text, through an excessive anxiety for verbal accuracy. See Introd. p. 62.

(III, c). v. 14. ὑμᾶς ἀμερίμνους ποιήσομεν " save you harmless"]. So Tynd. 2. Cran. Gen. This is clearer than " make you safe," of Tynd. 1. " ye shall be safe," of Cov. " Secure you," Auth. " make you careless," Bish. very absurdly (see Introd. p. 95). " Indemnify," Campbell; as if anything could indemnify the soldiers, should Pilate order them to be put to death. Again, πείσομεν is rendered by Tynd. "pease ;" " still," by Cov. " pacify," by Gen. I think " persuade," of Cran. Bish. Auth. need not be altered. Every one except Dr. Symonds will understand by persuasion, both here and in Acts xviii, 4 ; xix, 8; xxviii, 23, the *attempt*, and not its successful issue.

(II, b). v. 16. εἰς τὸ ὄρος, οὗ . . . " unto the mountain, where . . ."]. So the Rhemish version, Martin, Ostervald, and Campbell, nearly. " Into a mountain, where"...Eng. I conceive that the article is here employed by anticipation, with an immediate reference to the clause οὗ ἐτάξατο κ. τ. λ. Mr. Green, however, says "this use of the article presents an instance, in which his own familiarity with circumstances leads a writer unwittingly to adopt language which is not correct with regard to his readers"(Gram. N. T. p. 221). Possibly the explanation I have offered may be judged the more natural; but see notes on ch. v, 1; viii, 32.

(II, b. See Introd. p. 45). v. 17. οἱ δὲ ἐδίστασαν " but some had doubted"]. So Martin (mais quelquesuns avaient douté), Doddridge, Newcome, Boothroyd, and Fritzche. Boothroyd supposes that allusion is made to some of the five hundred brethren, to whom our Lord shewed himself after his resurrection (1 Cor. xv, 6). Grotius also takes the aorist in this place as a Latin pluperfect, but thinks that Thomas is the person chiefly glanced at. Such too seems to be the opinion of Ostervald, who translates, loosely enough, " même ceux qui avaient douté." The same question had been raised by Theophylact, who clearly sanctions the rendering I have proposed: ὀφείλεις οὕτω νοῆσαι, ὅτι εἰς μὲν τὴν Γαλίλαιαν ἐλθόντες προσεκύνησαν αὐτῷ· οὗτοι δὲ οἱ προσκυνήσαντες ἐν τῇ Γαλιλαίᾳ, ἐδίστασαν πρότερον ἐν τῇ Ἱερουσαλήμ (Luke xxiv, 11; 38; 41). Chrysostom, on the contrary, favors the interpretation " but some doubted," which is also that of Eng. Vulg. Beza, and Castalio. Syr. has ܘܕܢ ܐܬܪܠܝ, for which both Tremellius and Schaaf have " dubitaverant," and I believe correctly: though it is quite true that the Syriac verb-substantive, when added to the preterite, does not of necessity constitute the pluperfect tense.

I have observed this form of expression occur one hundred and four times in the Peshito version of the Acts, in about fifty of which passages it must be understood as a simple past tense. In the present instance, by assigning the pluperfect sense to ἱδίστασαν, the whole context is relieved of considerable difficulties. Nor is it quite fair to say, with a modern critic, that this explanation looks " too much like a device for the nonce." That such an use of the aorist, more especially in parenthetic clauses, is both legitimate and common, will hardly be denied. It is admitted even by Auth. in ch. xvi, 5 ; Luke viii, 29; John xviii, 24 : it *ought* to be adopted in ch. xxvi, 48 ; and probably in Luke xxii, 24. See also note on v. 2.

(I). v. 19. Griesbach and Scholz here omit οὖν. It is rendered by Syr. Vulg., but is not read in ten uncial manuscripts (A E F H K M S, and all three of Matthæi's) and numerous cursive copies of both families; so that it would be difficult to defend the particle, even were it worth contending for.

(II, a). *ibid.* μαθητεύσατε " make disciples of "]. So the margin of Auth. in the later editions, adding " or Christians," and Syr. (ܬܠܡܕܘ). " Proselyte," Doddridge ; " convert," Campbell. " Docete" of Vulg. Beza, Castalio, and "teach" of Eng. are very feeble and inadequate. Epiphanius (apud Suicer.) well explains the term by μεταβάλλετε τὰ ἔθνη ἀπὸ κακίας εἰς ἀλήθειαν. A similar change is very properly suggested by the same recent editors in the margin of Auth., Acts xiv, 21. Above, in ch. xxvii, 57, the verb had been used intransitively.

(I)°. v. 20. Ἀμὴν is cancelled by Griesbach and

Lachmann. It is omitted by Chrysostom, Vulg. and all Eng. previous to Auth.,* which contains the word, as also does Syr., and an immense majority of the manuscripts. Indeed it is found in all except B D (A is doubtful) 1. 22. 33. 102, and three of the least important of Matthæi's. Of the other authorities, the Coptic, Armenian, and a few Italic documents neglect it. The word might readily have been added by the scribes who prepared the ecclesiastical copies (see Mill *ad loc.*); but no sober critic should reject it on such evidence as has hitherto been alleged. Griesbach's decision is no less rash at the end of St. Luke's Gospel; where, however, Scholz, with admirable consistency, sides with him, although he *here* abides by the received text. The authenticity of ἀμὴν at the end of St. John is somewhat more doubtful. In Mark xvi, 20, though it is read in Stephens's third edition (see Introd. p. 8), it never obtained admission into those of Beza or the Elzevirs.

---

* This instance should be added to those enumerated in the note on ch. xxv, 2, in which Tyndal and his successors agree with the Vulgate readings in preference to those of the *present* Greek text. This passage also confirms us in the conclusion to which we there arrived; for ἀμὴν is wanting in the first edition of Erasmus, 1516.

APPENDIX A.

LIST OF THE PRINCIPAL GREEK MANUSCRIPTS WHICH CONTAIN THE FOUR GOSPELS.

The following tabular view of the most remarkable of the Greek Manuscripts which contain the Four Gospels, or portions of them, may be convenient to the reader of the present volume.

N. B. *Alex.* denotes the Alexandrian family; *Byz.* the Byzantine; *mut.* that part of a manuscript has been lost.

Manuscripts written in Uncial or Capital Letters.

A. CODEX ALEXANDRINUS, in the British Museum, contains the whole of the N. T., but *mut.* in Matth. i, 1—xxv, 6; John vi, 50—viii, 52. A facsimile edition of this MS was published by Woid in 1786. Its most probable date is the 5th century. In the Gospels it is chiefly *Byz.*, but where it agrees with the other recension, its testimony is of great weight (e. g. Matth. xxv, 13; xxvi, 39; xxvii, 64).

B. CODEX VATICANUS 1209, at Rome, contains the whole N. T. *mut.*, the Apocalypse being in a later hand. It is perhaps the most antient of all our extant MSS, being generally referred to the 4th century. It presents the *Alex.* text in its best and purest form. Codex B has been often, though hastily, collated. Cardinal Mai is preparing a facsimile edition, a work which has been long and greatly needed.

C. CODEX EPHREMI, of the King's Library at Paris, contains the whole N. T., sadly *mut.* This document is a palimpsest of about the 5th century, and a facsimile was published by Tischendorf in 1842. *Alex.*, as a standard of which text it is in value and accuracy second only to Codex B.

D. CODEX BEZÆ, of the Public Library at Cambridge, contains the Gospels and the Acts, *mut.* It was written not later than the 6th century, and a facsimile edition was published by Kipling in 1793. *Alex.* This is the most corrupt of all the great manuscripts. It is so full of interpolations, of Latinising, singular and improbable readings, that its solitary evidence deserves little or no attention.

E. CODEX BASILEENSIS B. vi, 21 (Bas. α, of Bengel), of about the 9th century, contains the Gospels, *mut.* *Byz.*

F. CODEX BOREELI contains the Gospels. *Byz.* It was used for Wetstein's edition, and after being missing for a century, was produced by Heringa in 1830. It is still very imperfectly known.

G. CODEX WOLFII A, or Seidelii, now Harl. 5684, British Museum, of the 11th century, contains the Gospels, *mut.* *Byz.*

H. CODEX WOLFII B, of the same age, also contains the Gospels, *mut. Byz.*, but its text is more mixed than that of G.

K. CODEX CYPRIUS, Reg. 63, Paris, of about the 9th century, contains the Gospels. This important MS has been carefully examined by Scholz. *Alex.*, but with many *Byz.* and peculiar readings of its own.

L. CODEX REG. 62, Paris, Stephani ή, of the 8th century, also contains the Gospels, *mut.* *Alex.* This copy had too great influence with Griesbach, and frequently agrees with Cod. D, in its worst corruptions.

M. CODEX REG. 48, Paris (Des Camps), of the 10th century, contains the Gospels. Text very mixed, but chiefly *Alex.*

P. CODEX GUELPHERBYTANUS A, ⎫ These Wolfenbuttel frag-
Q. CODEX GUELPHERBYTANUS B, ⎭ ments are palimpsests of the 6th century (P of the four Gospels, Q of Luke and John only). *Alex.* Their readings were published by Knittel.

S. CODEX VATICAN. 354, of the 10th century, contains the Gospels. It is the best *Byz.* of all the uncial MSS.

T. CODEX BORGIÆ 1, at Rome, *mut.* of the 5th century, contains John vi, 28—67; vii, 6—8; 31. *Alex.* Collated by Georgi.

U. CODEX NANII 1, in the Library of St. Mark, Venice, of the 10th century, contains the Gospels. *Byz.*

X. CODEX LANDSHUTENSIS (Vossii), of the 10th century, contains the Gospels, *mut.* *Alex.* Collated by Scholz.

Z. CODEX DUBLIN: much *mut.* a palimpsest of St. Matthew's Gospel, written about the 6th century. A facsimile edition was published by Dr. Barrett in 1801. *Alex.*, closely resembling Codd. B and P.

Γ. CODEX VATICAN. 3785, of the 7th century, contains a few fragments of St. Matthew. *Alex.* Collated by Marini.

Appendix A.

Δ. CODEX SAN-GALLENSIS, a Greek-Latin MS of the 10th century, contains the Gospels. A facsimile edition was published by Rettig in 1836. It has been hitherto very little used for critical purposes. *Alex.?*

The uncial manuscripts collated by Matthæi for his edition of the Greek Testament (1782—1788) are

B. CODEX SYNODI MOSQUENSIS 43, of the 8th century; it is an Evangelarium, or book of lessons from the Gospels, appointed for Divine Service in the Greek Church. *Byz.*
H. CODEX TYPOGRAPH. SYNOD. MOSQ. 12, also an Evangelarium, is considered by Matthæi the earliest MS of the N. T. now extant. Less sanguine critics refer it to the 8th century. *Byz.*
V. CODEX SYNOD. MOSQ. *mut.* of the 8th century, contains the Gospels down to John vii, 38. *Byz.* valuable.

Manuscripts written in Cursive or ordinary Letters.

1. CODEX BASILEENSIS B. vi, 27 (Bas. γ, of Bengel), of the 10th century, contains the whole N. T. except the Apocalypse. It was known to Erasmus, though little used by him. *Alex.*, much resembling Codd. D L.
2. BASILEENSIS B. vi, 25 (Bas. β, of Bengel), of the 15th century, contains the Gospels. *Byz.* Since this is the copy chiefly followed by Erasmus, it is of course nearly connected with the textus receptus.
5. REG. 106, Paris, Stephani δ', of the 12th century, contains all the N. T. except the Apocalypse. *Byz.* but mixed.
13. REG. 50, Paris, of the 13th century, contains the Gospels, *mut.* This document is very decidedly *Alex.*
17. REG. 55, Paris (Greek-Latin), of the 16th century, contains the Gospels. Usually *Byz.*, very like the received text.
22. REG. 72, Paris, of the 11th century, contains the Gospels. Manifestly *Alex.*
28. REG. 379, Paris (Colbert. 2, of Mill), *mut.* of the 10th century, contains the Gospels. *Alex.* with many peculiar readings.
33. REG. 14, Paris, of the 11th or 12th century, contains the whole N. T. except the Apocalypse, *mut. Alex.*
36. COISLIN. 20, Paris, of the 11th century, contains the Gospels. *Byz.* (41. COISLIN. 24, is of the same date.)

51. BODLEIAN. Oxford (Laud. 2, of Mill), of the 13th century, contains the whole N. T. except the Apocalypse. *Byz.* (See note on Matth. xxvi, 60).
61. MONTFORT. Dublin, of about the 15th century, contains the whole N. T. This manuscript was at one time suspected (unjustly, as it would seem) of having been forged in order to uphold the text of the Three Heavenly Witnesses, 1 John v, 7: which passage was inserted in the 3rd edition of Erasmus (1522) on the authority of the present document. Its text is so much corrupted by Latin readings, that it must not be depended on.
69. LEICESTRENSIS, of the 14th century, containing the whole N. T., is the property of the Corporation of Leicester. *Mut.* in Matth. i, 1—xviii, 5, &c. Like most other manuscripts deposited in England, it stands in urgent want of a fresh examination. *Alex.*, but not so exclusively so as D. 1. 13. 33.
71. EPHESIUS, at Lambeth, of the 12th century, contains the Gospels. It is an accurate *Byz.* copy.
72. HARLEIAN. 5647 (Johnson), in the British Museum, of the 11th century, contains the Gospels. *Alex.*, but mixed.
102. An unknown MEDICÆAN MS, containing Matth. xxiv—Mark viii. Its readings were extracted by Wetstein from the margin of Plantin's Nov. Test. 1591. *Alex.*, almost always with D L, &c.
106. The WINCHELSEA MS, of the 10th century, containing the Gospels, was used for Wetstein's edition. *Alex.*
118. BODLEIAN. MARSH 124, of the 13th century, contains the Gospels, *mut.* It is an important *Alex.* document.
120. REG. 185.a, Paris, Stephani ιδ', of the 13th century, contains Matth., Luke and John. *Byz.*
124. LAMBECC. 31, in the Imperial Library, Vienna, of the 12th century, contains the Gospels. Chiefly *Alex.*
130. VATICAN. 359 (Greek-Latin), of the 13th century, contains the Gospels. Its text is mixed. (Codd. 127—158 are all deposited in the Vatican Library).
131. VATICAN. 360, of the 11th century, contains the whole N.T. except the Apocalypse. It appears to have been used by Aldus Manutius for his edition (1518). *Byz.*, but it has many singular readings.
157. URBINO-VATICAN. 2, of the 12th century, contains the Gospels. Chiefly *Alex.* Scholz says of it " exscriptus est ex vetustissimis codicibus hierosolymitanis in monasterio quodam montis sancti servatis." By mons sacer he means Athos.

Appendix A.

183. LAURENTIAN. vi, 14, of the 12th century, contains the Gospels. *Byz.* (Codd. 182—198 are all at Florence).
208. VENETUS 9, of the 10th century, contains the Gospels. *Alex.*
209. VENETUS 10 (Bessarionis), of the 15th century, contains the whole N. T. *Alex.* in the Gospels.
218. LAMBECC. 1, Vienna, of the 13th century, contains the whole N. T. The text is very mixed. From this celebrated MS Alter printed his edition of the N. T. in 1786 —87, with various readings from other MSS in the Imperial library, viz. 3. 76. 77. 108. 123—125. 219—225., which (except 123—125. 225) are chiefly *Byz.*
235. HAVNIENS. 2, at Copenhagen, of the 14th century, contains the Gospels. *Alex.*
346. AMBROSIAN. 23, at Milan, of the 12th century, contains the Gospels. *Alex.* (Codd. 260—469 were first made known, and partially collated by Scholz. See Introd. p. 17.)

Matthæi's cursive manuscripts of the Gospels (including Evangelistaria, and portions of Scripture contained in copies of Chrysostom's Homilies), are about fifty in number. They are of various degrees of value and importance, and bear dates from the 10th to the 15th or even the 16th century. They are for the most part Byzantine, but the following exhibit a mixed text:

a. SYNOD. 45, at Moscow (259 of Scholz), of the 10th or 11th century, containing the Gospels. Chiefly *Alex.*
e. SYNOD. 48 (238 of Scholz), of the 11th century, containing Matthew and Mark only.
k. DRESDENSIS Matthæi (241 of Scholz), of the 11th century, containing the whole N.T. It has some peculiar readings.
x. TABULAR. IMPERIAL., at Moscow (251 of Scholz), of the 11th century, containing the Gospels.

⁎ The following manuscripts furnish the most characteristic readings of the Alexandrian family: D L. 1. 13. 33. 118. 124. 151. 235.

The reader will not feel surprised on observing that so many of the manuscripts in the preceding catalogue belong to the Alexandrian recension. It is obvious that these documents, which contain readings at variance with those of the great bulk of the authorities, will naturally attract a larger share of our attention, than they could claim on the score of intrinsic merit. In our studies, as in common life, the *exception* makes a deeper impression on the mind than the rule which it violates.

ERRATA.

Page 149, *line* 27, *for* Demosth. *read* Pseudo-Demosth.
Page 274, *line* 24, *for* Appendix I, *read* Appendix A.

DATE DUE

HIGHSMITH #45230

BS186 .S434
A supplement to the authorised English
Princeton Theological Seminary-Speer Library

1 1012 00059 4756

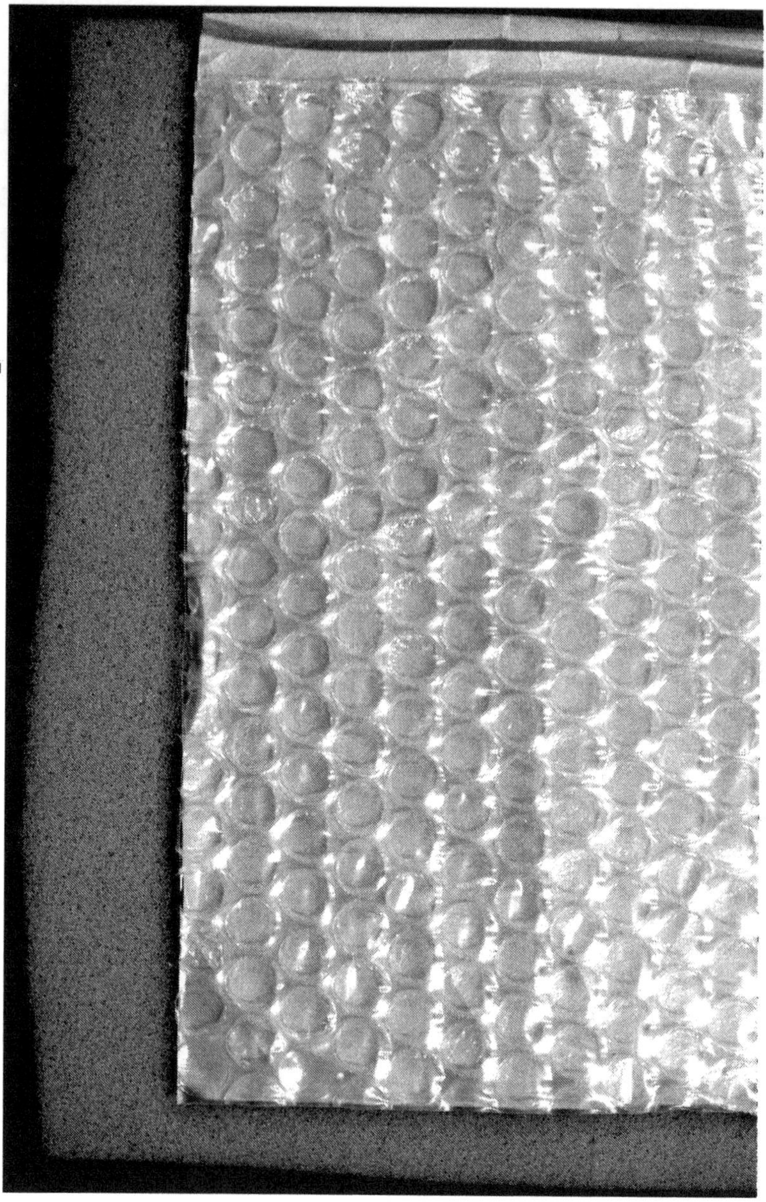

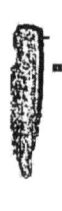

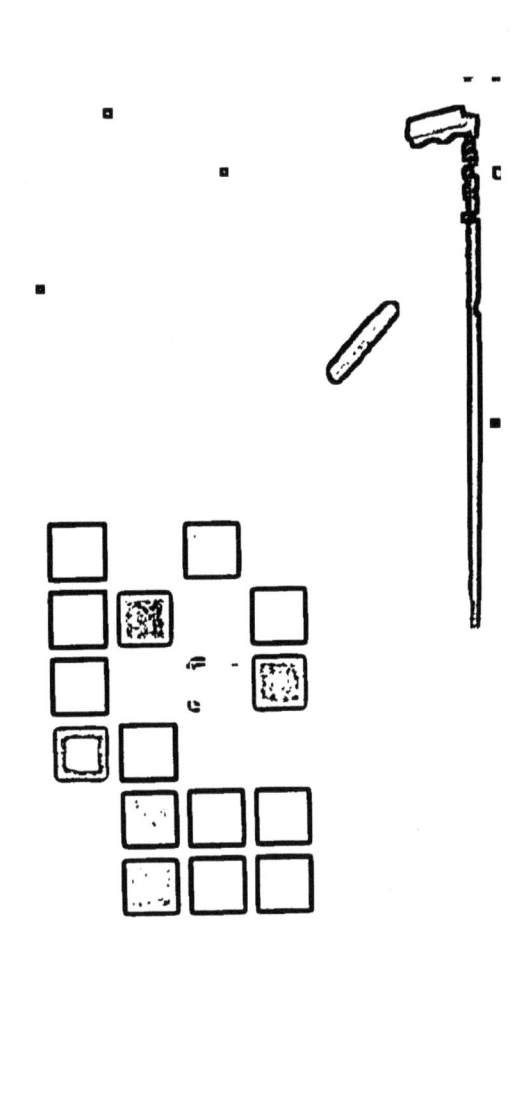

Lightning Source UK Ltd.
Milton Keynes UK
UKHW020820060123
414934UK00006B/55